LES BLANCS:

THE COLLECTED LAST PLAYS

OF LORRAINE HANSBERRY

Books by Lorraine Hansberry

A Raisin in the Sun
The Sign in Sidney Brustein's Window
To Be Young, Gifted and Black
The Movement

Les Blancs: The Collected Last Plays of Lorraine Hansberry

Les Blancs:

The Collected Last Plays of Lorraine Hansberry

EDITED, WITH CRITICAL BACKGROUNDS,
BY ROBERT NEMIROFF

INTRODUCTION BY JULIUS LESTER

Random House • New York

TO *Angela Davis,*

George Jackson

AND *the Men of Attica,*

WHOSE SPIRIT IS IN THESE PAGES

AND TO *Mili*

CONTENTS

Introduction BY JULIUS LESTER   3

LES BLANCS

A Critical Background   35
Les Blancs   47
Postscript   173

THE DRINKING GOURD

A Critical Background   189
The Drinking Gourd   217
Notes   311

WHAT USE ARE FLOWERS?

A Critical Background   317
What Use Are Flowers?   323

Introduction

On January 12, 1965, a little more than a month before the assassination of Malcolm X, Lorraine Hansberry died; she was thirty-four. Somehow it seems like more than coincidence that the two should die within less than a month and a half of each other and scarcely nine months before the "deferred dream" exploded in the streets of Watts. Each of them possessed an uncommon prescience. They knew that a plague was about to be loosed upon the land and they went down into Egypt and told Pharaoh to let their people go. To their people, they painted images of the bondage which entombed them and of the wilderness that lay between that bondage and the Promised Land. Each had a different vision of that Promised Land, but those visions did not clash because each was the possessor of an uncommon integrity and humanity, the kind which lives easily with differences and contradictions that would tear others apart. They came and told of what they saw in the world around them and of what they saw in their mind's eye. Then, they died and the manner of their dying reflected their living. Malcolm's presence among us had been like a detonation and he died in the sound of an explosion, lying on a public platform for all the world to see, his life flowing in crimson rivulets from bullet punctures. Lorraine Hansberry was no less fiery in her passage, but she was tempered by gentleness and laughter, and her effect on others was like the seepage of rain into the earth, nourishing roots which only the rain knew were there.

3

She died from cancer, slowly, methodically, life retreating cell by cell, fiber by fiber. From the blood of Malcolm a new people arose, as if it were Easter morning and the shedding of the blood itself had rolled away the stone from the tomb of the race. And, having risen, the people swept across the land, an avenging tornado of blackness. Now the storms have passed and, in the quietness, the voice and vision of Lorraine Hansberry needs to be heard. It was there all along, but we weren't ready to listen. Now perhaps we are.

At the time of her death, Lorraine Hansberry was recognized as one of America's leading playwrights. Her reputation rested on one play, *A Raisin in the Sun*. Her second play, *The Sign in Sidney Brustein's Window* (which closed on Broadway on January 12, 1965, the day of her death), was hardly understood by most critics and, because it was not a Broadway hit, did not serve to enhance the acclaim she had received from *Raisin*.

Until the off-Broadway production of *To Be Young, Gifted and Black* in January, 1969, Miss Hansberry had become a part of theatrical history, which is to say, almost forgotten. It was assumed, who knows for what reasons, that there was nothing in her work relevant to the late sixties. But that assumption could only be made by those who had not returned to her plays and retained only shadowy and impressionistic memories.

The subject matter of *A Raisin in the Sun* may make it appear outdated. The action taking place in what now seems like a long past time—the days before Black Power, antiwar protests, student uprisings and black rebellions. The play concerns itself with the Younger family: Mama Younger, who has survived and won; her son, Walter, the pivotal character of the play, the black male castrated by the blade of the American dream but who blames the castration on his wife; Ruth, Walter's wife, who sees the wound and is unable to stanch the bleeding and, like her Biblical namesake, can say, "Whither thou goest, I will go"—but Walter will not lead; Beneatha, Walter's sister, a college student, a black militant in a day before there was a name for her; and, Joseph Asagai, an African student, with a vision of a black-ruled Africa. Within one apartment, Lorraine Hansberry capsulized so much of black life on a myriad of levels. Here is the black male-black female conflict presented in all its painful rawness in Walter and Ruth; and here too is a history of black women, all of them beautiful in totally different ways, all of them strong in totally different ways.

Because the play ends with the Youngers moving into an all-white neighborhood, it is too easy to think that it is about integration and entering the middle class. Nelson Algren wrote that the play was about

> . . . the aspiration of the new, rising Negro mercantile class to own color TV, refrigerators that have two doors, sports cars, split-level homes, central heating, self-wiping dishes and air-conditioning. In short, it is not a play about human dignity, but how to invest wisely. . . . Dramatically, RAISIN does for the Negro people what hair straightener and skin-lightener have done for the Negro cosmetics trade. . . . As a social study, it is a good drama about real estate.

One would have expected a little more acumen from Mr. Algren.

The dramatic action involves what the Younger family will do with the ten thousand dollars insurance money from

Mr. Younger's death. Mama Younger wants to buy a house and move her family out of their South Side Chicago tenement Walter Lee wants to invest it in a liquor store. What is at stake here is not moving into a white neighborhood, as some would have it, nor is it the aspiration "to own color TV," as Mr. Algren would have it. What is at stake is the kind of human being Walter Lee Younger should be.

Walter is a typical black male of working-class parents. He has grown up in the ghetto, seen his parents work hard at menial jobs all their lives. He has married, has a son, works as a chauffeur; and his wife works as a maid. And he wants more. He sees the affluence of America around him every day. He comes into contact with it on his job and every time he goes downtown and sees white people in fine restaurants. America has defined life in material terms and Walter accepts the definition without question and, in an eloquent speech, he describes vividly the kind of life he wants. It is the American dream.

> . . . one day when you 'bout seventeen years old, I'll come home and I'll be pretty tired, you know what I mean, after a day of conferences and secretaries getting things wrong the way they do . . . 'cause an executive's life is hell, man . . . And I'll pull the car up on the driveway . . . just a plain black Chrysler, I think, with white walls—no—black tires. More elegant. Rich people don't have to be flashy . . . though I'll have to get something a little sportier for Ruth—maybe a Cadillac convertible to do her shopping in . . . And I'll come up the steps to the house and the gardener will be clipping away at the hedges and he'll say, "Good evening, Mr. Younger." And I'll say, "Hello, Jefferson, how are you this eve-

ning?" And I'll go inside and Ruth will come downstairs and meet me at the door and we'll kiss each other and she'll take my arm and we'll go up to your room to see you sitting on the floor with catalogues of all the great schools in America around you . . . All the great schools in the world! And—and I'll say, all right son—it's your seventeenth birthday, what is it you've decided? . . . Just tell me where you want to go to school and you'll go. Just tell me, what it is you want to be—and you'll *be* it . . . Whatever you want to be—Yessir! You just name it, son . . . And I hand you the world.

Walter has been taught that he should want the world, but because he is black he has been denied the possibility of ever having it. And that only makes the pain of the desire that much more hurting. As Paolo and Francesca are blown close to each other but never allowed to touch in Dante's *Inferno*, so Walter is allowed to see what America has to offer. It is held tantalizingly before him but, always, it is just out of reach.

Sometimes, it's like I can see the future stretched out in front of me—just as plain as day. The future, Mama. Hanging over there at the edge of my days. Just waiting for me—a big, looming blank space—full of *nothing*. Just waiting for *me*. Mama—sometimes when I'm downtown and I pass them cool, quiet-looking restaurants where them white boys are sitting back and talking 'bout things . . . sitting there turning deals worth millions of dollars . . . sometimes I see guys don't look much older than me.

But Mama Younger has not let America define her. She has defined herself. And she asks him: "Son—how come you talk so much 'bout money?"

WALTER   Because it is life, Mama!

MAMA   Oh. So now it's life. Money is life. Once upon a time freedom used to be life—now it's money. I guess the world really do change.

WALTER   No—it was always money, Mama. We just didn't know about it.

MAMA   No . . . something has happened. You something new, boy. In my time we was worried about not being lynched and getting to the North if we could and how to stay alive and still have a pinch of dignity, too . . . Now here come you and Beneatha—talking 'bout things we ain't never even thought about hardly, me and your daddy. You ain't satisfied or proud of nothing we done. I mean that you had a home; that we kept you out of trouble till you was grown; that you don't have to ride to work on the back of nobody's streetcar. You my children—but how different we done become.

And it is this difference in values that the play is about. Perhaps that would be clearer if Lorraine Hansberry had not chosen to write about material needs and aspirations so concretely. *A Raisin in the Sun* is no intellectual abstraction about upward mobility and conspicuous consumption. It goes right to the core of practically every black family in the ghettos of Chicago, New York, Los Angeles and elsewhere. Whether they have a picture of Jesus, Martin Luther King, or Malcolm X on the lead-painted walls of their rat-infested tenement, all of them want to get the hell out of there as quickly as they can. Maybe black militants don't know it, or don't want to admit it, but Malcolm X made a down payment on a house in a suburban community a few weeks before he was murdered. And one surely can't accuse Malcolm of bourgeois aspirations. He merely wanted what every black wants—a home of his own adequate to his needs, at a minimum, and the fulfillment of his desires, at the most. Contrary to Mr. Algren's interpretation, *A Raisin in the Sun* is most definitely about "human dignity" because Lorraine Hansberry is concerned with the attitude we must have toward material things if we are to be their master and not their slave. Is that attitude to be Mama's? Or is it to be Walter's? And, for blacks, locked out from these things for so long, the question is a crucial one. As blacks acquire more and more of America's material offerings, are they, too, going to be transformed by their acquisitions into mindless consumers like the majority of whites? Or are they going to continue to walk in the path of righteousness like their forebears? Lorraine Hansberry summarized it well when, in a letter, she wrote of the play:

> . . . we cannot . . . very well succumb to monetary values and know the survival of certain interior aspects of man which . . . must remain if we are to loom larger than other creatures on this planet. . . . Our people fight daily and magnificently for a more comfortable material base for their lives; they desperately need and hourly sacrifice for clean homes, decent food, personal and group dignity and the abolition of terroristic violence as their children's heritage. So, in that sense, I am certainly a materialist in the first order.
>
> However, the distortion of this aspiration surrounds us in the form of an almost maniacal lusting for "acquisitions." It seems to have absorbed the national mentality and Negroes, to be sure, have certainly been affected by it. The young man in the play, Walter Lee, is meant to symbolize their number.

9

Consequently, in the beginning, he dreams not so much of
being comfortable and imparting the most meaningful gifts
to his son (education in depth, humanist values, a worship
of dignity) but merely of being what it seems to him the
"successful" portion of humankind is—"rich." Toward this
end he is willing to make an old trade; urgently willing. On
the fact that some aspect of his society has brought him to
this point, the core of the drama hangs.

Walter blames himself, his wife and his mother for what he
sees as his personal failure. And only at the end of the play
does it become possible for him to realize that there is a
puppeteer manipulating him, a puppeteer who brought him
dangerously close to destroying his family and himself.

The climax of the play comes after Walter's deal to get
a liquor license falls through. Mama Younger has made a
$3500 down payment on a house and gives the remaining
money to Walter to do with as he wishes after he deposits
$2500 in a savings account for Beneatha's education. Wal-
ter, however, takes the entire $6500 and gives it to one of
his two future "partners." One of the "partners" absconds
with the money. A Mr. Lindner, a white man from the
neighborhood into which they are to move, comes and offers
to buy the house from them for more than they would
eventually pay. The whites in the neighborhood do not want
a black family moving in. Previously, Walter had scornfully
turned the man down. However, when he learns that his
money has been stolen, he calls Mr. Lindner on the phone
and tells him that they will sell the house. Mr. Lindner
comes over and Walter finds that he is unable to go through
with it. There is something in him—a little bit of self-
respect is still left; he tells Mr. Lindner that they are going

to move in. And with Walter making his first step toward being a man, a *black* man, the play ends.

Few see the heroism in Walter's simple act of assertion. Indeed, how many who have seen the play or the movie have not thought that Walter was a fool for *not* accepting the money? How one views Walter's act is a direct reflection of how much one accepts the American dream. And there is the significance of the fact that the play ends with the Youngers moving into a "white" neighborhood. To see this as a confirmation of the American dream is to accept the myth that blacks have wanted nothing more than to be integrated with whites. In actuality, the fact that the neighborhood is white is the least important thing about it. It merely happened to be the neighborhood in which Mama Younger could find a nice house she could afford. And it is this simple, practical element which has always been mistaken by whites as a desire on the part of blacks to be "integrated." But why, the question could be raised, would the Youngers persist in moving into a neighborhood where they are not wanted, where they may be subjected to harassment or even physical violence? They persist, as all blacks persist, not because it is any great honor to live among whites, but because one cannot consider himself a human being as long as he acquiesces to restrictions placed upon him by others, particularly if those restrictions are based solely on race or religion. If Walter had accepted the money, he would have been saying, in graphic language, You are right, we are niggers and don't have the right to live where we can afford to. But, with that earthy eloquence of a black still close to his roots, Walter says, "We have decided to move into our house because my father—my father—he earned it." And, in that realization, Walter learns also that it was not a black woman who castrated him. It was America and his own acceptance of America's values. No woman can make him a man. He has to do it himself.

He is a hero, a twentieth-century hero. We still long, of course, for the heroes who seemed to ride history as if it were a bronco and they were champion rodeo riders. But those heroes—if they were ever real—come from a time when life, perhaps, was somewhat less complex. But the problems that face man in the latter twentieth century are large, larger than any one of us, and the sword of a knight in armor is laughable to the dragons roaming our countryside. Our heroes are more difficult to recognize only because they appear so small beside the overwhelming enemies they must slay. But because they appear small does not mean that they are, and it does not make their acts less heroic. Walter Lee Younger has his contemporary historic counterpart in the person of a small, quiet black woman named Rosa Parks who refused to get out of a seat on a bus in Montgomery, Alabama. It would have been so easy for her to have relinquished her seat to a white person that day—as it would have been easy for Walter to have taken the money. But something in her, as in him, said No. And in that quiet dissent, both of them said Yes to human dignity. They said No to those who would define them and thereby deny their existence, and by saying No, they began to define themselves. There have been many Rosa Parks, but few of them have mysteriously set in motion a whole movement for social change. Walter Lee Younger is one of those whose act probably set nothing in motion. And that only increases its heroic dimension. In an article in *The Village Voice*, which compared Walter to Willie Loman, Lorraine Hansberry described the hero she saw in Walter Younger:

> For if there are no waving flags and marching songs at the barricades as Walter marches out with his little battalion, it is not because the battle lacks nobility. On the contrary, he has picked up in his way, still imperfect and wobbly in his small view of human destiny, what I believe Arthur Miller once called "the golden thread of history." He becomes, in spite of those who are too intrigued with despair and hatred of man to see it, King Oedipus refusing to tear out his eyes, but attacking the Oracle instead. He is that last Jewish patriot manning his rifle in the burning ghetto at Warsaw; he is that young girl who swam into sharks to save a friend a few weeks ago; he is Anne Frank, still believing in people; he is the nine small heroes of Little Rock; he is Michelangelo creating David, and Beethoven bursting forth with the Ninth Symphony. He is all those things because he has finally reached out in his tiny moment and caught that sweet essence which is human dignity, and it shines like the old star-touched dream that is in his eyes.

Part of the unrecognized genius of Lorraine Hansberry was a compassion for people that allowed her to see that there is no difference between Michelangelo, Beethoven, Oedipus and a black chauffeur on the South Side of Chicago. To our minds, besotted with self-righteous intellectuality, her comparisons are absurd and ludicrous. But heroes abound in our society—the teacher who endures the soul-killing bureaucracy of boards of education because he/she loves the children who enter the room each morning; the lunch-counter waitress who cares that your fifteen or twenty minutes at lunch are good ones; the cab driver who wants each passenger to leave his cab feeling a little better than when he entered. The heroes are with us; we simply have to learn to recognize them.

As a dramatist, Lorraine Hansberry had the gift of making us see the extraordinary in those who society had decreed were merely ordinary. The Younger family *is* black America, and the way she handles them as a dramatist is a good example of Mama Younger's advice in the play to her daughter:

> When you starts measuring somebody, measure him *right*, child, measure him right. Make sure you done taken into account what hills and valleys he come through before he got to wherever he is. . . .

Lorraine Hansberry "measures" all of her characters "right," even Mr. Lindner, of whom she once wrote in a letter:

> I have treated him as a human being merely because he is one; that does not make the meaning of his call less malignant, less sick. All that he stands for in his meandering, uncertain and polluted quest for "a way out" is detrimental to the best interests of the future of this nation and of the human race.

In the play he is not a caricature, but a person and we see and experience him for who he is. Lorraine Hansberry was an artist, not a preacher—which too many seem to think is the principal role the black artist should play today. She did not simplify the complexities of human beings, whether she agreed with them politically or not. Lesser artists are so concerned with communicating their "message" that their

characters never get off the ventriloquist's knee. Lorraine
Hansberry always had a message; she wouldn't have been a
writer if she hadn't. But she was aware that "whatever is said
must be said through the living arguments of human beings
in conflict with other human beings, with themselves, with
the abstractions which seem to them to be 'their society.' "

The Younger family is one particular black family living
in a very particular place. And because she draws them with
such precise fidelity, they are true to the social, cultural and
political environment in which they live and, by being so,
they become universal—as Leopold and Molly Bloom
become universal. Yet Lorraine Hansberry quite rightly re-
sented those whites who, in grasping the universality of the
play, wanted to diminish the significance of the black par-
ticulars.

> People are trying to say . . . that this is not what they consider
> the traditional treatment of the Negro in the theatre.
> They're trying to say that it isn't a propaganda play, that it
> isn't something that hits you over the head; they are trying
> to say that they believe the characters in our play transcend
> category. However, it is an unfortunate way to try and say
> it, because I believe that one of the most sound ideas in
> dramatic writing is that in order to create the universal, you
> must pay very great attention to the specific. Universality, I
> think, emerges from the truthful identity of what is.
>
> In other words, I have told people that not only is this a
> Negro family, specifically and definitely culturally, but it's
> not even a New York family or a southern Negro family. It
> is specifically Southside Chicago . . . that kind of care, that
> kind of attention to detail. In other words, I think people,
> to the extent we accept them and believe them as who

they're supposed to be, to that extent they can become everybody. So I would say it is definitely a Negro play before it is anything else.

To try and deny that *Raisin* is a black play is to deny the very particular ways in which blacks express their humanity (and what is culture if it is not a particular expression of humanity?).

Essential to any understanding of Lorraine Hansberry is the comprehension of her profound humanity and infinite respect for Man and sense of awe at the possibilities inherent in him. She cared about people and because she did, she refused to hate and refused to people her world exclusively with blacks. The new "black aesthetic" decrees that black writers must write only for and about blacks. This "aesthetic," however, overlooks the fact that anyone who writes with integrity about blacks is going to be writing for everyone who will open himself and listen.

In July 1964, Lorraine Hansberry was part of a historic forum at Town Hall in New York City called "The Black Revolution and the White Backlash." On that forum, among others, were LeRoi Jones and John Killens, blacks who, more and more, would articulate a degree of militancy which would almost make Malcolm X look like a moderate. That night Lorraine Hansberry said something which was unpopular then and is still totally unacceptable to many now:

Some of the first people who have died so far in this struggle have been white men. And I, for one, would be prepared, I must say in exception to anything said, to accept the leadership of a person who gives that much devotion as against someone who would exhibit the traitorous characteristics of, say, a Moise Tshombe. I don't think we can decide ultimately on the basis of color. The passion that we express should be understood, I think, in that context. We want total identification. It's not a question of reading anybody out; it's a merger . . . but it has to be a merger on the basis of true and genuine equality. . . .

She had a humanity which too few have today. She loved people and hated injustice and did not *define* a person as unjust because he acted unjustly.

Her next play, *The Sign in Sidney Brustein's Window*, was about whites, and it must have taken a lot of courage to follow *A Raisin in the Sun* with this drama about a white liberal intellectual in New York's Greenwich Village. It was a risk of the highest order for the most eminent living black playwright to take. It would only disorient and confuse critics and playgoers to have to confront a black writing about something other than "the problem." Many are still confused by the play, but it is an important one and a logical successor to *A Raisin in the Sun*.

Sidney Brustein is an intellectual who no longer cares. At one time he was politically active and involved—an idealist, if you will. It is never made explicit, but it is clear that he went through the McCarthy period, was anguished about the persecution and eventual execution of the Rosenbergs, then succumbed to the ennui of the Eisenhower years. Yet he has been trying to make a new life for himself, to give his life a meaning as significant as that which it once had. Instead, he has merely drifted from one failing endeavor to another. He has adopted a mask of cynicism but, unlike

Mort Sahl or Lenny Bruce (of whom Sidney's humor is reminiscent), he is unable to lash out at anything except his wife, a young aspiring actress who works as a waitress and is the constant target for Sidney's bitterness and self-hatred. The play delineates the reconstruction of Sidney through his involvement in a political campaign.

The Sign in Sidney Brustein's Window is a call to arms to white liberals and intellectuals. Lorraine had come to womanhood during the fifties and, though she identified as a black, she identified also as a Western intellectual. Writing in the last year of her life in *The New York Times*, she said:

> Few things are more natural than that the tortures of the *engagé* should attract me thematically. Being 34 years old at this writing means that I am of the generation which grew up in the swirl and dash of the Sartre-Camus debate of the postwar years. The silhouette of the Western intellectual poised in hesitation before the flames of involvement was an accurate symbolism of some of my closest friends, some of whom crossed each other leaping in and out, for instance, of the Communist Party. Others searched, as agonizingly, for some ultimate justification of their lives in the abstractions flowing out of London or Paris. Still others were contorted into seeking a meaningful repudiation of *all* justifications of anything and had, accordingly, turned to Zen, action painting or even just Jack Kerouac.

> Mine is, after all, the generation that had come to maturity drinking in the forebodings of the Silones, Koestlers and Richard Wrights. It had left us ill-prepared for decisions that had to be made in our own time about Algeria, Birmingham or the Bay of Pigs. By the 1960's few enough American

intellectuals had it within them to be ashamed that their discovery of the "betrayal" of the Cuban Revolution by Castro just happened to coincide with the change of heart of official American government policy. They left it to TV humorists to defend the Agrarian Reform in the end. It is the climate and mood of such intellectuals, if not these particular events, which constitute the core of a play called *The Sign in Sidney Brustein's Window.*

Elsewhere she once wrote that "American intellectual thought has been pretty much fractured by the Great Retreat. From everything. From everything, that is, that smacks of passionate partisanship." Her second play was an attempt to stop the retreat. It was produced a year and a half before white liberals were to be confronted with the specter of black power so well-augured at the Town Hall forum. It was written at a time when liberals still refused to acknowledge that there was a war in Vietnam which could not be ignored or apologized for. Perhaps Lorraine Hansberry did not know in specifics what the late sixties were to bring, but she had been an associate of Paul Robeson and W.E.B. Du Bois. And, like them, she had had her passport taken away by the U.S. State Department. She had lived long enough to have been involved with the Student Non-Violent Coordinating Committee and to have written the text for a book of photographs about the civil rights movement, called *The Movement;* she had lived long enough to have been affected by Malcolm X, whom she had met and talked with on several occasions; to have confronted an uncomprehending Attorney General named Kennedy. And because she was an artist, because she was, as Ezra Pound defined the artist, "the antennae of the race," she had a real sense of what was to come. There is a remarkable element of prognostication in her plays. There are Beneatha and Joseph in *A Raisin in the Sun*, foretelling the political involvement of black youth of the sixties. There is the remarkable scene in the same play when Walter becomes an African warrior, foretelling the black identification which will come with dashikis, black studies and black pride. There is Sidney Brustein, who would march against the Vietnam war in the later sixties. And when we come to *Les Blancs* we have Tshembe Matoseh, the black intellectual who becomes a revolutionary, Dr. Willy DeKoven, the white liberal who has been radicalized and the black warriors. Her sensitive antennae made her plays seismographs of social upheaval. But few could respond to this element in them, because to respond was to change—And change is a process we are unwilling to begin until our very lives are threatened and, even then, we do not change as much as we merely seek to camouflage ourselves. *The Sign in Sidney Brustein's Window* was a conscious warning, a plea to her white intellectual counterparts to prepare to pick up the gauntlet and return to the field. (*A Raisin in the Sun* is a conscious warning to the black middle class and those of the lower class with middle-class aspirations not to exchange the lessons bequeathed them by their parents for a mess of pottage.) But the Sidney Brusteins who saw the play didn't realize they were seeing themselves in it; and by this time Lorraine lay dying.

The Sign in Sidney Brustein's Window is also a look into the future for those of us who are now as young as Sidney once was and who will be growing older, as Sidney was. Where will we be ten, fifteen years from now, with our books, our record collections, our memories and our dreams?

We are young now, but one day we will have been to one demonstration too many, heard the same speeches once too often. One day we, too, may be frightened as more and more people who believe as we do are jailed, killed or disappear into the "underground." We may find ourselves with no way to express the passionate caring which is a part of us and, like Sidney, begin to drift, with clouds of marijuana smoke marking our stopping places. Will we be able to resurrect ourselves, like Sidney, and to declare as he did that we are "fools" who believe

> that death is waste and love is sweet and that the earth turns and men change every day and that rivers run and that people wanna be better than they are and that flowers smell good and that I hurt terribly today, and that hurt is desperation and desperation is—energy and energy can *move* things. . . .

Lorraine's idealism is of a kind that was always rare. She believed in the ultimate goodness of people, believed

> that one cannot live with sighted eyes and feeling heart and not know and react to the miseries which afflict this world. . . . What I write is not based on the assumption of idyllic possibilities or innocent assessments of the true nature of life. But rather . . . that, posing one against the other, I think the human race does command its own destiny and that destiny can eventually embrace the stars.

She had faith in Man during a time when others only had faith in Man's ability to destroy and either reinforced that ability or despaired because of it. Her faith existed as a bulwark against the inevitable death that will come when such a faith does not exist. Her faith was at the core of what motivated and shaped her as an artist. She refused to abstract or dehumanize the world; she refused to be a mere reflector of an increasingly technologized society. In answer to a letter from a stranger she wrote what constitutes an important part of her *raison d'être*.

> . . . people are generally better than their circumstances.
> . . . I think that the glorious thing about the human race is that it does change the world—constantly. The world or "life" may seem to more often overwhelm the human being, but it is the human being's capacity for struggling against being overwhelmed which is remarkable and exhilarating. In my opinion all fine drama should rest on some aspect of that recognition.

> I should be very unhappy though if that were taken to mean that I have some peculiar notion of a rosy world. On the contrary, there are days when I should, like most persons of conscience, utterly like to clear out of this terrifying world. And yet I see so much to affirm. Some of us who think of ourselves as "artists" have, in fact, grown fond of observing, perhaps arrogantly so, that it is actually easier, in art, to try to approximate the dead, dying or decadent. And that one can lose one's very mind trying to first discern and then recreate the healthy, the Insurgent, the fine. Naturally, great art has always circumscribed both. But "great" is a luxurious adjective and has little to do with the present output of some of my fellow writers and myself who have to content ourselves with trying to create even a measure of truth—let alone "great truths." However, as I started to say above, we have begun to suspect that the ever recurrent vogue of "de-

spair" as literature and art have their origins in the profound difficulty in creating literature and art of "affirmation." We think, perhaps, and not without some rather snide amusement, that some of the "abstractionists" and "non-objectivists" about have merely decided that they cannot compete with the Renaissance and have therefore flown to the dots, dashes, spilled paint and twisted metal of contemporary painting (and the equivalent in the drama and novel). Clearly man has grown very, very tiny in the modern drama (some, not all) and virtually disappeared from the canvas. We think it is the cheap way out and will not prevail; man, after all was not "finer" when Leonardo or Michelangelo perceived his magnificence or Shakespeare or Shelley discerned the largeness of his spirit!

. . . I personally believe that the possibilities of man are infinite. So, indeed, is his cruelty and backwardness and it is a long march about. But all these things are dynamic and not static. The little family in *Raisin* tried to reflect this and changed their world a little bit. Few of us, I think can do more; none of us have the right to do less.

Sometimes, this enormous faith could lead her to indulge in sentimental excesses, as with *What Use Are Flowers?*, a short play about a hermit who returns to the world and finds a group of children to be the only survivors of an unnamed holocaust. The children are worse than wild animals, and he endeavors to teach them the rudiments of civilization before he dies; but, as he dies, the children are fighting, just as they had been when he first saw them, before they begin to rebuild the wheel. It is not a good play, but it helps us all the more to appreciate how good Lorraine Hansberry was when she was good. Perhaps one of the most

difficult things an artist can do is write a literature of "affirmation," as she called it. Pete Seeger once said to this writer,
"It is all too easy to write about despair." No one perhaps
knew that better than Lorraine Hansberry, surrounded as
she was by a generation of artists who made despair and
alienation the theme of a generation of literature. (And how
ironic that a theater of "affirmation" should come from a
black woman who, one would think, would have plenty to
despair about.) The audience of a Lorraine Hansberry play
left the theater feeling a little better than when it entered.
They left with a little more hope; and while *What Use Are
Flowers?*, is a momentary failure of craft, it is not a failure
of vision.

Lorraine Hansberry's faith did not, however, blind her to
the hard political realities of the world in which she lived.
Throughout *To Be Young, Gifted and Black*, she shows her
awareness of the impending black revolution, of what we
now call the Third World, of imperialism and capitalism.
She was a political radical, a revolutionary, who could calmly
say that night at Town Hall, "If anybody comes and does
ill in your home or your community—obviously, you try your
best to kill him . . ." She was a revolutionary who understood
that "only . . . when the white liberal becomes an American
radical will he be prepared to come to grips with . . . the basic
fabric of our society—which, after all, is the thing which
must be changed to really solve the problem: the basic
organization of American society is the thing that has
Negroes in the situation they are in and never let us lose
sight of it!"

The genius of Lorraine Hansberry lies in her ability to

meld her revolutionary commitment with her artistic skill and integrity. And she was able to do this because her commitment was to people, not to ideology. She could never have committed the sin of "socialist realism" or its contemporary counterpart, "black nationalist realism." She knew that people were more than the summation of their political beliefs.

This is evident in *The Drinking Gourd*, a television drama commissioned by NBC and never produced. In it she describes slavery from the point of view of its participants— the slave, the poor white, and the slave owner, his wife and son. She does not stereotype the slave owner as a lusting, bloodthirsty villain, but presents him as a person. The white overseer is shown in all the frustration and wretchedness which poor whites, then and now, live in. There is never any doubt, of course, about whom she identifies with, but to identify with one group of people does not necessarily mean you must cease to acknowledge the existence of others. Lorraine Hansberry lived on a level of identification with black people that could only lead her to feel the souls of those who opposed her.

This identification gets its most complex treatment in *Les Blancs*, her finest play. The spiritual setting is people in a time of revolution. The play seems to have its inspiration in the Kenya of the mid-fifties during the time of the Mau Mau rebellion, taking place as it does in a white-ruled African nation when white settlers are being attacked by black natives. The principal character is Tshembe Matoseh, a young African who left his country years before and settled in England, where he married a white woman by whom he has a son. Because his father is dying, Tshembe returns. But he arrives the day after his father's death and finds himself in the middle of the rebellion, of which he wishes no part. He wants only to return to England, to his wife and son.

The action of the play takes place at the home of Tshembe's father, where his half brother now lives, and at the Mission compound, a hospital established many years before by a European minister, Reverend Neilsen, a character obviously suggested by Albert Schweitzer.

As usual, the range of characters is wide. There is Charlie Morris, a good white American liberal, a reporter who has come to the Mission to do a story on the "good" Reverend; Major George Rice, a soldier, a white settler, who is busy trying to stop the "terrorists" and preserve the nation which he now considers his home; Dr. Willy DeKoven, a doctor who came to the Mission a do-gooder liberal and has become radicalized by his experiences there. There are the blacks: Abioseh Matoseh, Tshembe's brother, who has become a Roman Catholic priest and is a "responsible" Negro; Peter, a black servant at the Mission during the day and a warrior at night; Eric, the half brother of Tshembe and Abioseh, living in anguish because of his mixed blood. The most remarkable character, aside from Tshembe, is Madame Neilsen, the wife of the Reverend, a woman of great humanity who is able to see her husband's paternalism for what it is and yet continue to love him; a woman who is able to understand the need for Tshembe to become a revolutionary and urges him to do so.

Les Blancs is the story of a group of individuals caught in a very particular situation, a situation to which they must respond, regardless of their desire not to. And who they are as human beings will be determined by how they respond to that situation—black liberation.

Tshembe, the black intellectual, is Sidney Brustein's counterpart; but the fact that he is black compounds the intellectual's disease of alienation. He is suspended between the part of him rooted in Africa and the part of him which has set down roots, personal and cultural, in Europe. And, as an intellectual, he resents history's imposing itself on him, demanding that he view himself and his life in terms of the African liberation movement. And he rebels.

> . . . one day, sitting on a bench in Hyde Park—watching the pigeons, naturally—it came to me as it must to all men: I won't come this way again. Enough time will pass and it will be over for me on this little planet! And so I'd better do the things I mean to do. And so I got up from that bench and went to meet the girl I had been wanting to marry but had not, you see, because of—the liberation! The Movement! AH-FREEKA!—and all the rest of it. Well, I was, as Camus would have it . . . a "free man" in that moment because I "chose" freely. *I chose.* And so, you see, it is all over with me and history. This particular atom has discovered himself.

But Tshembe knows that he cannot stand outside history without mutilating himself, and his own sensibilities will not allow him to do that. Like Sidney, he knows that it hurts too much "not to care." There is no way out of the dilemma. He exists, as all of us do, in the chasm between despair and joy. And, unlike most of us, he knows it.

Some of the sharpest and most pointed dialogue Lorraine Hansberry wrote occurs between Charlie Morris, the reporter, and Tshembe. Charlie, like all white liberals, does not want to recognize his share in the collective responsibility for a radically defined society. He insists that he is not all white men, but simply Charlie Morris. And it is on that basis that he wants to have a relationship with Tshembe, unaware that no relationship between a black and a white can be that simple. Tshembe knows that Charlie is a person, an individual in his own right. He also knows, however, that Charlie *is* all white men and, sadly, there is nothing either of them can do about it. Not unless Charlie becomes radicalized. Tshembe does not accept his offer of friendship and Charlie accuses him of hating all whites. Tshembe could resolve it easily by saying Yes. But hating whites is such an easy way out, almost too easy, and Tshembe has too much self-respect to allow himself to take it. If he does, then he allows whites to avoid the confrontation with themselves that they must have. Tshembe recognizes that whites want to be hated, because they can then wallow in their own feelings of guilt, or they can feel justified in expressing in retaliation their hatred of blacks, which was there all the while.

> I shall be honest with you, Mr. Morris. I do not "hate" all white men—but I desperately wish that I did. It would make everything infinitely easier! But I am afraid that, among other things, I have *seen* the slums of Liverpool and Dublin and the caves above Naples. I have *seen* Dachau and Anne Frank's attic in Amsterdam. I have seen too many raw-knuckled Frenchmen coming out of the Metro at dawn and too many pop-eyed Italian children to believe that those who raided Africa for three centuries ever "loved" the white race either. I would like to be simple-minded for you, but—I cannot. I have—*seen*.

Later, Charlie and Tshembe try to communicate with each other again. Charlie accuses Tshembe of being obsessed with race. Tshembe denies it, saying that "racism is a device that, of itself, explains nothing. It is simply a means. An invention to justify the rule of some men over others." Charlie couldn't agree more: "Race hasn't a thing to do with it actually," he exclaims, relieved. The African knows, however, that the American has not understood him; he replies, "Ah—but it *has.*" Charlie throws up his hands in disgust and accuses Tshembe of "playing games." Tshembe responds:

> I am not playing games! I am simply saying that a device is a device, but that it also has consequences: once invented it takes on a life, a reality of its own. So, in one century, men invoke the device of religion to cloak their conquests. In another, race. Now, in both cases you and I may recognize the fraudulence of the device, but the fact remains that a man who has a sword run through him because he refuses to become a Moslem or a Christian—or who is shot in Zatembe or Mississippi because he is black—is suffering the utter *reality* of the device. And it is pointless to pretend that it doesn't *exist*—merely because it is a *lie!*

But Charlie Morris doesn't understand.

The warriors come to Tshembe and tell him that his father, whose funeral he attended the day before, was their organizer and leader. They ask Tshembe to assume that leadership. He refuses, saying, quite simply, ". . . there are men in this world . . . who see too much to take sides." But he has no choice but to take sides. In fact, the decision was made for him long before he was born. History picked his side. Events will force him to acknowledge it.

The climax of the play comes when Abioseh, learning from Tshembe that Peter is a warrior, betrays him and tells Major Rice. The Major comes to the Mission compound and kills Peter in the presence of Tshembe and the whites there. The Major also announces that the body of Reverend Neilsen was found that morning; he has been murdered along with a number of other whites.

In the final scene, Abioseh is sitting with Mme. Neilsen beside Reverend Neilsen's coffin. Tshembe, Eric and a group of warriors come in. Tshembe kills Abioseh, and then, in a burst of gunfire, Mme. Neilsen is killed. Tshembe kneels beside her body, takes it in his arms and "emits an animal-like cry of grief." And the curtain falls.

In the Broadway production, James Earl Jones played the role of Tshembe, and from his performance it is clear that that final cry is more than an expression of sorrow by Tshembe for the woman who taught him in school and was the mother of his other self. Tshembe cries for her, for himself, for his brother, whom he has just murdered. He cries because it *had* to be, all of it, and there was nothing anyone could do. He cries, knowing that when History makes one group of people victims, the time will eventually come when the victims will become the executioners. And when that time comes, the guilty and the guiltless will die indiscriminately. It is not right. It is not just. But that is the way it is. Tshembe cries, not for one old white woman, but for the blindness of Man, which is responsible for the needless deaths that have been and will be. But unlike the liberal who only cries, Tshembe has acted and will act again. If lamentation is one's only response to injustice, then one indulges in self-pity, an act of indulgence which, at a certain point, will not be tolerated. Tshembe's cry is not one of pity, but of anger and sorrow.

Lorraine Hansberry had no illusions about revolution. She had no illusions about people. In some way or another, all of the characters in *Les Blancs* have a little of the truth. None of them are all bad or all good. We must recognize both the humanity and inhumanity of Major Rice as well as of Peter. But, above all, we must recognize that the necessity of black liberation takes command of the lives of its bearers and its victims. And, because it does, one "emits an animal-like cry of grief." One does not glorify or romanticize revolution. One cries.

Les Blancs is no catharsis for bloodthirsty blacks or masochistic whites. One leaves it with a profound sorrow in the soul. Yet because of the magnificent examples of humanity in Tshembe and Madame Neilsen, one also leaves saying Yes, that is the way it is and, maybe, I have a little more strength to accept it now. Tshembe does what he must and kills his brother. Madame Neilsen, whose husband has just been killed by warriors, tells Tshembe, "Our country *needs* warriors." Both of them are people who "see too much to take sides," but they do, never ceasing to see too much.

It is a masterful play, an almost pure distillation of Lorraine Hansberry's personal/political philosophy. My God, how we need her today! She knew that politics was not ideology, but caring. Politics is that quality of becoming more and more human, of persuading, cajoling, begging, and loving others to get them to go with you on that journey to be human—and defending yourself against those who seek to prevent that journey.

Perhaps the greatest irony is that so much humanity should have come from the life and work of a black woman. Then again, it is quite logical. She had been tempered by the fire and emerged briefly to let her own light shine. She knew that blackness was the basis of her existence, not the totality, and that if it becomes the whole, one can only be consumed by the fires of one's own rage and frustration. Lorraine Hansberry is the black artist who lived beyond anger, which is not to say that she wasn't angry. Her plays are an expression of rage against the outrages perpetrated against humanity. Anger did not define her art, but motivated and informed it. The quality which pervades her plays is compassion, the kind of compassion which can slap a face as easily as it can kiss a cheek, which can curse as easily as it can tease. She didn't make the mistake of hating white people. She hated what people did to each other.

She stands as the quintessential model, not only for her vision, but for her skill and integrity in the expression of that vision. Man's relationship to his time was her theme and she described that time, the many relationships people had to it, and the way people could respond to it. That was Lorraine Hansberry, and a young, gifted and black writer could do no better than to set himself the goal of being worthy of this woman.

Julius Lester

Les Blancs

A CRITICAL BACKGROUND

"Some ancestor of mine came from that self-
same coast I trust and begat with some Eng-
lishman who was a blacksmith I hear. Thus—
my English name—and 'my African loyalty.' "

—LORRAINE HANSBERRY,
notes on the anniversary of
Ghanaian independence

I do not know when, specifically, Lorraine Hansberry's
abiding interest in Africa began, but it is certain that by the
time I met her she was, at twenty-one, one of a handful of
Americans who could be said to be truly knowledgeable in
the subject. Africa had been a conscious part of her almost
as far back as consciousness itself. And this was no accident.

She remembered vividly seeing newsreels of the Italian
conquest of Ethiopia when she was five, and crying over
them and, when the Pope blessed Mussolini's soldiers, being
told by her mother "never to forget what Catholicism stood
for." She recalled hours as a girl spent "postulating and
fantasizing . . . over maps of the African continent." In an
unfinished partly autobiographical novel she wrote:

In her emotions she was sprung from the Southern Zulu and
the Central Pygmy, the Eastern Watusi and the treacherous

35

slave-trading Western Ashanti themselves. She was Kikuyu and Masai, ancient cousins of hers had made the exquisite forged sculpture at Benin, while surely even more ancient relatives sat upon the throne at Abu Simbel watching over the Nile. . . .

She recalled studying news photos out of modern Africa and turning to the mirror—"searching, searching for a generality." But Lorraine said of the heroine: "She did not find it and therefore did the next best thing: she embraced *all* Africa as the homeland."

It is possible that her earliest serious influence in this regard was that of her uncle, William Leo Hansberry, one of the world's foremost scholars of African antiquity, whose preeminence is only now beginning to emerge out of imposed academic darkness as the once Dark Continent itself moves toward the center of world events. Through Professor Hansberry's classes and living room in the nineteen forties passed such students as Nnamdi Azikewe, first president of Nigeria, Kwame Nkrumah of Ghana, and others soon to become the founders and leaders of new African nations. In 1963, Nigeria dedicated the new Hansberry College of African Studies at Nsakka in honor of Professor Hansberry.

In 1951 Lorraine Hansberry was a young woman on fire with black liberation not only here but in Africa, an insurgent with a vision that embraced two continents—and notebooks filled with jottings like the following:

> Sometimes in this country maybe just walking down a Southside street. . . .
> Or maybe suddenly up in a Harlem window. . . .

Or maybe in a flash turning the page of one of those
picture books from the South you will see it—
Beauty . . . stark and full. . . .
No part of something this—but rather, Africa, simply
Africa. These thighs and arms and flying wingèd cheek-
bones, these hallowed eyes—without negation or apol-
ogy. . . .
A classical people demand a classical art.

She was voracious reader of everything in African studies
she could lay her hands on: such works as Jomo Kenyatta's
great sociological study of the Kikuyu, *Facing Mt. Kenya*;
Melville J. Herskovits' *The Myth of the Negro Past*; W. E.
B. Du Bois' *Black Folk Then and Now*; Lorenzo D. Turner's
Africanisms in the Gullah Dialect, which traced the survivals
of West African languages in the Carolina and Georgia Sea
Islands; and Basil Davidson's *Lost Cities of Africa*, which
described the great civilizations that were to surface in
Beneatha Younger's brash (but factual) announcement in *A
Raisin in the Sun* that her "people . . . were the first to smelt
iron on the face of the earth . . . performing surgical operations when the English were still tatooing themselves with
blue dragons!"
At the time, she was completing a year's seminar on
African history under Dr. Du Bois, who, among his innu-
merable accomplishments, was the father of Pan-African-
ism, the man who, as a disillusioned delegate to the
Versailles Peace Conference, initiated the first world Pan-
African Congresses. Under Du Bois' tutelage, she wrote a
research paper on "The Belgian Congo: A Preliminary Report on Its Land, Its History and Its Peoples." References

in *Les Blancs* to "chopping off the right hands of our young men by the hundreds, by the tribe" were, in fact, based upon the actual "preventive" methods King Leopold employed to eliminate resistance. And when in the play she mentions Stanley and Livingstone, the point of reference was not characters seen in a movie, but in Stanley's case a man whose work she had actually studied.*

As first a reporter, then associate editor, of Paul Robeson's monthly, *Freedom*, Lorraine shared offices in the early fifties in the building at 53 W. 125th Street, with, among other instrumentalities of the black freedom struggle in that day, the Council on African Affairs, and thus found herself a frequent close working associate of such men as Du Bois, W. Alpheus Hunton, Director of the Council, and Robeson himself. Through the offices of *Freedom* and into our home in those years (and after) came incredible young men and women, exiles from South Africa and the Rhodesias, exchange students from Kenya, the Gold Coast (as colonial Ghana was known then), Sierra Leone and Nigeria, not a few of whom were to become leaders in the fight for independence, and some no doubt to die in colonial prisons. And often we would find ourselves by their sides on picket lines before the United Nations or one or another European consulate in protest of South Africa's Sharpeville massacre, the French war in Algeria, or—uppermost in all our minds in those days—the British campaign in Kenya, where mass

*The bibliography included Sir H. M. Stanley's *The Founding of the Congo Free State*, as well as such works as Sir Harry Johnston's *George Grenfell and the Congo*, Guy Burrows' *The Curse of Central Africa*, the Belgian Tourist Bureau's *A Traveler's Guide to the Belgian Congo and Ruanda Urundi*, and *Belgian Colonial Policy* by Albert de Vleeschauer, Colonial Minister of Belgium.

concentration camps, terror bombing and the strafing and burning of villages were employed a dozen years before Vietnam. Lorraine was a close observer of the five-month trial of Jomo Kenyatta, spokesman of the demand for land restitution and self-government in Kenya. At street-corner meetings in Harlem, as in the pages of *Freedom* and frequent letters to the press, she questioned whether the trial, and in fact the entire British campaign, was in fact directed at the sporadic and, until Kenyatta's arrest, quite isolated incidents of so-called "Mau-Mau" terror (as Lorraine would point out, the words "Mau-Mau" do not exist in any East African language), or at Kenyatta's powerful and fast growing Kenya-African union, whose mass public meetings were attracting hundreds of thousands in the months preceeding his incarceration. She circulated petitions for Kenyatta's release from banishment to a remote desert village, and later shared with the visiting Tom Mboya her sense of triumph when Kenyatta at last stepped from exile to the prime ministership of his nation.

I remember how odd it seemed to some in those early years to hear Lorraine talk with absolute certainty of the "coming" upsurge for independence. For in those days not much had changed in a continent that seemed as Dark and remote from twentieth-century revolution as ever. There was occasional talk of plebiscites, promised in unheard of places and, of course, the wars in Kenya and Algeria—about which Albert Camus was predicting, in the unthinkable event of independence, "a land of ruins and dead which no force, no power in the world, will be capable of reviving in this century." But apart from that, not much. The African in shirt and tie, much less with gun or Constitution or governmental robes, remained an "exotic" stranger on Western horizons, while few indeed were those Americans, black or white, who linked their destiny to Africa.

Thus, when *A Raisin in the Sun* opened in 1959, it must have puzzled many—though not those who knew the author —that out of the lips of a Southside chauffeur in his first moment of envisioned (if drunken) grandeur on the Broadway stage, should suddenly spurt the call to greatness of an African chieftain to his "Black Brothers . . . [who] meet in council for the coming of the mighty war!" Or that the chauffeur's teen-age sister should march on stage in a full-fledged Afro. Or that, most baffling of all, into their ghetto tenement home should stride an African student with talk-dreams of "freedom," "revolution," and the solidarity of colored peoples—to sweep the sister off her feet and become, in the process, the playwright's most articulate spokesman.

But *Raisin* was only the precursor. For, two weeks before it opened, Lorraine Hansberry, in her first formal public address as a writer, defined the course that, for her, lay ahead:

> . . . more than anything else, the compelling obligation of the Negro writer, as writer and citizen of life, is participation in the intellectual affairs of all men, everywhere. The foremost enemy of the Negro intelligentsia of the past has been and in a large sense remains—isolation. . . . The unmistakable roots of the universal solidarity of the colored peoples of the world are no longer "predictable" as they were in my father's time—they are here. And I for one, as a black woman in the United States in the mid-Twentieth Century, feel that I am more typical of the present temperament of my people than

not, when I say that I cannot allow the devious purposes of white supremacy to lead me to any conclusion other than what may be the most robust and important one of our time: that the ultimate destiny and aspirations of the African peoples and twenty million American Negroes are inextricably and magnificently bound up together forever.

From these words to *Les Blancs*—the first major work by a black American playwright to focus on Africa and the struggle for black liberation—the path was inevitable.

Les Blancs first began to form in the playwright's mind sometime in the late spring or summer of 1960. Her earliest workbook jottings refer to "the return of Candace for her mother's funeral" and the confrontation between her brothers Shembe (as she spelled it then) and Abioseh over the funeral. (Interestingly, "Candace" was also the name she gave the heroine of her semiautobiographical novel *All the Dark and Beautiful Warriors*.) The notes indicate that Tshembe was a committed revolutionary as first conceived; they describe a confrontation with an American newspaperman, and conclude with a projected scene in which Eric, the youngest brother, "chooses Shembe and with sister blows up Mission—and the past."

It was not, however, until May 1961 that the elements began to move into focus and the play to find its final shape and title. This was in immediate visceral response to Jean Genêt's celebrated drama *Les Nègres (The Blacks)*, which had its American premiere that month. The title was chosen half in jest, for the work-in-progress bore no direct relation to the Frenchman's tour de force, not in style or technique, nor certainly in the events and characters depicted. Yet the pun masked a deeper concern. More than anything else, she considered *The Blacks* "a conversation between white men about themselves." A *needed* conversation perhaps, important in that for the first time it dared to face the depths of the problem and the hatred which three hundred years of the rape of Africa had produced. But nonetheless a conversation haunted by guilt, and too steeped in the romance of racial exoticism to shed much light on the real confrontation that was coming:

> The problem in the world is the oppression of man by *man;* it is this which threatens existence. And it is this which Genêt evades with an abstraction: an elaborate legend utilized to affirm, indeed, entrench, the quite *different* nature of pain, lust, cruelty, ambition presumed to exist in the blacks. . . .

> In *The Blacks* the oppressed remain *unique.* The Blacks remain the exotic in "The Blacks." And we are spared thereby the ultimate anguish—of *man's* oppression of man.

Whereas:

> To have had to deal with *human beings* . . . would have been to confront Guilt with a greater imperative: the necessity for action—that is, to *do* something about it. The too easy purgation of the Whites—self-condemning and self-absolving—the untouched remoteness of the Blacks—would be nullified by a drama wherein we were *all* forced to confrontation and awareness.

In *Les Blancs*, Lorraine undertook to write that drama. As much as anything in life, and increasingly in these years, she felt the urgent need for dialogue and concerted action if the coming struggle for power in the world, the struggle for liberation, were not to degenerate into, in effect, a racial war.

It is part of the point of *Les Blancs* that, in spite of the three hundred years, men must talk; they must establish a dialogue whose purpose is neither procrastination nor ego-fulfillment but clarity, and whose culminating point is action: to find the means, in an age of revolution, to reduce the cost in human sacrifice and make the transition as swift and painless as possible.

At the turn of the century, Du Bois had written the words which ironically undergird and echo through every agonizing moment of contemporary history: "The problem of the Twentieth Century is the problem of the color line." *Les Blancs* was an effort to examine in dramatic terms—in terms of individual human responsibility—precisely what that meant. It was an effort to come to grips on the highest possible level with the problem of color and colonialism not just here in America, not even in Africa, but on a world scale: to determine to what degree color was—and was *not* —the root cause of the conflict. And thus to confront head-on the impending crisis between the capitalist West and the Third World.

Lorraine considered *Les Blancs* to be potentially her most important play and hoped originally that it might precede *The Sign in Sidney Brustein's Window* to the stage. Yet though a number of drafts were written, the strict demands of craftsmanship sufficient to the theme were, in her eyes, not satisfied.

In 1963, what was to remain essentially Act One, Scene Three, was staged for the Actors Studio Writers' Workshop by Arthur Penn, with Roscoe Lee Browne as Tshembe, Arthur Hill as Charlie, Rosemary Murphy as Marta and Pearl Primus as the Woman Dancer. The stunned response of the audience of actors and writers—I am told it was one of the most extraordinary sessions ever held at the Studio—confirmed some of her doubts. A good deal remained to be done.

At the same time, Africa itself was changing from what had been yesterday's dreams into today's reality. Clearly this did not affect the perspective, but it did change the shadings, bringing to the fore, for example, conflicts of method between the capitals of Europe and the white settlers of Africa, and putting into bolder relief internal antagonisms among the blacks as the struggle for formal independence, once achieved, became transformed into a more fundamental struggle for control of one's own economy, resources, destiny. The character Abioseh loomed larger in the scales as the death of Lumumba in the Congo, and the rise of men like Moise Tshombe, Kasavubu and Mobuto, made inescapable what had always been implicit: the tenacity of Western capital interests and the fact that blacks could be as opportunistic and dangerous in serving them as whites.

All through her last year and a half, then, as *Sidney Brustein* proceeded toward production, Lorraine kept at *Les Blancs*—at the typewriter when she could, in notes and discussion when she couldn't. She carried the manuscript with her into and out of hospitals—polishing, pondering, rethinking a scene here, refining a relationship there, but above all, seeking a multileveled structure, taut yet flexible enough to contain and focus the complexity of personalities, social forces and ideas in this world she had created. In her last working months she cracked the problem to her own satisfaction and outlined in our discussions (during these sessions, I acted as soundingboard-advocate-critic) the major structural and character developments she envisioned. After her death, as literary executor, I continued the work: synthesizing the scenes already completed throughout the play with those in progress, drawing upon relevant fragments from earlier drafts and creating, as needed, dialogue of my own to bridge gaps, deepen relationships or tighten the drama along the lines we had explored together.

In 1966, a preliminary draft was completed. Then, as the play moved toward production, I was fortunate in having the assistance of a number of friends and associates whose critical and creative contributions proved invaluable: Ossie Davis, actor, playwright, activist, who worked with me in preparation for a first—and as it turned out, abortive—production; Charlotte Zaltzberg, who came as a secretary but, in short order, became an incisive collaborator in the preparation of all of Lorraine's work for production and publication; Konrad Matthaei, the producer who, with his wife Gay, brought the play to the stage out of a deep and unstinting belief in what it had to say; Joseph Stein, author of *Fiddler on the Roof*, whose vast skill helped to solve crucial problems in the final weeks of production; Sidney Walters, the director who cast the play, gave it its overall look and interpretation and was responsible for some of its most memorable moments; and John Berry, the director who brought tremendous vitality and artistry to the process of compression and heightening out of which the play emerged in its final form on stage.*

Somewhere in these pages each of these individuals has left his mark. Yet, except in the sense that all theater is—to one degree or another—collaborative, neither their contributions nor my own should obscure the paramount fact that *Les Blancs* in its conception, characters, events and ideas, its most penetrating speeches, the great bulk of its dialogue —and in the vision that informs it throughout—is the work of Lorraine Hansberry.

Robert Nemiroff

*It should be noted that, for reading purposes at least, the present edition restores some materials which—to better serve the overall concept—were not included in the Broadway production.

LES BLANCS:

THE COLLECTED LAST PLAYS

OF LORRAINE HANSBERRY

"If there is no struggle there is no progress. Those who profess to favor freedom and yet deprecate agitation, are men who want crops without plowing up the ground, they want rain without thunder and lightning. They want the ocean without the awful roar of its many waters.

"This struggle may be a moral one, or it may be a physical one, and it may be both moral and physical, but it must be a struggle. Power concedes nothing without a demand. It never did and it never will. Find out just what any people will quietly submit to and you have found out the exact measure of injustice and wrong which will be imposed upon them, and these will continue till they are resisted with either words or blows, or with both . . . Men may not get all they pay for in this world, but they must certainly pay for all they get. If we ever get free from the oppressions and wrongs heaped upon us, we must pay for their removal. We must do that by labor, by suffering, by sacrifice, and if needs be, by our lives and the lives of others."

—Frederick Douglass

"But what exactly is a black?
First of all, what's his color?"
—Jean Genet

LES BLANCS *was first presented by Konrad Matthaei at the Longacre Theatre, New York City, on November 15, 1970, with the following cast:*

THE WOMAN	Joan Derby
AFRICAN VILLAGERS (AND WARRIORS)	Dennis Tate
	George Fairley
	Bill Ware
	Joan Derby
	Charles Moore
DR. MARTA GOTTERLING	Marie Andrews
AFRICAN CHILD	Gregory Beyer
PETER	Clebert Ford
CHARLIE MORRIS	Cameron Mitchell
DR. WILLY DEKOVEN	Humbert Allen Astredo
MAJOR GEORGE RICE	Ralph Purdum
SOLDIERS	Garry Mitchell
	Gwyllum Evans
PRISONER	Bill Ware
MADAME NEILSEN	Lili Darvas
ERIC	Harold Scott
TSHEMBE MATOSEH	James Earl Jones
ABIOSEH MATOSEH	Earle Hyman
OLD MAN	Dennis Tate
NGAGO	George Fairley

Final Text Adapted by   ROBERT NEMIROFF
Directed by   JOHN BERRY
Scenery Designed by   PETER LARKIN
Costumes Designed by   JANE GREENWOOD
Lighting Designed by   NEIL PETER JAMPOLIS
Ritual Dances Created by   LOUIS JOHNSON
Sound Created by   JACK SHEARING
Script Associate   CHARLOTTE ZALTZBERG
Drummers   LADJI CAMARA, CHARLES PAYNE
Production Stage Manager   MARTIN GOLD
General Manager   PAUL B. BERKOWSKY

ACT ONE
PROLOGUE

Five minutes before curtain time the sounds of the African bush are heard stereophonically around the audience from the sides and rear. They begin quite softly, sounds of crickets, frogs and "bush-babies." The stage is open, and a cyclorama, enveloping the entire stage, is seen emanating a gray-green glow which is African twilight. During the next five minutes the cyc will gradually change to deep blue-black with an occasional star.

The sounds of the bush grow louder and, after about three minutes, we hear drums, at first sporadic, from speakers on the sides being answered by drums on the other sides. These are not at all the traditional "movie drums" but distinct, erratic and varied statements of mood and intent. They get louder and just before curtain, as the houselights go to black, they reach a crescendo which moves up through the audience with a rush to the speakers on stage.

Suddenly there is silence. A WOMAN *dancer is seen suspended in the sky in a characteristic African dance pose. Black-skinned and imposing, cheeks painted for war, her wiry hair rounded by a colorful band, she wears only a leather skirt and, about her waist, a girdle of hammered silver. From her wrists and ankles hang bangles of feathers and silver. Before her, planted in the earth, rests a spear.*

As the sound of the bush reasserts itself, we hear the unearthly "laughter" of a hyena—three times. The WOMAN *begins to move in place to slowly mounting staccato drumbeats, her focus on the spear. At the climax, she pulls it from the earth with great strength and raises it high in symbolic appeal to resistance.*

Blackout

ACT ONE
SCENE 1

*In the darkness the sound of a river-boat whistle is heard
several times in the distance and—abruptly—brilliant, almost blinding sunlight envelops the stage, and the sky turns
intense blue.*

It is mid-afternoon at a Mission compound in Africa.

On the veranda down left, DR. MARTA GOTTERLING *is
examining a small black boy. She is a handsome, blond,
self-assured woman in her mid-thirties, in surgical gown,
white headcloth and stethoscope. Down right several* AFRI-
CAN VILLAGERS *squat in the dust awaiting their turn.*

PETER *enters from over a rise up right, followed by* CHARL-
IE MORRIS. PETER, *an African porter in shorts and undershirt,
is a man of middle years, with graying hair and a profoundly
subservient manner. He is barefoot, bareheaded and carries
two heavy valises.* CHARLIE *is an American in his late forties.
He wears a pith helmet and carries a battered portable typewriter and attaché case.*

As they come on, CHARLIE *hangs back the least bit, as if
to fix the scene in memory.* PETER *goes directly up the
Mission steps at center and sets the valises down with relief.*

PETER (*Singsongy*)   You wait here, Bwana. You sit, make
self cool. Doctor be with you soon.

(CHARLIE *notes the man's excessive subservience with disapproval and hauls out a couple of coins*)

CHARLIE   All right, thanks . . . er—?

PETER   Peter, Bwana.

CHARLIE   Thanks, Peter.

MARTA (*Calling out—she is listening to the* AFRICAN CHILD*'s chest*)   Hello there. I shall be with you in a moment.

PETER   You sit, be cool. (CHARLIE *pays him and he backs away, out the door and down the steps*) Thank you, thank you, Bwana! Doctor be with you soon. Soon, Bwana. Thank you.

CHARLIE   Yes, I'm sure. Thank you. Thank you. (*As the man disappears*) Peter, old man, you have seen one "Bwana" movie too many.
       (*He crosses onto the veranda*)

MARTA (*Looking up*)   Mr. Morris? We've been expecting you. I'm Dr. Gotterling. Marta Gotterling. Welcome to the Mission. (*To the boy—examining his eyes, ears, throat during the following*) Open up.

CHARLIE   All the comforts of the Mayo Clinic.

MARTA   Not quite.

CHARLIE   What's wrong with the boy?

MARTA   Just a little tonsillitis.

CHARLIE   That all? I don't know why I'm surprised. I suppose I was expecting a rare tropical disease!

MARTA (*Smiling*)   Rare tropical diseases are also rare in the tropics! I'm sorry Reverend Neilsen isn't here to greet you. He had to go cross river.
(*She gives the boy an injection and a comforting pat*)

CHARLIE   Oh? Too bad. Well, I'll be here for a while. I want to really get to know this place before I start putting words on paper. What's happening cross river?

MARTA   Among other things, a wedding, a funeral, twelve baptisms . . .

CHARLIE   Twelve—that's rather a handful even for the Reverend, isn't it?

MARTA (*Smiles*)   They are done *one* at a time, Mr. Morris! (*Leads the boy across to one of the* AFRICANS *and holds up a vial of pills*) Give him this three times a day. (*Indicating with fingers*) Three—day. Any first impressions, Mr. Morris?
(*She motions the next patient to follow her*)

CHARLIE   Well, yes. I was a little curious . . . Isn't the —(*He hesitates*)—lack of sanitation here somewhat of a problem?

MARTA (*Smiling matter-of-factly*)   "Sanitation," Mr. Morris? We're not that sensitive. You mean the dung—goat dung? (*She takes the patient's pulse*) Actually it's less of a problem than too *much* sanitation. Here we have to give up some things for others. The African feels much more at home with goats and chickens wandering about the wards. It's the only way they'd come. (*To the patient*)

57

Breathe in. Out. (*He doesn't understand; she demonstrates and he follows suit—making a great show of it*) Please help yourself to a drink, Mr. Morris. It's right there.

CHARLIE   Thanks, I can use it.
(*He pours one and looks about uncertainly*)

MARTA   Sorry, no ice.

CHARLIE (*Remembering*)   Of course. No refrigeration . . .

MARTA (*With curious pride*)   That's right, Mr. Morris. No electricity, no phones, no television, no movies . . .

CHARLIE (*He drinks a good one and, closing his eyes, leans his head back and savors*)   When you've been traveling a day and a half without a drink there's nothing as good as Scotch—without ice!
(*An* AFRICAN *runs on, whispers to the* AFRICAN *being examined, and both suddenly run off, followed by the others*)

MARTA   Wait!

CHARLIE   What was that?

MARTA (*Shrugs*)   Mr. Morris, I've been here five years and I'm afraid I still have a great deal to learn about the African.

CHARLIE   Well, you've got the best possible teacher. It's been my impression—in fact, the world's impression—that Reverend Neilsen is practically one of the natives himself by now.

MARTA   Not really one of them. More like their father. Like our father, too. We are *all* his children.

CHARLIE   What's he like, Doctor?

MARTA   What's he like? He's a good man. When Reverend Neilsen came here forty years ago, he came with a particular great idea: here the native should feel that the hospital and the church are a part of the jungle, an extension of his own villages. If you are open-minded, you will learn what he has done here—and be deeply rewarded. I can promise you that. I know, because—

CHARLIE (*Finishing it for her*)   —because *you* have been. Doctor, you give me the extraordinary impression of being a happy woman.

MARTA (*Lightly*)   Yes. Something went "wrong" in my life, Mr. Morris: it has been unutterably satisfying!

CHARLIE (*Smiling knowingly*)   I've come a long—long way to hear those words. (*Moving about, absorbing the scene*) What makes some men do it, Doctor? What makes some men do what the rest of us spend our lives thinking we should do and don't? Do you know what this place is? You're probably so used to it you don't even think about it. It's a temple: a way station in the darkness. Nobody really believes that such things even exist any more. And you know something? Until I came paddling down that river I didn't even know that I had stopped believing it either. (*Quizzically, softly*) But you people *are* here, aren't you? You really are . . .

(DR. WILLY DEKOVEN *enters, a slight, deeply browned man in surgical dress, without pith helmet*)

DEKOVEN   Marta—

MARTA   Oh, Willy, good. (*She pronounces the "W" in middle-European fashion—with a "V" sound*) This is Mr. Morris from the United States. Dr. DeKoven.

DEKOVEN   How do you do? Would you have a look at Keito, Marta? I would like your opinion.

MARTA (*Starting out quickly*) Of course. (*To* CHARLIE, *charmingly: a hostess as much as a surgeon*) Excuse me. I know you don't believe it, but we really will send someone sooner or later to show you to your room.
    (*Without warning there are several loud rifle shots offstage. They spin around*)

CHARLIE   What the hell was that?

DEKOVEN (*Sharply, taking several steps in the direction of the shots*) That was no more than a hundred yards away—
    (MARTA *stiffens and closes her eyes and as promptly regains composure*)

MARTA   I'll see to Keito.
    (*She exits.* MAJOR RICE *enters hurriedly—a Colonial Reserve Officer in his fifties*)

DEKOVEN   What were those shots, Major?

RICE (*To* CHARLIE)   Who are you?

DEKOVEN (*Performing the introductions*) Major Rice of the Colonial Reserve. Mr. Morris, from the United States.

RICE   Oh, Mr. Morris. I have been looking forward to this. How do you do, sir?
(*Extending his hand*)

CHARLIE   How do you do? What's going on, Major?

RICE (*Ignoring the question*)   Come to do a piece on *our* "New World," eh? No place on earth like it.

CHARLIE   I'm beginning to believe that. What's happening here?

RICE   Is the Reverend about?

DEKOVEN   No, he went cross river. What were those shots, Major?

RICE   We flushed out a couple of terrorists in the bush. I think one used to work around here.

CHARLIE (*Incredulous*)   Terrorists—*here?* We've had no news—

DEKOVEN (*Dryly*)   The authorities think it helps for some reason if the world doesn't hear about it.

CHARLIE   It's not just—well—an outbreak of banditry or something?

RICE (*Cutting it short*)   One tends to think not, Mr. Morris, if nothing is stolen. And nothing is. Except whatever guns there are. (SOLDIERS *enter, leading a prisoner with a long rope about the neck—his mouth gagged, face bloodied—whom they throw to the ground*) I'd appreciate your help in this, Doctor.

DEKOVEN (*With sudden sharpness*)   You know better, Major!

RICE   This one—(*Jerking the prisoner's head around*)—I believe he's worked here, isn't that right?

DEKOVEN   I really couldn't say.

RICE   Or wouldn't?

DEKOVEN (*Evenly*)   I don't know the man, Major.

RICE (*Furious*)   I hope that we don't all have the enormously illuminating experience of being butchered in our beds thanks to those like you, Dr. DeKoven! (*He motions to the* SOLDIERS *to take the man off. They exit*) As you can see, Mr. Morris, we've got a bit of an emergency going here. May I ask that you let me have a look at any dispatches you send out? You understand, I'm sure.

CHARLIE   No, I'm afraid I don't.

RICE   All the same, would you mind?

CHARLIE   Yes, I would mind.

RICE (*Stiffening*)   Well—I hope you enjoy your visit.
       (*He exits*)

CHARLIE   What will they do to him?

DEKOVEN (*A meaningful shrug.* CHARLIE *stares at him horrified*)   Mr. Morris, there is a *war* going on here. Everyone else that you talk to will call it a bit of an emergency, pacification, police action—I'm sure your country is familiar with such phrases? But I assure you that what we have here is a war.

CHARLIE   And what about—the leader of the independence movement? . . . Kumalo?

DEKOVEN Kumalo?

(*Offstage* MAJOR RICE *'s jeep starts up and roars off*)

CHARLIE Well, it's been my impression that the West was using its head for a change—here. I mean Amos Kumalo *is* still in Europe? They *are* talking?

DEKOVEN Oh, yes. They are talking.

CHARLIE Then why—just when some hope for progress—

DEKOVEN Progress, Mr. Morris? For *whom?* The settlers are outraged because the Foreign Office is talking at all—and the blacks, because talk is no longer enough. Kumalo—

(*They are interrupted as an old woman in antiquated European dress, leaning heavily on a cane and supported by* MARTA, *is ushered on from behind the Mission up left. She is fragile in appearance, genteel in manner; underneath there is sharp intelligence*)

MADAME NEILSEN Willy? Where are you? (DEKOVEN *rises and holds out an arm which she leans upon in the manner of the badly sighted*) Ah, yes, it is you. Who do you suppose has been butchered today, Willy?

MARTA We have a guest, Madame.

MADAME (*Her face lighting*) Oh, so? Where indeed is the guest?

DEKOVEN (*Gestures for* CHARLIE *to come nearer*) Mr. Morris is going to visit with us for a while.

CHARLIE It's a great honor, Madame Neilsen.

MADAME   Mr. Morris—Mr. *Charles* Morris. You have come to write about us. How nice. How very nice. I know your work well. Now I shall come to know you. Marta, darling, I must sit.
>   (DEKOVEN *and* MARTA *help her to the couch. Congo drums of basso intensity start up offstage*)

CHARLIE   What's that—?

DEKOVEN (*Smiling*)   *All* drums are not war drums . . . Not yet.

MADAME (*To herself*)   No, not war drums at all . . . Marta, you and Willy can get back to your work. Mr. Morris and I will be able to entertain each other nicely, I am sure.

MARTA   Very well. (*To* CHARLIE, *looking about*) Sooner or later Eric will finally be here to see to you.
>   (MARTA *exits*)

MADAME   Yes, first will come the liquor fumes and then will come Eric.

DEKOVEN (*At the door*)   The boy can't help it! Why must you pick after him about it!

MADAME   No, he can't help it any more than you can help giving it to him, can he—my dear, tortured Dr. DeKoven!

MARTA (*Plaintively*)   Madame!

DEKOVEN   I'm sorry.
>   (*He turns and exits abruptly and* MARTA *follows*)

MADAME   It is wrong of me to taunt Willy. He is a good man. Willy DeKoven is among the best of men, Mr. Morris.

CHARLIE   But I take it, he has a weakness for slipping a little liquor to the natives.

MADAME   Well—he doesn't give it to the natives—he gives it to Eric, which is something of a different matter. (CHARLIE *is, of course, confused by this*) Well, Mr. Morris, I am so sorry that you had to come at such an unhappy time. And now, the drums announce a funeral. Someone important has died.

CHARLIE   Oh, you can read the drums?

MADAME   Oh, mercy yes! In the old days, I used to spend most of my hours with the women of this village. With Aquah in particular. Yes, Aquah. She was the dearest friend that I have had in Africa. It was she who taught me the drums and to speak the language of the Kwi people. I taught her a little English in return and a smattering of French. We were just getting on to Norwegian when she died. Dear Aquah! (*She saddens and then lightens again*) We used to go for long walks in the woods.

CHARLIE   (*Smiling incredulously*)   You went strolling in that jungle out there with only a native woman?

MADAME   Heavens yes. We used to pick herbs and berries —Aquah taught me how to make quinine. Do you know how to make quinine, Mr. Morris? It is a wonderful thing to be able to know how to do. Of course, I taught her a few things too. (*Leaning over and whispering a little devilishy*) Certain matters concerning feminine hygiene, you know . . . And then the change came.

CHARLIE   What change?

MADAME   The change. Some cold wind blew in over our people here and chilled their hearts to us. It is the times, you know. I'm afraid he'll never understand it—the Reverend. And what hurt him most was that Abioseh was the first to change. Old Abioseh, the husband of Aquah, my friend—a truly remarkable man. First Abioseh—and after him the village—then the tribe. Oh, they still come to the clinic, some of them. But to this day, virtually no Kwi attend Reverend Neilsen's services. In almost seven years I have not set foot in a hut in this village. (*Sadly*) And today someone important has died and no one has come to tell me. For a few years Aquah's children came. But they have grown up and gone away and now—no one comes. (*A young boy appears behind the Mission up left and looks quickly about to make certain he is unobserved: a sodden, fairskinned youth in the late teens, in shorts, filthy undershirt and sneakers, and—incongruously—a clean white pith helmet.* MADAME *stiffens and stares straight ahead*) Now, sir, "Caliban" is almost upon us. He has turned on the generator and now the river breeze tells me—(*He crosses swiftly to a tree stump down right*)—he is crossing the compound to make certain—(*He looks from right to left, stoops and reaches into the tree stump*)—that Dr. DeKoven has left him a bottle. (*He comes up with the bottle, drinks, recaps and replaces it, and heads for the Mission*) This, sir, is Eric.

ERIC (*In the door*) I am here, Madame.

MADAME (*Without turning her head*) Eric. Show Mr. Morris to his room.

CHARLIE Hello, Eric.

ERIC Mr. Morris.
(*Manipulating his pith helmet under his arm, he picks up the American's bags and exits left.* CHARLIE *is about to follow when* MME. NEILSEN *takes his arm*)

MADAME I shall think you an exceedingly poor journalist, Mr. Morris, if you allow me to believe that you are in the least confounded by either the name or the complexion of our Eric. (*Settling back with finality*) Now I have said enough. Now I shall sit on the veranda and merely be quiet and old and invalid, and leave the world to its deceptions. (CHARLIE *looks at her, hesitates—and is about to speak, when:*) I'm sure your room is ready, Mr. Morris.
(CHARLIE *exits. The old lady sits staring dead ahead*)

Dimout

ACT ONE
SCENE 2

Dusk. The Matoseh hut.

As the lights slowly darken in the parlor, they come up on a Kwi hut down right, the great house of an elder. ERIC *sits on a mat with a bottle before him. He drinks a good one, adjusts his pith helmet and studies himself in a hand mirror as he whistles an African tune. Offstage the drums are constant.*

Over the rise up left comes TSHEMBE MATOSEH, *a handsome young African in worn and rumpled city clothes, his tie loosened, jacket slung over his shoulder, a traveling bag in one hand. At center, he sets it down, wipes his brow, then hearing the whistle comes up behind* ERIC *and joins in the tune.*

ERIC (*Looking up with startled apprehension and joy*)
Tshembe! You came!

> (TSHEMBE *throws his arms together straight out over his head and claps three times in the Kwi "sign" of greeting.* ERIC *reciprocates and the two brothers embrace*)

TSHEMBE   Where is my father?

ERIC   He died last night.

TSHEMBE (*He crosses away to look out at the dying sun*) So I missed the last goodbyes.

ERIC (*Slips the mirror out of sight*)   Each day for a month I told him you would come and then last night he no longer believed.

TSHEMBE   "Sons, sons: hurry, hurry. Do not dawdle—(*A man deeply moved*)—or you will miss your last goodbyes."

ERIC   When I wrote you, I didn't think that you would come at all.

TSHEMBE   As the whites say: There are ties that bind. There are ties that bind. (*A beat*) Where is our brother?

ERIC   We never see Abioseh any more. After you went away, he went off to St. Cyprian's.

TSHEMBE   Did you send word to him of our father?

ERIC   Yes, but I don't think Abioseh will come.

TSHEMBE   You also didn't think that *I* would come. (*Brightening*) Eric, you've become a man.

ERIC   It's been five years. . . !

TSHEMBE   Five years . . . You smoke?
(*Crosses in, opens his bag and tosses the boy a few packs of cigarettes and some newspapers*)

ERIC   American cigarettes! (*He eagerly breaks a pack*) Willy almost never has American cigarettes.

69

TSHEMBE Willy—? (*A long pause, to remember*) Dr. DeKoven? (*He regards* ERIC, *the pith helmet, filthy clothes and whiskey bottle; the other averts his eyes. He fingers the bottle, drinks, puts it down, then snatches the helmet from* ERIC's *head*) He gives you things—

ERIC Yes.

TSHEMBE Cigarettes? (ERIC *nods*) Whiskey even?

ERIC Tell me about Europe. About your life there . . . Tshembe, please!

TSHEMBE (*Softening. He smiles*) Well—you are an uncle. I had a son just before I left. (*Fist in the air for proud emphasis*) Eight pounds of son!

ERIC (*Clasping his hands with delight*) You got some girl in trouble!

TSHEMBE (*Amused*) I have a wife, Eric; and we have a son.

ERIC (*Wide-eyed*) You are married?

TSHEMBE (*Dryly*) Yes, people are doing it everywhere.

ERIC You have her picture? (TSHEMBE *tosses it, gets up, takes off his shirt and fills a basin to wash*) She—she is European!

TSHEMBE Very.

ERIC How old is she?
        (*He is studying the photo critically*)

TSHEMBE (*Amused—at both* ERIC *and the custom*) That is something one is not supposed to ask.

ERIC   Why?

TSHEMBE   It is a custom among her people not to.

ERIC   Why?

TSHEMBE (*Absurdly*)   Because it is.

ERIC   She's not very handsome.

TSHEMBE (*Shaking water from his head and taking the photo back*)   It is also not the custom to say such things about other people's wives!

ERIC   She looks older than you do.

TSHEMBE   She isn't. Europeans—wrinkle faster. (*Looking at the photo*) She is handsome. And she has eyes that talk. (*He kisses the picture fondly and puts it away*)

ERIC   What color are they?

TSHEMBE   Gray.

ERIC   Ugh. Like Reverend Neilsen's.

TSHEMBE   And like your own. What is wrong with gray eyes?

ERIC   It is no color at all.

TSHEMBE   Gray eyes are all colors and hers have a lot of green in them and they are very, very beautiful.

ERIC   What color is her hair?

TSHEMBE   Red like the sunset.

ERIC It sounds ugly.

TSHEMBE It is striking.

ERIC Can you see her veins?

TSHEMBE Her what?

ERIC Her veins. When you stand close to Dr. Gotterling, you can see her veins through her skin. Like a chicken.

TSHEMBE (*Rubbing his body dry with raffia*) You don't think Dr. Gotterling is strange-looking, do you?

ERIC No, why should I? She is very—serious for a woman —but she is handsome.

TSHEMBE Blue eyes, yellow hair, veins and all?

ERIC (*Puzzled*) Yes.

TSHEMBE (*Delighted at the universal absurdity of it*) What we *know*—is what we accept. (*He laughs and boxes the boy's head*) It is like that everywhere!

ERIC Wouldn't you like a towel?

TSHEMBE Raffia works up the blood better!

ERIC (*Shrugs and opens the newspaper*) They say that Kumalo is coming home. To Zatembe.

TSHEMBE (*Sighing*) Yes. Kumalo is coming home.

ERIC What will he do in Zatembe?

TSHEMBE What has he done in Europe? *Talk!* Talk, talk, talk. That is what the African does in Europe. He wanders around in the cold in his thin suits and he *talks.* You would like that part, Eric. There is a great deal of pomp. In Europe the European is—(*Playing it*)—*very* civilized. When our delegations are ushered in, and our people have said what they came to say, the Europeans have a way of looking very hurt as if they have never heard of these things before . . . and presently we sit there feeling almost as if it is *we* who have been unreasonable. And then they stand up—it is always the Europeans who stand up first— and they say (*With exaggerated Oxford accent and the dignity of a minuet*): "Well. There are undoubtedly some valid things in what you have had to say . . . but we mustn't forget, must we, there are some valid things in what the settlers say? Therefore, we will write a report, which will be forwarded to the Foreign Secretary, who will forward it to the Prime Minister, who will approve it for forwarding to the settler government in Zatembe"— (*Abruptly sobering*)—who will laugh and not even read it. *That* is what Kumalo has been doing in Europe. *That* is what he will do in Zatembe.

(TSHEMBE *proceeds to change into native garb, a skirt of handsome leather*)

ERIC   Are they really sending him home for that?

TSHEMBE   The government in Europe has persuaded the government here to talk to him, and he agreed to come.

ERIC   What will happen?

TSHEMBE   Talk!

ERIC   Will he support the terrorists?

TSHEMBE   When did you become interested in politics, Little Toy? Does your doctor whisper politics when he pours your whiskey?

ERIC (*Bitterly, lifting his head above it*)   He discusses many things with me.

TSHEMBE (*Somewhat chastened*)   How should I know what Kumalo will do? And don't call them terrorists: that's for the settlers. Call them rebels, or revolutionaries. (*Looking off with his own sad irony*) Or fools. But never terrorists. (*A beat*) Tell me about my father in his last hours. Of what things did he speak?

ERIC (*Curtly—to hurt in return*)   Only of his ancestors, what else?

TSHEMBE   Why do you say it like that, Eric?

ERIC   Because it's true. He was just an old savage who went to his death rubbing lizard powder on his breast and chanting out his kula or some damn thing!

TSHEMBE (*Grabbing the boy violently*)   So did our mother! Do you despise her memory too? Have they finally turned the world upside down in your head, boy? (*They stare hard at one another.* TSHEMBE *releases him*) Does Madame Neilsen know about my father?

ERIC (*Shaking his head*)   I thought that you would want to tell her.
> (*During this a third man, unnoticed, has approached the hut and stands now at some distance: taller, older, wrapped in a great African blanket*)

ABIOSEH   You are as our mother said you would be, Tshembe—lean, handsome, with the face of a thinker! (*The brothers turn with astonishment*) So were you named, so have you come to be. Greeting!
(*He raises his arms in the "sign" of greeting and* TSHEMBE *returns it*)

TSHEMBE   Abioseh!
(*It is a shout of joy as the two rush together and embrace fully, then stand back and look at one another*)

ABIOSEH (*Turning at last to the younger one*)   And you, Eric. Are you well?

ERIC (*Blurting it out in his nervousness*)   Tshembe has a wife with gray eyes and red hair and they have a son eight pounds . . .

TSHEMBE (*To* ERIC, *saluting*)   Thank you!
(*The three brothers laugh*)

ABIOSEH   Is it so?

TSHEMBE   It is so. Ah, Abioseh, Abioseh! It is a long time. I have seen both Europe and America since last we met.

ABIOSEH (*Smiling tenderly*)   The Wanderer, my brother called Tshembe, who is Ishmael. Tell me of your doings.
(*The three brothers sit as of old*)

TSHEMBE   Well—I worked in the mines on the coast for a while. (*He offers his brother a cigarette but* ABIOSEH *declines*) And then I got a job on a newspaper. But when the resistance began the government closed it down.

75

Poof! (ABIOSEH *looks at him curiously*) So I scraped together some cash and went off to Europe. At first I roomed with Titswali Okele. You'd approve of Okele, Eric. He got *two* girls in a fix: one European and one black American. And sent them both to an East Indian abortionist.

(*He laughs and settles back*)

ABIOSEH "Resistance," Tshembe? You mean the terror. (*With obvious concern for his brother*) You are not involved in this trouble—are you?

TSHEMBE (*Carelessly, an assumption*) All Africa is involved in this trouble, brother.

ABIOSEH (*Smiling*) I can see that you have learned the philosophical reply.

ERIC He talks funny now.

TSHEMBE I think funny.

ABIOSEH You are different than when you went away, Tshembe.

TSHEMBE Inside and out! (*Bending his head over*) How do you like my part? Something, huh?

ABIOSEH (*Ruffles his brother's hair fondly. Then, searching his eyes*) I hope you have not been swallowed up in the fanaticism. It is everywhere. The killing. You have heard?

TSHEMBE I have heard.

ABIOSEH (*With great enthusiasm—pouring it forth*) Tshembe, these are new times. There are those in London—some even in Zatembe—who recognize that this is our country too. We have had feelers—

TSHEMBE   "Feelers"?

ABIOSEH   Nothing official, you understand—

TSHEMBE   "We"?

ABIOSEH   We have a group—responsible, educated, enterprising. Men like ourselves who want to build—not destroy. But the settlers won't budge, of course, while fanatics give them the least excuse—

TSHEMBE   I don't recall that the settlers ever needed excuses. (*Shrugging mightily as the other starts to answer*) Oh, dear brother, what does it matter! I worried about such things for years and then, one day, sitting on a bench in Hyde Park—watching the pigeons, naturally—it came to me as it must to all men: I won't come this way again. Enough time will pass and it will be over for me on this little planet! And so I'd better do the things I mean to do. And so I got up from that bench and went to meet the girl I had been wanting to marry but had not, you see, because of—(*On his fingers, deliberately mocking the words*)—the liberation! the Movement! "AH-FREE-KA!"—and all the rest of it. Well, I was, as Camus would have it . . . (*Ironically, with a small introspective laugh, for he does not in any sense feel the "freedom" he boasts about*) . . . "a free man" in that moment because I "chose" freely. *I chose.* And so, you see, it is all over with me and history. This particular atom has discovered himself. (*He gets up and signals to* ERIC *to fetch the funeral robes and pulls out a pot of ceremonial paint*) In any case, we should get ready for the ceremony.

(ABIOSEH *watches with disbelief*)

ABIOSEH   And what do you propose we do at the ceremony, my disenchanted, world-traveled young intellectual? (ABIOSEH *rises and stands very tall, still holding the blanket about him*) Should we also paint our cheeks?

TSHEMBE (*Holding the pot of paint out to him*)   Yes.

ABIOSEH (*Staring hard at him*)   And dance?

TSHEMBE   Of course.

ABIOSEH   With yellow ochre on our cheeks and the rattle in our hands?

TSHEMBE   We should.

ABIOSEH (*His voice rising with hostility*)   To chase away the spirits of evil that have taken our father away?

(TSHEMBE *starts to paint his own face*)

TSHEMBE   Why do you ask these things, Abioseh?

ABIOSEH   Do you believe in any of it?

TSHEMBE   Of course I don't believe in it!

ABIOSEH   Then why?

TSHEMBE   We are our father's sons. Our people expect it. What great harm is there in lizard powder, Abioseh? (ERIC *hands him the ceremonial robe, a great imposing garment of animal skins, and he advances, holding it out to* ABIOSEH) It is your place to wear the robe now. . . .

(*He reaches out and pulls the blanket from his brother—who stands revealed in the cassock and crucifix of the Roman Catholic Church.* ERIC *gasps.* TSHEMBE *regards him in silence*)

ABIOSEH   I take the final vows in the spring.

TSHEMBE (*Donning the robe himself*)   And what will be your name then, my brother?

ABIOSEH   Father Paul Augustus. (TSHEMBE *and* ERIC *exchange looks*) I thought to tell you of this in a different way.
   (*The two are confronting each other; one in the mystical robes of ancient and contemporary Africa—the other in the mystical robes of medieval and contemporary Europe.* TSHEMBE *laughs*)

TSHEMBE   I see. Such is the marketplace of Empire! You, the son of a proud elder of the Kwi, are now pleased to change your ancient name for that of a Roman Emperor! You came home not to pay respects to your father but to rail against a few pots of innocent powder.

ABIOSEH   Some day, Tshembe—

TSHEMBE   You have found Reason in a bit of dirty ash— (*Hotly touching his forehead*)—and Humiliation in the rattles and feathers of our ceremonies!

ABIOSEH   Some day a black man will be Archbishop of this Diocese, a black African Cardinal. Think of what that will mean!

TSHEMBE   It will mean only the swinging jeweled kettle of incense of another cult—which kept the watchfires of our oppressors for three centuries! (*Gesturing impatiently to* ERIC*'s own robe, which is far less imposing*) Eric, get dressed!

ABIOSEH   You were raised by Christians, Eric!

TSHEMBE (*Simply, without passion*)   And maimed by them!

ABIOSEH   Some dreadful thing has happened to you, Tshembe. (*Coming towards him with hand outstretched*) But it is not too late—

TSHEMBE (*Drawing violently away*)   The sale, dear brother, has been completed and you are wearing the receipts!

ABIOSEH (*With determined gentleness*)   Ah, Tshembe, Tshembe . . . you dare to equate my faith, my acceptance of the supreme morality of humankind—with purchase?

TSHEMBE (*Reaching out and taking the silver crucifix in his hands*)   I know the value of this silver, Abioseh! It is far more holy than you know. I have collapsed with fatigue with those who dug it out of our earth! I have lain in the dark of those barracks where we were locked like animals at night and listened to them cough and cry and swear and vent the aching needs of their bodies on one another. I have seen them die! And I think your Jesus would have loved those men—

ABIOSEH   I see that you remember at least *part* of your teachings—

TSHEMBE —but I think He would have cared nothing for those who gave you this!
>   (*He flings the cross back at him, and* ABIOSEH *passionately falls to his knees*)

ABIOSEH You are ravaged by things that will destroy you, Tshembe!

TSHEMBE (*Quietly, evenly*) I am ravaged.
>   (*He turns to go*)

ABIOSEH (*Clutching the crucifix to his lips*) Tshembe, come and kneel and pray with me!

TSHEMBE (*At the door, rattle and headpiece in hand: it is a great imposing affair of furs and animal horns*) Abioseh, I know the tale of Jesus. But I think now if there was such a man he must have been what all men are: the son of man who died the death of men. And if the legend is true at all that he was a good man, then he must have despised the priests of the temples of complicity! I am going out to our people.
>   (*Looking from one brother to the other, he dons the headpiece*)

ABIOSEH You are condemning yourself to hell, Tshembe Matoseh!
>   (TSHEMBE *throws back the door flap, and a sudden shaft of yellow light glints on the silver crucifix as* ABIOSEH *raises it above his head and intones a prayer in ringing liturgical Latin.* TSHEMBE *throws back his head and begins, with all his power, to join in the offstage funereal chant. The two barbaric religious*

cries play one against the other in vigorous and desperate counterpoint. The lights come down on the novice Paul Augustus on his knees and the terrified ERIC, *still clutching his robes as* TSHEMBE *sweeps out)*

Blackout

ACT ONE
SCENE 3

Evening. MME. NEILSEN *sits alone on the veranda taking the night air.* CHARLIE *appears in the parlor doorway and regards the night, momentarily caught up in the distant funeral chant offstage.*

CHARLIE "And it shall follow as the night the day—" (*Calling inside*) Say, Doctor Gotterling, you know this is the only place I've ever been where the night really *does* follow the day. Whatever happened to your twilights here?
　　(MARTA *joins him in the doorway. They are not aware of the old lady*)

MARTA (*Tongue-in-cheek*) Well, Mr. Morris, I shall tell you: Since they serve no useful purpose at the Mission— we have eliminated them entirely!

CHARLIE Shall we stroll by the river, Doctor?

MADAME Excellent, Mr. Morris! Marta is romanced so seldom!
　　(*They start and then laugh*)

CHARLIE (*Extending his arm*) Doctor—shall we?

MARTA (*Not unpleased*) No, I think not.

CHARLIE (*With a courtly turn toward* MME. NEILSEN) Madame?

MADAME (*Delighted*)   No, I think not!

CHARLIE   Won't change your mind, Doctor? I've always wanted once in my lifetime to stroll through the African jungle in the moonlight, arm in arm with a lovely lady.

MARTA   Have you really?

CHARLIE   No, but I thought it sounded good.

MARTA (*Not moving*)   It could be dangerous.

CHARLIE   Doctor, I'm not that dangerous!

MARTA   Really, Mr. Morris, it's not wise to go wandering at this hour. The terror isn't a joke—as much as we all wish it were.

CHARLIE   It's almost . . . impossible . . . to associate terror with that incredible moonlight.

MARTA (*Tightly*)   They found the Hokinson family murdered in the very same incredibly beautiful moonlight. (*A beat*) They had three children.

CHARLIE   And is there no way —?

MARTA   This country is almost a quarter the size of the United States, Mr. Morris. The patrols have to come from wherever they are when the alarms go off. And sometimes they don't go off at all. Sometimes the first thing they do is cut the flare signal wires. Sometimes the servants are in on it. But then—(*With sudden bitterness, scanning the darkness*)—they *all* are.

MADAME   Marta! You know better than that, my dear . . . Ah, how I should like a bit of music! Do you perhaps play an instrument, Mr. Morris?

CHARLIE (*Stirring from preoccupation*)   Oh? Ah—no, I'm afraid that I don't.

MADAME   What a pity that Torvald did not get back in time to play for us this evening. You will love the austerity of the cello in this lush, tropical atmosphere.

MARTA (*Rather blurting*)   I think it's maddening of him to stay away like this.

MADAME   Torvald has been trampling around these villages for forty years, my dear. When he has done whatever he has to do, he will come home.
    (*A jeep slams to a stop offstage, followed by the rushed steps of men*)

CHARLIE   Now what—?

MADAME (*Coolly, dryly*)   It is the sound of the nerve ends of frightened men, Mr. Morris.
    (RICE *enters with two* SOLDIERS—*rifles borne at the ready—who patrol slowly back and forth as the scene continues*)

MARTA   Major Rice.

RICE   There's been another attack.
    (DEKOVEN *comes out of the parlor*)

MARTA   Dear God.

RICE   The Duchesne family. Wiped out.

MARTA   Why? Why?

RICE   All of them.

MADAME   No, no.

RICE   Including the servants. Where is the Reverend?

DEKOVEN   He hasn't returned.

RICE   What has to happen before you people finally understand security measures!

MADAME   (*Quietly, reflectively*)   The Duchesnes . . . the Duchesnes . . . they were decent people . . .

RICE   And these are the savages they want us to sit and "talk" with—

CHARLIE   Major Rice, I'd hardly call Kumalo a savage.

RICE   No. Of course not. The blacks are always "civilized" in the next man's country, aren't they, Mr. Morris?

CHARLIE   Injustice in my country, Major, does not excuse it in yours.

RICE   "Injustice," Mr. Morris! How unfortunate that the Duchesnes are not available to benefit from your objectivity. I would like to speak to you alone, DeKoven.
(*He moves briskly up the steps and exits into the parlor.* DEKOVEN *follows*)

CHARLIE (*To* MARTA) I didn't mean that the killing was justified.

MARTA I'm afraid that's rather the way it sounded.
(*At exactly this moment* TSHEMBE *appears out of the darkness up right, dressed in African garb.* CHARLIE *starts violently and moves forward instinctively to interpose himself before* MARTA. *At the same time the* SOLDIERS *whirl and cock their rifles.* TSHEMBE *halts*)

MARTA (*Peering at him. To the* SOLDIERS) It's all right.
(*They resume their pacing.* TSHEMBE *moves forward, looks* CHARLIE *in the eye and—very deliberately— curtsies in mock deference to the American's courage in the face of him, then comes calmly past him*)

MADAME Who is it?

TSHEMBE (*Softly*) Good evening, Madame.
(*He squats before her*)

MADAME Tshembe! Why, you've come home, you rogue!
. . . Let me touch your face!
(*He leans forward and she feels his features eagerly*)

TSHEMBE (*Playfully, familiarly*) I am come fully to manhood since last you saw me.

MADAME Yes, yes! These are a man's features. Are you handsome as the devil?

TSHEMBE Some women around the world have thought so, Madame.

MADAME But where is your hair? That marvelous bush—

TSHEMBE   I wear it short now—in the way of city men.

MADAME   (*Laughing*)   And with one of those dreadful parts!

TSHEMBE   Some women around the world have voiced no complaints!

MADAME   Oh, Tshembe! Well, did you have time to get yourself a decent education at least?

TSHEMBE   I am fashionably well spoken, I think, Madame.

MADAME (*Delighted with him*)   And fresh as the wind still! Where have you been, you incorrigible?

TSHEMBE   Waltzing around the world, Madame.

MADAME   Not the waltzes I taught you!

TSHEMBE   To Europe and America. In Europe, I found the town where you were born. I saw your beautiful mountains . . .

MADAME   Ah, so you saw my mountains . . . my beautiful mountains.

TSHEMBE   They were as you told me. I brought you a gift from there.
> (*He pulls out a thing in flimsy tissue. She tears the paper away and accidentally trips the spring which sends a "cuckoo" bird out of its clock house. They both laugh*)

MADAME   (*Sobering*)   Tell me. Have you seen Eric?

TSHEMBE   (*Understanding*)   I have seen Eric.

MADAME   It is good you have come. And where is your brother Abioseh? Ah, he was such a good student. So stiff-faced and serious. Not like you, constantly raising your impudent eyes to me and saying, "But, Madame, you have not told me *why* it is so."

(*She boxes his head and they laugh as* RICE *and* DEKOVEN *reemerge*)

RICE (*Continuing, to* DEKOVEN)   I repeat: we shall require cooperation for the duration. Your personal attitudes— (*Noticing* TSHEMBE) Who's the kaffir?

MADAME   We do not have "kaffirs" here, Major Rice. We have friends who are Africans.

(TSHEMBE *turns*)

RICE   Tshembe!

DEKOVEN   Welcome home!

TSHEMBE (*Rising and nodding to* DEKOVEN)   Doctor.

RICE (*Routinely*)   Your papers . . .

TSHEMBE   I don't have them with me.

(*He starts to walk away—the* SOLDIERS *cock their rifles in warning. He halts*)

RICE (*Crossing towards him*)   Why not?

MADAME (*With restrained outrage*)   Major Rice, Tshembe was born here—as *you* well know! Why should he have to carry those ridiculous papers?

MARTA   Madame, it is the emergency . . .

(TSHEMBE *looks at her swiftly; she averts her eyes*)

RICE   Why has he suddenly reappeared?

TSHEMBE   I have come home—

RICE   Yes. That much is clear. Now up with your sleeves! (*He gets out his flashlight.* TSHEMBE *stiffens and at last obeys.* MADAME *sits rigid and* DEKOVEN *turns away as the* MAJOR *runs the light over* TSHEMBE'*s arms*)

MARTA (*To* CHARLIE)   When they take the oath, they're marked.

RICE (*To* TSHEMBE)   All right. That will do.

MADAME   I shall report you to someone, Major! I shall find someone in this country gone mad to whom it is possible to report you!

RICE (*Ignoring her*)   Why are you in the regalia?

TSHEMBE   I came home . . . (*Turning to the old woman*) . . . to my father's funeral, Madame.

MADAME (*A deep gasp of hurt*)   Ahhhh . . . The drums! The drums . . . Abioseh, dear stubborn old man . . . he has left us.
(*It is the last straw: completely outside himself,* DEKOVEN *advances*)

DEKOVEN   Well, it would appear that you may now go protect civilization someplace else, Major! This particular "terrorist" has turned out to be a son in mourning!

RICE (*Wheeling in fury*)   I will hope, Doctor, that had you seen those little children lying in their own blood tonight, you might finally be able to get your sympathies in order.

Whatever the nature of your attachments—*elsewhere!*
My condolences, Tshembe. (*Then, to all of them*) As of
tonight, this entire area is under martial jurisdiction. I
must order everyone, male and female, to wear side-arms.
I am sorry, Dr. Gotterling, but at this point—

MARTA   I understand, Major.

RICE   Mr. Morris?

CHARLIE   Are you "ordering" *me*, Major?

RICE   I am making a suggestion that well might save your
life.

CHARLIE (*Drawing up his sleeve*)   Major, would you like to
check my arm?

RICE   Mr. Morris, this is Africa—

CHARLIE   Yes, I know. Where Stanley met Livingston!

RICE   Precisely. And where one does not conduct an enqui-
ry on the ethics of resisting cannibalism while being sea-
soned for the pot! (*To* DEKOVEN) Doctor—?

DEKOVEN   Who will order me to *fire* it, Major?
        (*He throws down his cigarette and strides out*)

RICE   If this Mission persists—

MADAME (*Interrupting wryly*)   I trust, Major Rice, you
don't expect *me* to wear one. After all— (*Peering at
him*)
        —I might hit *you*.
        (RICE *turns to* TSHEMBE)

RICE Why don't some of you educated chaps talk sense
into these murderers? What do they think they are going
to accomplish? Murdering people who never did them a
moment's harm—and their own people to boot? We
don't pretend that it's been all jolly on our side—but this
business—what's the good of it, boy? 'Tisn't going to
solve a bloody thing! And they can't win, you know. Why
don't the fellows like you *do* something . . . *talk* to them?
(*They gaze at one another—the European with almost
plaintive urgency; the African without expression. At last*
RICE *turns—a man perplexed and embarrassed, who
desires, like all of us, sympathy*) There—you see, Mr.
Morris: the response to reason. And it will be no different
with Kumalo. It may surprise you, sir, but I do not enjoy
my present role. I am not by temperament an adventur-
ous sort. Or a harsh one. I have become a military man
only because the times demand it. (*A curious, urgent and
almost sad defensiveness*) This is my country, you see. I
came here when I was a boy. I worked hard. I married
here. I have two lovely daughters and, if I may presume
an immodesty, a most charming and devoted wife. At
some other time I should have liked to have had you out
to our farm. This is our *home*, Mr. Morris. Men like
myself had the ambition, the energy and the ability to
come here and make this country into something . . .
(*He turns ever so slightly from time to time to catch*
TSHEMBE*'s expression*) *They* had it for centuries and did
nothing with it. It isn't a question of empire, you see. It
is our home: the right to bring up our children with
culture and grace, a bit of music after dinner and a glass

of decent wine; the right to watch the sun go down over our beautiful hills—(*Looking off with a surge of appreciation*) And they *are* beautiful hills, aren't they? We wish the blacks no ill. But—(*Simply, matter-of-factly, a man confirmed*)—it is our home, Mr. Morris. (*A beat. He looks up, a little embarrassed*) I should be grateful if, whatever other impression you may have received, you would try to remember that when you write of this place.

MADAME Marta, I must go to bed. (*Pointedly*) Do you know, in some ways I think I am quite glad to be going blind? The less one sees of this world, I am convinced, the better . . .

> (RICE *shoots* MADAME *a look.* MARTA *rises to assist her*)

RICE (*To* TSHEMBE) There is an eight-thirty curfew for all natives. (*He looks at his watch*) It is now eight-fourteen. (*To all, crisply*) Good night.

> (*He exits.* CHARLIE *stands looking after him*)

MARTA (*Her arm about* MADAME) Good night, Mr. Morris. Good night, Tshembe.

CHARLIE Good night, Doctor.

MADAME (*Pausing before* TSHEMBE) You must come back and tell me all about your travels, Tshembe. I am so pleased that you got to see my mountains. I should have loved to have seen them again . . . Ah yes . . . (*She reaches out to touch him, but instead balls up her fist as if to compress all the emotion that is in her and lightly touches his chest.*) Good night, child.

(*They exit.* CHARLIE *and* TSHEMBE *regard each other across the veranda*)

CHARLIE   Well, Mr. —

TSHEMBE (*Turning, crisply*)   Matoseh.

CHARLIE (*Hand extended*)   Morris. (*They shake. It is cursory, abrupt; the pace set by the African's disinterest*) How's about a drink? I know where they keep the liquor and it's pretty decent stuff. Even without ice.

TSHEMBE (*As if stirring from a preoccupation*)   Thank you, no. In fact, I will say good night also.

CHARLIE (*Swiftly, to stop him*)   I think I know everything you were feeling when that ugly scene was happening, Mr. Matoseh.

TSHEMBE (*Halting, with restrained hostility*)   Do you?

CHARLIE   Yes. It's easier when you are outside a situation to see the whole. I felt very sorry for *both* you men, you and Rice, then. It's a particular kind of vantage point given to an outsider.

TSHEMBE (*Crisply*)   Yes, it was precisely the "vantage point" I had in your country.

CHARLIE (*Getting it and smiling easily*)   I'm sure. How about that drink?

TSHEMBE   I think you heard. There is a curfew here for— "natives."

CHARLIE   I don't think either one of us cares one hell of a lot about that curfew. (*Pointing to the veranda roof and grinning*) Besides, you are indoors technically.

TSHEMBE   Men die here on account of such technicalities.

CHARLIE (*Simply, looking at the other*)   I really would like to talk. (TSHEMBE *says nothing but remains*) I'll get the bottle. (*He does so. Smoothly, engagingly: a man practiced at setting others at ease*) I'll tell you right off, Matoseh, I know you are trying to decide: which *kind* am I? One of the obtuse ones who is sure to ask you all about rituals and lions? Or one of the top-heavy "little magazine" types who is going to engage a real live African intellectual in a discussion of "negritude" and Senghor's poetry to show that I am—(*He winks;* TSHEMBE *smiles back the least bit, warming*)—really—"in." Well, I am neither. I am a man who feels like talking. Sit down.

TSHEMBE (*Sits*)   American straightforwardness is *almost* as disarming as Americans invariably think it is.
      (CHARLIE *grins and lifts his glass in friendly salute;* TSHEMBE *reacts in kind and they drink*)

CHARLIE   You married?

TSHEMBE   Yes. I have, however, only *one* wife!

CHARLIE (*Annoyed*)   Look, I thought we had decided to assume that the other was something more than an ass, Matosch.

TSHEMBE   It may be, Mr. Morris, that I have developed counterassumptions because I have had—(*Mimicking lightly but cruelly*)—too many long, lo-o-ong "talks" wherein the white intellectual begins by suggesting not only fellowship but the universal damnation of imperialism. But that, you see, is always only the beginning. Then the real game is begun. (*With mock grandiloquence*) The game of plumbing *my* depths! Of trying to dig out *my* "frustrations"! And of finding deep in my "primeval soul" what *you* think is the secret—quintessential—"root" of my nationalism: "SHAME"! (*As swiftly dropping it*) But, you see, I have already had those talks and they bore me.

CHARLIE   I see that you are outraged by others' assumptions but that *you* are full of them! Let's get a simple thing understood: I am not a hundred other people. Are you? (*They glare at one another; by his silence and barely perceptible smile* TSHEMBE *concedes*) Cigarette?

TSHEMBE   Thank you.

CHARLIE   What parts of the States were you in?

TSHEMBE   Most of your urban capitals: Boston, Los Angeles, Chicago . . . New York, of course.

CHARLIE   Man, you really got around. I hope the shortness of your visit didn't distort your view? That happens, you know.

TSHEMBE (*Dryly*)   I believe I understood what I saw in America.

CHARLIE (*Laughing*)   Well now, it's the damnedest thing —everybody seems to come with preconceptions. You know, America is a lot more than supermarkets, instant coffee and the fast buck.

TSHEMBE   I don't believe that America is misunderstood because of its instant coffee, Mr. Morris. But then I don't believe it is very often misunderstood.

CHARLIE (*Turning his cigarette about*)   Did you get down to our . . . tobacco country at all?

TSHEMBE   Yes, I was in *the South!* (*With deliberate impatience*) And yes, I did find the situation there absolutely enraging!

CHARLIE (*Openly frustrated*)   You really can't come off it, can you! Why the hell should it be so hard for us to talk, man?! Christ, all I want to do is talk!

TSHEMBE (*Whirling on him, words flying*)   And just why should we be able to "talk" so easily? What is this marvelous nonsense with you Americans? For a handshake, a grin, a cigarette and half a glass of whiskey you want three hundred years to disappear—and in five minutes! Do you really think the rape of a continent dissolves in cigarette smoke? Or the mutilation of whole peoples on a few ounces of amber! (*He rises*) This is Africa, Mr. Morris, and I am an African, not one of your simpering American Negroes sitting around discussing admission to country clubs!

CHARLIE (*In kind*)   I see you know even less about American Negroes than you think you know about me!

TSHEMBE   Perhaps my obsessions have made me myopic! In this light, for instance, I really cannot tell you from Major Rice! (*Playing it heavily*) You all really do

9 7

look alike, you know . . . (*He starts out*) There, I have given you a first sentence for your notebooks!

CHARLIE (*Rather shouting*)   What—will happen if we cannot . . . talk to one another, Matoseh? (TSHEMBE *halts and their eyes meet.* CHARLIE *grins disarmingly*) You know, I really cannot shoulder my father's sins . . . I have quite enough of my own to contend with. (TSHEMBE *comes back and sits. A beat*) Did you know Kumalo?

TSHEMBE   Know him? I worked as his second-in-command for a year . . . until they kicked me off the committee. I know him well.

CHARLIE   Oh? Why were you kicked off?

TSHEMBE (*Leaning back, blowing smoke rings*)   They said that I lacked—ah—"passion" . . . for "freedom"! And other things. (*With amused pride*) There were several *large* reports drafted about me. (*Then, turning his eyes on the other*) I am so sorry to disappoint you, Mr. Morris.

CHARLIE (*The American*)   Oh, come on now, to hell with all this "Mister" stuff. You call me Charlie and I'll call you Tshembe.

TSHEMBE   No.

CHARLIE   What?

TSHEMBE   I said "No." I prefer to be addressed formally. And if we decide to change it you won't decide by yourself. (*Smiling*) We will have to hold a referendum which includes me!

CHARLIE   Now, isn't that silly!

TSHEMBE (*Knowing it is*)   Of course.

CHARLIE   But it has something to do with a principle?

TSHEMBE   I'll think of one.

CHARLIE (*Mystified, but accepting it*)   About Kumalo—

TSHEMBE (*Sighs, looking off*)   Kumalo . . . is a scholar, a patriot, a dreamer and a crazy old man. If you ask him the time of day he looks at you without seeing you and says with passion glistening at the corners of his lips (*Cruelly, mockingly*) *"Independence!"* If you ask him the weather he says, *"Free-dom, now!"* If you ask him has he a woman, he says (*Raising his hand in the salute*) "AH-FREEKA!" They are all like that, the sincere ones. And the others, those for whom it is all a pose—drive themselves just as hard to ensure themselves a position when the day comes!

CHARLIE (*Intently*)   Then it really doesn't matter, does it, once you get under the skin? White rule, black rule— they're not so very different?

TSHEMBE   I don't know, Mr. Morris. We haven't had much chance to find out.

CHARLIE   Oh, come on, Matoseh. You'll get your chance. We both know that. The question is what will you do with it? (*Crossing up he refills his drink*) Look, let me tell you something. (*Confidentially*) Have you ever heard of —Twin Forks Junction?

TSHEMBE (*Dryly*)   Somehow, Mr. Morris, I missed it.

CHARLIE (*A deliberate put-on*)   Twin Forks Junction, *Nebraska.*

TSHEMBE (*Amused*)   Oh. *That* Twin Forks Junction!

CHARLIE (*Playing it big*)   Twin Forks Junction, Nebraska, is the fifth-largest town in Boone County—except at harvest time when the influx of farm laborers swells the population to . . . twenty! It has the largest silo east of Albion. An all-year movie house. A jim-dandy Federal Agricultural Station. And there's something else about Twin Forks Junction—

TSHEMBE (*With bated breath*)   Yes, Mr. Morris?!

CHARLIE   When I was a boy the two darkest faces within sixty miles were . . . a "black Irishman" and a sunburned Greek! And one day (*He sits on the edge of the veranda, looking off*) a contingent of colored troops came through —and you know what? Some of us played hookey so we could go down and see—don't laugh, Matoseh—what a black man looked like. I'll never forget it. They marched along in perfect formation, their eyes looking straight ahead, and it was the damnedest thing: I could feel their eyes on me, even though it was *I* who was watching *them.* And then they were gone and it was too late . . . and I kept wanting to call them back, to reach out and say, "Hey! . . . Lookit me! I never knew you were. Did you know *I* was. . . ?"

> (*He sits silently: for a moment he is in that other time*)

TSHEMBE Yes?

CHARLIE (*Turning to him as if the point should be self-evident*) Well, don't you see—? (*But* TSHEMBE *merely waits, blankly*) Matoseh, we cannot spend our lives like this! Sometime, the contingents have got to stop—and look at each other. Tshembe, if we can't find ways to build bridges—to transcend governments, race, the rest of it—starting from whatever examples we have—then we've had it. (*Smiling thoughtfully*) Which, in fact, is why I came here.

TSHEMBE To this Mission. . . ?

CHARLIE To this Mission.

TSHEMBE (*Sincerely*) Mr. Morris, I am touched, truly. But tell me, did you just happen to come by way of Zatembe? Then you must have seen the hills there and the scars in them? (CHARLIE *stares at him uncomprehendingly*) The great gashes from whence came the silver, gold, diamonds, cobalt, tungsten? Tell me, Mr. Morris, are there scars in the hills of Twin Forks Junction—cut by strangers? Well, that, you see, is the difference: we *know* you are, and we have known it for a very long time! I like your glistening eyes, dear man, and your dream of bridges, but the fact of the matter is that those great gashes have everything to do with this Mission—and human transcendence virtually nothing!

CHARLIE (*Incredulous*) Matoseh, I don't believe it—that you can sit here, under this very roof where you learned to read and write—and deny the evidence of your own eyes! The dedication of those who came here—

TSHEMBE (*Utter dismissal*) I do not deny it. It is simply that the conscience, such as it is, of imperialism is . . . irrelevant.

CHARLIE (*Clutching his head in despair*) Oh, for Christ's sake, man! "Imperialism!" Can't we, even for five minutes, throw away yesterday's catchwords?! The sacrifice that these people—

TSHEMBE (*Jumping up, afire*) "Sacrifice!" There, you see, it is impossible! You come thousands of miles to inform us about "yesterday's catchwords"? Well, it is still yesterday in Africa, Mr. Morris, and it will take a million tomorrows to rectify what has been done here—

CHARLIE (*Intently*) *You hate all white men*, don't you, Matoseh?

TSHEMBE (*Casting his eyes up with a sigh of utter resignation*) Oh, dear God, *why?* (*He crosses down and away*) Why do you all *need* it so?! This absolute *lo-o-onging* for my hatred! (*A sad smile plays across his lips*) I shall be honest with you, Mr. Morris. I do not "hate" all white men—but I desperately wish that I did. It would make everything infinitely easier! But I am afraid that, among other things, I have *seen* the slums of Liverpool and Dublin and the caves above Naples. I have *seen* Dachau and Anne Frank's attic in Amsterdam. I have seen too many raw-knuckled Frenchmen coming out of the Metro at dawn and too many pop-eyed Italian children to believe that those who raided Africa for three centuries ever "loved" the white race either. I would like to be simple-minded for you, but—(*Turning these eyes that have "seen" up to the other with a smile*)—I cannot. I have—(*He touches his brow*)—seen. (*And suddenly, wearily, closes his eyes*) Mr. Morris, mostly I am tired. I came home for sentimental reasons. I should not have come. (*A beat. Smiling with his own thoughts*) My wife is European, Mr. Morris . . . a marvelous girl. We have a son now. I've named him Abioseh after my father and John after hers. And all this time I have, mainly, been thinking of them. In the future when you tell some tale or other of me, will you take the trouble to recall that as I stood here, spent and aware of what will probably happen to me, most of all I longed to be in a dim little flat off Langley Square, watching the telly with my family . . .

CHARLIE   Then all this talk about freedom and Africa is just that . . . talk!

TSHEMBE   Isn't that what you wanted, Mr. Morris, to "talk"?

CHARLIE   Yes, but I thought . . .

TSHEMBE   You thought! You thought because I am a black man I have answers that are deep and pure. I do not!!
(*A villager runs on upstage and without breaking his speed hurls a piece of bark at* TSHEMBE *'s feet and exits into the darkness*)

CHARLIE (*Dryly*)   This is some curfew.

(TSHEMBE *does not reply. He stands rigid.* CHARLIE
moves to retrieve the bark)

TSHEMBE   No! (*He picks it up but does not look at it*) It is
for me.
    (*The distant, haunting strains of a chant are heard.*
    TSHEMBE *listens. The lights begin to assume a surreal*
    quality and the Mission and CHARLIE *to dim out*)

CHARLIE   What the devil is it?

TSHEMBE (*A quizzical smile on his lips*)   It's an old problem, really. (*Looks, at last, at the writing on the bark*)
. . . Orestes . . . Hamlet . . . the rest of them . . . (*He puts*
it away. Wistfully) We've really got so many things we'd
rather be doing . . .
    (*It is as if he has been awaiting something all along*
    and now at last it comes: in the sky above him the
    WOMAN *dancer appears, as in the Prologue.* TSHEMBE
    is instantly transfixed, his senses alerted, eyes far
    away, though he cannot see her. The stage has ac-
    quired a fantastical look. The Mission moves off or
    dims out and when CHARLIE*'s voice is heard again,*
    it, too, is unreal, reverberating as in a dream)

CHARLIE   What's the matter with you?

TSHEMBE   Ssh! . . . Soon she will come for me . . .

CHARLIE   "She?" "*She,*" Matoseh?

TSHEMBE   Ssh! . . . She will materialize out of the bush; she
will waft up from the savannahs. (*The* WOMAN *begins to*
move in place) She will rise from the smoke outside the

huts. I have known her to gaze up at me from puddles in the streets of London; from vending machines in the New York subway. Everywhere. And whenever I cursed her or sought to throw her off . . . I ended up that same night in her arms!

(*The* WOMAN *fades out*)

CHARLIE   Who?

TSHEMBE (*Possessed, fighting her*)   Even when I held my bride, she lay beside me, her arms on my thighs caressing, insisting that I belonged to her!

CHARLIE   *Who,* Matoseh?

TSHEMBE (*Passionately, crying out*)   Who! Who! When you knew her you called her Joan of Arc! (*She comes up again on another level, closer to him, more distinct*) Queen Esther! Columbia! La Passionara! And you did know her once, you did know her! But now you call her nothing, because she is dead for you! She does not exist for you! (*Her movements quicken*) Will you go now, Mr. Morris?

CHARLIE   What?

TSHEMBE   I said, will you excuse yourself . . . will you go now? (*Her movements quicken and she takes the stage and he addresses her directly—but still without ever turning to look at her, for there is no need to: she has overrun the terrain of his mind*) No! I will not go! It is not my affair any more! (*She circles in movements symbolic of the life of the people, binding him closer*) I have a wife and son now! I have named him Abioseh after my father and John after hers. (*She signifies the slaughter, the enslavement*) I know all of that! But it is not my affair! (*He sinks to his knees*) I don't care what happens here—anywhere! (*She writhes in agony*) I am not responsible! (*Then stillness: the "sleeping lioness" of the lore. She rises; a tremor of wakefulness possesses her and she reaches out for him and dances an unmistakable dance of the warriors—beckoning urgently, insistently*) It is not my affair! (*Abruptly she sweeps up a spear and thrusts it before him and he clutches it, automatically, to stop it from falling, then sees it in his hand. Screaming*) I HAVE RENOUNCED ALL SPEARS!!!

Blackout

ACT TWO

SCENE 1

Two days later, mid-morning. Outdoors, in the shade of a building or tree.

CHARLIE *is emptying the last of a case of drugs onto a table upon which is a stack of great banana leaves.* MARTA *stands wrapping the bottles in the leaves and placing them in a large low-slung box. About her waist is a holstered pistol.*

MARTA   And so you see, Mr. Morris, it's quite simple really. For *my* father—in those times—medicine just wasn't enough. (CHARLIE *joins her in the wrapping*) And so Papa took those stubby, miraculous hands of his to Spain—and died there, fighting Franco. (*Smiling wistfully*) I was twelve years old.

CHARLIE (*Gently*)   You loved him very much. (*She nods*) Hey—how'm I doing?

MARTA (*Critically surveying his handiwork*)   As a mission doctor, Mr. Morris, I'd say you make a first-rate interviewer! (*Leaning over to demonstrate*) There—tuck in the edges a bit more here . . .

CHARLIE   Mmm-hmm.

MARTA   . . . to make sure that the bottle is covered completely.

CHARLIE (*With appreciation*) Aha! Yes, that does help . . . Please go on.

MARTA But what else is there to say? Years later, when I'd finished my residency, I heard about the Reverend, the work he was doing here, and suddenly it all fit. I just packed up and came. (*Suddenly looking anxiously at her watch*) I do wonder what's keeping him. He should have been back well before now.

CHARLIE You've never regretted it?

MARTA Not at all. Oh, I get irritated sometimes, infuriated even, but regret? No . . .

CHARLIE (*Suddenly struck again by the wonder of where he is and what he is doing, moves his hands sweepingly over the leaves and drugs*) Tell me, Doctor, does this really *work?*

MARTA (*Eying his efforts with amusement*) Well, it has until *now*, Mr. Morris . . .

CHARLIE Incredible. And to think that all these years hospitals in the States and Europe have been wasting all that money on refrigeration . . . when they could have been storing their drugs wrapped in banana leaves under the buildings!

MARTA You're laughing at us, Mr. Morris—

CHARLIE (*Genuinely*) No, Dr. Gotterling. Not laughing. Marveling . . . (*She says nothing*) And the fact is—it really . . .

MARTA (*Finishing it for him*)   Yes, Mr. Morris, I assure you, it really *does* act as a substitute for refrigeration. Well, that is, for *most* drugs.

CHARLIE   And the others?

MARTA   Those we don't stock. (*He looks at her*) As I told you, it's a question of choices. Giving up some things for others.
(PETER *enters*)

PETER   You called, Dr. Gotterling.

MARTA   They go under Ward Six. (PETER *picks up the box*) Thank you, Peter.

PETER (*Nods. To* CHARLIE)   Bwana.
(*He exits*)

MARTA   And thank you, Mr. Morris. (*Looks at her watch*) And now I really must get back.

CHARLIE   Oh, please, we haven't finished—

MARTA   Oh, but we have—that's it. "My life." (*A slight satisfied shrug*) There just isn't any more.

CHARLIE   Not anywhere? There's never been . . . another part?

MARTA (*Looking up quizzically*)   Another part? Oh . . . I see. "The Man." (*Smiling impudently*) Well, I hadn't thought my life was over!

CHARLIE (*Meeting her eyes*)   I hadn't thought so either, Doctor . . .

MARTA (*Returning the look*)   Am I still being interviewed?

CHARLIE   Yes, but if I play my cards right it will turn into a conversation.
(*He motions her to sit on the ground. She does, and he joins her*)

MARTA   The question, then, is what do I do for love—for romance? (*Smiles*) It has a way, Mr. Morris, of coming wherever one is.

CHARLIE   Good.

MARTA   If one doesn't work at it too hard.

CHARLIE (*Grins*)   I'll make a note of that. I take it that Dr. DeKoven isn't . . .

MARTA (*Smiling*)   Dr. DeKoven *isn't*. Look, Mr. Morris, I know it's the tradition in your country to publish the most extraordinary personal details of—

CHARLIE   Oh, it's not for publication.

MARTA   Ah? Then I am *not* still being interviewed?

CHARLIE   Let's say we are gently sliding into a conversation.

MARTA (*Leaning forward very confidentially*)   Well, I won't tell you for any reason. I've lived without a confidant for years: it really isn't the strain it's painted to be.

CHARLIE   I see.
(*He opens his mouth to speak, hesitates, then closes it again, then opens it—just enough to begin chewing on his pencil*)

MARTA Yes?

CHARLIE I didn't say anything—

MARTA Oh. Sorry. My error.

CHARLIE Well, actually—you don't ever feel that your life is in some ways wasted here?

MARTA Wasted, Mr. Morris—?!

CHARLIE Well, as far as I can see, this place isn't exactly exploding with appreciation.

MARTA I can only give you a professional answer.

CHARLIE And the professional answer is, of course, that you didn't come here to be appreciated.

MARTA Exactly.

CHARLIE And to get an unprofessional answer one has to know you much, much better.

MARTA Oh—*much.*
  (*It hangs for a moment, then*)

CHARLIE *How* much?

MARTA Mr. Morris . . .

CHARLIE Hmm?

MARTA You're working too hard. (*He grins. She looks at her watch*) Was there something else?

CHARLIE Yes. (*Leaning forward intently. He hesitates*) Please understand. If I am to write the truth about this place, I have to question everything. Even Reverend Neilsen.

MARTA (*Suddenly wary*) Oh?

CHARLIE Have you ever wondered—I am being devil's advocate now—if just possibly he hadn't "capitalized," so to speak, on the backwardness he found here?

MARTA (*Tightly*) Mr. Morris, I am not a very complicated person. I believe that people are what they do. You may think it simple-minded of me if you like—but if you don't understand the *depth* of his sacrifice merely by being here—

CHARLIE Well, I agree. But—look, I spoke with that fellow Matoseh last night. He has such a different point of view I'm beginning to wonder if there is any place where the two join.

MARTA (*Overreacting*) Why should you listen to Tshembe Matoseh? What possible difference does it make what he says—or any of them for that matter?

CHARLIE (*Quick to pursue the point*) Why not?

MARTA Because they haven't earned the right to criticize yet—

CHARLIE Oh . . . I see. (*Indicating the pistol at her waist*) The gun . . .

MARTA Yes—?

CHARLIE   Would you *use* it?

MARTA (*With a failing effort at restraint*)   Mr. Morris, one could hardly call me a racialist, but there are some things one cannot get out of one's mind when you hear all this new nationalist blood and thunder—the Duchesne family, for example! (*They are distracted momentarily as* ERIC *and* DR. DEKOVEN, *assisting a woman, enter and cross the compound*) Ah—Willy. Is there any word of the Reverend?
    (*He shakes his head*)

DEKOVEN (*Turning to her by way of comfort*)   Marta, you *know* his ways . . .
    (*He follows the others off*)

CHARLIE (*Looking after them. Abruptly*)   Doctor—who was Eric's father?

MARTA (*Staring at him*)   Mr. Morris, I cannot imagine what that has to do with what you say you came here to write . . .

CHARLIE   Oh? Well, actually I'm not sure that it does, but . . . the fact is that there are some things that give insight to a writer, and the frailties of strong men is one of them.

MARTA   I see. Well, I'm afraid, Mr. Morris, that you'll have to look for your insights elsewhere, because the frailties of those who settled here are not my business. (*She rises*) Being a doctor *is*. And now if you'll excuse me . . . (*She starts out, then turns for a parting shot*) Oh—and as for Reverend Neilsen: after forty years I'd say it is a bit late

for you—or Tshembe Matoseh—or anybody to be check-
ing his credentials! Good morning.

>   (*She exits left.* CHARLIE *stands looking after her and
>   then, on an impulse, exits swiftly up right, as the
>   lights—*)

Dimout

ACT TWO
SCENE 2

Shortly after. The hut.

TSHEMBE *sits on the floor beside a box of old odds and ends. He is regarding* ERIC*'s mirror curiously, as the boy enters, quite drunk, and bemusedly makes the sign of greeting.*

TSHEMBE (*Pulling an African robe from the box*)   Our father wore this the last time he went to the Mission. He never wore it again. (*A beat. He holds up the mirror*) Eric, did our father take to staring at his image in his old age?

ERIC   It's mine.
(*He reaches for it, but* TSHEMBE *holds it back*)

TSHEMBE   A gift?
(ERIC *ignores the question and pulls out an old, worn blanket*)

ERIC   The blanket Madame gave you, Tshembe. Remember how we used to sit by the fire and talk . . . you and me and Abioseh. When the fire went out you'd wrap me in it and I'd fall asleep. Remember, Tshembe?

TSHEMBE   I remember, Eric.
(TSHEMBE *is leafing through a battered Bible*)

ERIC   And the Bible the Reverend gave you!

TSHEMBE   It started Abioseh huffing and puffing his way to heaven. Have you studied it, Eric? All those "thou shalt nots"?

ERIC   Sometimes. The names are strange.

TSHEMBE   What names?

ERIC   Abraham, Isaac, Jacob.

TSHEMBE   Strange names for Kwi warriors.

ERIC   . . . Eric.

TSHEMBE   (*Picking up the mirror again and turning it about*)   "Made in Holland." Also from Dr. DeKoven?

ERIC   Willy.

TSHEMBE   Willy! (*Grabs* ERIC *'s bag and angrily empties it*) . . . A woman's cosmetics! So, Eric, if you cannot quite be a white man you have decided to become a white woman? (*Cruelly knocking the pith helmet from the boy's head*) And toys like this! What else does he give you to make you his playtime little white hunter?

ERIC   He is kind. No one else is kind. You and Abioseh were gone.

TSHEMBE   Our father—was he gone too?

ERIC   He was not *my* father!

TSHEMBE   (*Tenderly. Reaching out to embrace him*)   Oh Eric, Eric . . . what does it matter . . . (ERIC *turns away, rigid*) We will be leaving here soon. Do you hear me, Eric? Look at me. I am taking you back with me. Would you like that, Eric? My son needs an uncle. Eric, listen to me—

(CHARLIE MORRIS *enters and* ERIC *runs off*)

CHARLIE   May I come in?

TSHEMBE   It's not a good idea.

CHARLIE (*Coming on in*)   Well, I'll just pretend that it is. I've never been in—

TSHEMBE   —"a native hut before." Did you bring your camera? Would you like me to pose making a basket?

CHARLIE (*Ignoring it, he produces the bottle*)   I brought some of the Reverend's whiskey. Is it too early for you?

TSHEMBE   How can it be too early?
      (*He holds out his hand*)

CHARLIE (*Gives him the bottle*)   Exactly my sentiments. Tell me, Matoseh. Why *are* you so hostile?

TSHEMBE (*Stops in mid-motion and gives him a look*)   The world is hostile, isn't it?
      (*He drinks*)

CHARLIE   What are your plans? (TSHEMBE *raises a quizzical eyebrow*) For your life.

TSHEMBE (*Displaying some African fabrics*)   It is my expectation to go into the textile business!

CHARLIE   Ah, a capitalist to the marrow.

TSHEMBE   Incipient, but to the marrow, yes. I think Reverend Neilsen and I shall get out a line of resort wear. Do you know any New York buyers, Mr. Morris?

CHARLIE   Not offhand. But you might try the Major—I hear he's got all kinds of connections. (*A beat*) Actually, I've been thinking about Mr. Rice . . .

TSHEMBE   So have I, Mr. Morris.
    (*He is seized by sudden inspiration and begins, methodically and with great flair through what follows, to lay out swatches of fabric on the floor in a great circle about him, each time forcing* CHARLIE *away as the barrier forms between them. At the moment* CHARLIE *ignores it*)

CHARLIE   I'm not surprised. You know, Matoseh, the fact is you and I probably share the same opinion of the Major, but there was one thing he said the other night that did seem to make sense.

TSHEMBE (*Coolly*)   To whom?

CHARLIE   Well . . . to me anyway. (TSHEMBE *shoots him a look*) And just possibly to you—and that is that a man of your background could do a great deal for your people.

TSHEMBE   The Major is too kind.

CHARLIE   . . . *if* you chose to.

TSHEMBE (*Indicating the fabrics*)   Oh, but I have—I shall be the first Minister-in-Exile of *Cloth!*

CHARLIE (*Annoyed*) That's very funny, Matoseh. Look, for Christ's sake, you're hardly an ordinary man in these parts. You've worked with Kumalo. You know your way around. Why don't you speak out?

TSHEMBE About what, dear man?

CHARLIE Why the terror, of course. (TSHEMBE *looks at him blankly*) Against the terror.

TSHEMBE "Against the terror." *Which* terror, Mr. Morris?! . . . Ah, this will make a beautiful stole for some lovely back, don't you think?

CHARLIE Now, come on, Matoseh. No matter what the provocations against your people you know damn well you can't expect the settlers to talk while fanatics go on butchering babies. I don't like it any more than you do, but in the world out thére one white life taken counts for more than the murder of blacks by the hundreds!

TSHEMBE (*Quietly*) Thousands, Mr. Morris.

CHARLIE (*Advancing on him*) Then, for God's sake, why don't you use your influence? And Kumalo—if *he* were to denounce the terror—

TSHEMBE Mr. Morris, if you don't mind I have a business to build! (*Holding a swatch up*) Midi, mini, or pants suit, what's your feeling?

CHARLIE Midi! *Why the hell not?*

TSHEMBE Because the moment Kumalo did that his bargaining power would vanish.

CHARLIE   Would it? I should think that the man's moral stature—

TSHEMBE   I do not recall that the Europeans have ever been exactly overwhelmed by morality—black or white. Or do you think they have suddenly become impressed because Kumalo is *saying* the black man wishes freedom? We have been saying that for generations. They only listen now because they are forced to. Take away the violence and who will hear the man of peace? (*He sits on the box, an island in a sea of cloth*) It is the way of the world, hadn't you noticed?

CHARLIE (*Looking off*)   I am thinking of a time when revolutionaries tended to be made out of idealism rather than cynicism . . .

TSHEMBE   Maybe that's what's botched up all the revolutions so far! Mr. Morris, your concern for nonviolence is a little late, don't you think? Where were you when we protested *without* violence and *against* violence? We did not hear from you then! Where were you when they were chopping off the right hands of our young men by the hundreds—by the tribe?

CHARLIE (*Sadly*)   I was just entering kindergarten, as I recall it . . .

TSHEMBE (*With contempt*)   Yes. I know. In Twin Forks Junction!

CHARLIE (*Shaking his head*)   You really can't get rid of it, can you? The bitterness. No matter how you try, we've done it to you: you do hate white men.

TSHEMBE (*Gazing at him with open disgust*)   Mr. Morris, I told you I do *not*, but have it your way! No matter what delusions of individuality infect *my* mind, to *you* I am not an individual but a tide, a flood, a monolith: "The *Bla-a-acks!*"

CHARLIE   Nonsense! To me you are no more "the Blacks" than I am "the Whites"—(*In his excitement* CHARLIE *steps on a swatch and* TSHEMBE, *flicking his wrist, motions him back*) That is, I can't speak for *you*—but *I* am myself.

TSHEMBE   And *that* of course is nonsense! *You* are a tide, a flood—a tide, yes, I like that, a receding tide.

CHARLIE   And you, the oncoming tide—? (TSHEMBE *nods, smiling*) There, you see! You are obsessed with it! And not just race either—vengeance!

TSHEMBE (*Swiftly, to end it*)   It is not *I* but you who are obsessed. Race—racism—is a device. No more. No less. It explains nothing at all.

CHARLIE   Now what the hell is that supposed to mean?

TSHEMBE (*Closing his eyes, wearily*)   I said racism is a device that, of itself, explains nothing. It is simply a means. An invention to justify the rule of some men over others.

CHARLIE   But I agree with you entirely! Race hasn't a thing to do with it actually.

TSHEMBE   Ah—but it *has!*

CHARLIE (*Throwing up his hands*)   Oh, come on, Matoseh. Stop playing games!

TSHEMBE   I am not playing games. (*He sighs and now, drawn out of himself at last, proceeds with the maximum precision and clarity he can muster*) I am simply saying that a device *is* a device, but that it also has consequences: once invented it takes on a life, a reality of its own. So, in one century, men invoke the device of religion to cloak their conquests. In another, race. Now, in both cases you and I may recognize the fraudulence of the device, but the fact remains that a man who has a sword run through him because he refuses to become a Moslem or a Christian—or who is shot in Zatembe or Mississippi because he is black—is suffering the utter *reality* of the device. And it is pointless to pretend that it doesn't *exist*—merely because it is a *lie!*

CHARLIE (*Deeply affected*)   You know something, Matoseh? I don't think I'll ever understand you: on the one hand you go completely beyond race, on the other you wrap yourself in it! One minute the purest lucidity, and the next—"the scars in the hills of Zatembe!" (*He is circling the perimeters of the cloth. Now he starts in towards* TSHEMBE, *thinks better of it, folds back a passageway and goes up to him*) Now if only you could drop the devices *yourself* you might find out we're on the same side—(TSHEMBE *throws him a look and abruptly turns away and snatches up the fabrics furiously*) For Christ's sake, man, we want the same things! We're both searching! Only, I respect your anguish. Now, if you could just try to respect mine—

TSHEMBE (*Whirling on him*) *"Respect,"* Mr. Morris? What is there to conceivably respect about the fact that your so-called "anguish" has brought you thousands of miles across rivers, mountains, whole oceans, to rapturize about a dirty, smelly little hospital which, presumably, must distribute one new germ for every one it almost accidentally exterminates!

CHARLIE Now, just a minute, Matoseh—

TSHEMBE (*Riding over him*) . . . And brings to life a new superstition for every old one it shames! *"Respect"?!* Those are vile and expensive vanities. In your own country you would not be paying tribute to this place, you would be campaigning to get it closed!

CHARLIE (*White heat*) The fact of the matter is that it is better than nothing and that is what you had before: *Nothing!*

TSHEMBE And even if that were true—billions and billions of dollars, pounds, francs, marks, have long since paid whatever debt we—

CHARLIE And you really think Marta Gotterling came here for gold—? Or was it cobalt! (*Advancing on him. The two stand jaw-to-jaw*) I'd like you to answer that, Matoseh. Do you?

TSHEMBE (*Smiling easily*) Of course not. She came to find fulfillment. Just as you came for salvation, and I to find— *cloth!* Here's hoping each of us finds what he is seeking. At Africa's expense, as always! (*He drinks*) Now take your stolen liquor and go, please. This conversation will never get any further.

(*He gets down on his knees with his back to* CHARLIE *and turns his full attention to the box of odds and ends*)

CHARLIE (*Not moving*)   It has to.

TSHEMBE   For whose sake . . . ?

CHARLIE   For both our sakes.

(CHARLIE *is about to pursue the point but hesitates with sudden apprehension as he notices that* PETER *and two* WARRIORS, *one with a spear, have approached the hut*)

PETER   Bwana.

CHARLIE   Peter.

(CHARLIE *exits.* PETER *and the* WARRIORS *step swiftly into the hut and surround* TSHEMBE, *who looks up uneasily from one to the other, still on his knees. The* WARRIORS *listen intently and respond throughout what follows. Even at his most "relaxed" and indifferent,* TSHEMBE *is acutely aware of their every move*)

PETER   You did not answer the summons yesterday, cousin.

TSHEMBE   Summons?

PETER   From the Council.

TSHEMBE   What do *you* know about that?

PETER (*Takes out a strip of bark*)   I know about it.
(*He hands it to him*)

TSHEMBE (*With slow realization*)   You, too—!

PETER (*Squats beside him to talk*)   Why did you not come?

TSHEMBE   What would I have done there?

PETER   You would have heard what is happening to our people.

TSHEMBE (*With a great sigh*)   I know what is happening to our people, Peter.

PETER   Then why did you not come? And in your father's house I am not "Peter"—I am Ntali, the name our people gave me.

TSHEMBE   Well, Ntali, the truth is, I can no longer think of myself as a Kwi. (*The* WARRIORS *stir with impatience and regard each other*) Only as a man.

PETER (*Dubiously*)   You took part in the funeral service as one who knows who he is.

TSHEMBE   It was a way of saying "goodbye."

PETER   Tshembe, I speak for the Council. There is a need for leaders.

TSHEMBE   I thank the Council but I am going back. I have a family in Europe.

PETER   Your father was a great Kwi—

TSHEMBE   And I am not. Ntali, there are men in this world —I don't know how to say this so you will understand— who *see* too much to take sides.

(*The* WARRIORS *respond with displeasure and one of them grips his spear.* PETER *motions him back*)

PETER (*Gently*) I understand, cousin—that such men have forgotten the tale of Modingo, the wise hyena who lived between the lands of the elephants and the hyenas. Tshembe, hear me. (*What follows is not merely told but acted out vividly in the tradition of oral folk art*) A friend to both, Modingo understood each side of their quarrel. The elephants said they needed more space because of their size, and the hyenas because they had been *first* in that part of the jungle and were accustomed to running free. And so, when the hyenas came to him, Modingo counseled (PETER *rises to become the "wise hyena"*): "Yes, brothers. True. We were first in this land. But they *do* need space—any fool can see that elephants are very *large!* And because I was born with the mark of reason on my brow—on which account I am called Modingo, 'One Who Thinks Carefully Before He Acts'—I cannot join you on our side while there is also justice on the other. But let me think on it." (*He sits, brow furrowed, chin in hand*) And thereupon Modingo thought. And thought. And thought. And the hyenas sat and waited. And seeing this, the elephants gathered their herds and moved at once—and drove them from the jungle altogether! (*Turning to* TSHEMBE) That is why the hyena laughs until this day and why it is such terrible laughter: because it was such a bitter joke that was played upon them while they "reasoned." (*There is silence for a moment, and then he leans forward to place his hand upon* TSHEMBE*'s*) Tshembe Matoseh, we have waited a thousand seasons for these "guests" to leave us. Your people need you.

TSHEMBE (*Sadly*) Ntali, the Europeans have a similar tale which concerns a prince . . .

PETER You are very full of what the Europeans have. Your people need you.

TSHEMBE If they need a Modingo to study the tides while the sea engulfs them—I am their man! But a leader I am not.

PETER Then become one! Tshembe, your father—was my commander in the Freedom of the Land Army.

TSHEMBE (*Staring at him, incredulous*) My father? You mean my father approved—?

PETER (*Smiling*) —conceived, Tshembe.

TSHEMBE My . . . father . . . !

PETER (*Rises*) We meet in the forest within the hour.
(*He turns to go, followed by the* WARRIORS. *Abruptly,* TSHEMBE *throws the bark back*)

TSHEMBE I am not interested in killing. Anyone. Especially harmless old missionaries and their wives.

PETER Nor I. But they are a part of it.

TSHEMBE They sing hymns and run a hospital!

PETER (*Ending it*) Within the hour, Tshembe.
(*He starts off*)

TSHEMBE Ntali, wait! You know Kumalo is coming home? (PETER *halts, nods*) For talks—

PETER   There has been enough talk. The Council speaks for the people. Not Kumalo.

TSHEMBE   But this is what the people have been fighting for—to force the settlers to negotiate . . .

PETER   Why did he not consult us?

TSHEMBE   Did you consult him before you took arms? Think, Ntali: you have only a few rifles and the long knives of our fathers . . .

PETER (*Perplexed*)   I know the whites. There is only contempt in their "negotiations."

TSHEMBE (*Crossing to him*)   Ah, but also *fear*, cousin . . . *fear!* These are new times, man. All Africa turns against them—the world turns against them! Your long knives have pushed them to the table. Now keep them poised—but steady!

PETER (*Abruptly, to end it*)   Too late. Too many have died.

TSHEMBE   But for a *reason*, Ntali. Perhaps now no more need die. Give Kumalo his chance.

PETER   His chance—for what? To trade white overseers for black!

TSHEMBE   Amos Kumalo is no puppet—

PETER   No, of course not. But will he control the Army? The mines? His own ministers? (*Shaking his head*) A government office . . . a government car . . . a white government secretary to warm his bed—"*who fears the lion after his teeth are pulled?*" No, Tshembe. In the past when invaders came we killed them. When we do so again, we will have peace. Only then.

(*He and the* WARRIORS *start out*)

TSHEMBE   Ntali! (*He sighs and does not even look at them as—wearily, the words coming almost automatically—he assumes the burden in spite of himself*) I will go to Zatembe—to speak with Kumalo. I will tell him the mood of our people. I will tell him the settlers have *one* season to grant our demands . . . *One* season, Ntali . . .

PETER   We have waited a thousand seasons—

TSHEMBE   Then what can it hurt to wait a thousand and one?

PETER (*Conflicted*)   You understand, we are determined to rule? (TSHEMBE *nods*) By whatever means necessary. . .

TSHEMBE (*Slyly reversing the emphasis*)   By *whatever* means necessary . . . !

PETER (*Studying him. With the slight edge of wonder and the faintest smile*)   Tshembe Matoseh, the Wanderer— who has come home from Europe with the white man's tongue . . . (*Searching his eyes*) I hope you do not have his heart . . . (*A beat. He decides*) I will speak to the Council.

(*Without warning, the* WARRIORS *suddenly vanish —as* ABIOSEH *approaches over the rise up left.* TSHEMBE *draws* PETER *aside and indicates* ABIOSEH)

TSHEMBE   Aren't you going to try to recruit him?

PETER   We do not recruit—Europeans.
   (*He exits*)

ABIOSEH   What did he want?

TSHEMBE   What did he "want"? He came to remind us
   that we are supposed to be our father's sons.
      (*They look at each other . . .*)

Dimout

ACT TWO

SCENE 3

Late that afternoon. The Mission.
There is a sudden burst of voices offstage.

RICE (*Offstage*) We have adopted these measures for ex-
tremely good reasons—(DEKOVEN, *perspiring and winded,
comes out of the jungle, a boy in his arms.* RICE *marches
behind him shouting. Two* SOLDIERS *follow*)—and I will
have them obeyed!

DEKOVEN Marta! *Fever!*

RICE I am responsible for every life in this district including your own—

DEKOVEN Thank you, Major. Marta! Peter! Someone!
(CHARLIE *enters down right and stands absorbing the
scene*)

RICE The life of a single native child cannot justify endan-
gering the security of the entire European community!
(DEKOVEN *kicks open the door and puts the boy
down, while the* SOLDIERS *post themselves outside*)

DEKOVEN Marta! For God's sake, hurry!

MARTA (*Offstage*) I am coming, Willy.

RICE   Even you must understand that, DeKoven!
(MARTA, PETER *run onstage*)

DEKOVEN   It's little Modeke. Fever . . .
(*He sits finally and mops his brow*)

RICE (*An unbroken crest on deaf ears*)   And if this Mission
continues to disregard precautions I shall have to close
down the hospital! HAVE I MADE MYSELF CLEAR,
DEKOVEN?

MARTA (*Turning, hypodermic needle in hand*)   This is neither a gymnasium nor a military barracks, Major. Please
lower your voice or leave.
(*She gives the boy a shot*)

RICE (*An angry look—but lowered voice*)   Have I made
myself clear?

MARTA (*To* PETER, *indicating the boy*)   Take him to Ward
Two. Isolation.

RICE   I said, Have I made myself clear?

DEKOVEN   About what, dear man?

RICE   About the fact that alone out there you were a perfect target, and every time a white man is killed the whole
idea of killing whites is made that much more attractive!
(PETER *stands listening between them, the child in
his arms*)

CHARLIE   I'd have thought he couldn't have been safer
than with that boy in his arms, Major. But then I'm sure
you know much more about it than I do.

RICE (*Sharply*)   Yes, I do. I know, for instance, that authority in this colony has always depended on the sacred-
ness of a white life—(PETER *exits*)—and once that
authority is undermined—well, if four million blacks
should ever take it into their heads to start killing white
men . . .

   (MME. NEILSEN *enters with* ERIC)

MADAME   Ah, George, I am glad to see you are your usual
cheery self!

RICE (*Shoots her a look*)   In any event, it is my duty to
inform you—(*Looking from one to the other*)—that as of
this moment I am assuming full command here. Kumalo
has been arrested.

DEKOVEN   Kumalo?!

CHARLIE   Jesus.

MADAME   Amos Kumalo?! Why?

RICE (*Taking out a telegram*)   I received this this morning.
"At 0100 hours, 19 May, Zatembe Airport, Dr. Amos
Kumalo was taken into custody by local authorities."

CHARLIE   On what charge?

RICE   Conspiracy.

CHARLIE   Have you gone out of your mind? Your own government invited him here . . .

RICE (*Reads*)   ". . . plotting and organizing an insurrection
against the peace and well-being of the colony. Protective
measures—including the detention of all disruptive ele-

133

ments—are to be instituted—(*Pointedly looking from one to the other*)—at the discretion of the *local* command."

MADAME   May God protect us.

RICE   I expect God will be in a better position to protect us now, Madame.

CHARLIE   No doubt. You have just put the one man in jail who offered a shred of hope that—

RICE   In jail, sir, which means that at last we can sleep in our beds without fear of murderers!

CHARLIE   Are you seriously suggesting that Amos Kumalo—

MARTA   I don't think the Major is suggesting anything of the sort, Mr. Morris—

CHARLIE   I was talking to the Major.

RICE   What say we leave that for the trial, eh, Mr. Morris?

MARTA   Yes, we do have courts of law here . . .

CHARLIE (*Sharply, to* MARTA)   I'm sure you do!

RICE   And I expect *our* standards of jurisprudence in matters of race will compare favorably with America's any day! (MARTA *glares at* CHARLIE *and storms off.* RICE *turns to* MADAME) In any case, Madame Neilsen . . .

CHARLIE   Incidentally, Major—what makes you think the world will sit still for this?

RICE   The *world*, Mr. Morris, will react *de*-cisively as always—with a U.N. resolution! But you don't actually think they'll send their sons against blood relatives over some half-demented darkie prophet? Now do you? (*He turns back to the old lady*) Madame, I'm afraid we shall have to quarter troops here.

MADAME *Here*, Major . . . ?

CHARLIE (*Outraged*) Major Rice—

DEKOVEN (*With ironic suavity*) Mr. Morris. For—the "peace and well-being of the colony."
    (PETER *returns with a broom and busies himself within easy earshot outside*)

MADAME (*To* RICE) I would appreciate it if you would postpone this decision until the Reverend returns.

RICE Where is he? When will he be back?

MADAME He should have been back by now . . .

RICE I'm sorry. This cannot wait. I will appreciate it if the staff would provide such emergency accommodations as possible.

MADAME The Reverend didn't build this Mission to be a base for military operations, George.

RICE Please inform the Reverend that if there are no military operations there will be no Mission.

DEKOVEN (*Bitterly*) The Major is right! We must listen to the Major!

MADAME Do we have a choice, Major?

DEKOVEN   In fact why stop there? We have lots of room here. Move the lepers in with the malarials in Ward One! Ward Two—"Disruptive Elements"!

RICE   Madame, we would never take these disagreeable measures if it—

MADAME   Do we have a choice, George?

RICE   I assure you we will not interfere with the Mission in any way . . .

DEKOVEN   And *we* will not interfere with the military! We must listen to the Major—

MADAME   Do we have a choice!

RICE   No. (DEKOVEN *turns on his heel and strides out*) Madame, I *am* sorry. Perhaps when this darkness is over you will thank me. Good day. (*He turns to go—and sees the eavesdropping* PETER. *Calling out*) Peter!
　　(*The African freezes*)

PETER   Yes, Bwana.

RICE   Would you wait? (PETER *looks from* RICE *to the* SOLDIERS *and measures the chances for escape*) Mr. Morris. I'd like you to see this. There is a reason why we do things the way we do here. Peter, step over here please. (PETER *hesitates*) Lively now!
　　(PETER *hastens to his side*)

PETER   Bwana.

RICE (*Studying him*)   How is everything going, Peter?

PETER   Everything just fine, Bwana.

RICE   "Just fine," is it?

PETER   Yes, Bwana.

RICE   No complaints then, Peter?

CHARLIE (*Sharing* PETER*'s humiliation*)   Major Rice, I really don't see—

RICE   You *shall*, Mr. Morris. Nothing in Africa is quite as it seems. Peter and I understand this—*do we not, Peter?* (PETER *smiles foolishly—not knowing what to make of it, but knowing enough not to say anything*) I do not hate the African. I simply know the proper relationship. I am devoted to the blacks who work for me and whom I have helped to civilize. There are no more loyal people. Isn't that so, Peter?

CHARLIE   Major—for Christ's sakes!

PETER   Yes, Bwana.

RICE   As I told you, Mr. Morris, I am going to illustrate a case in point. Peter is a part of—Africa—that you must not forget in times like these. There is a relationship here, something natural and fine. Peter's children will have something else . . . Have I spoken fairly, Peter?

PETER   Yes, Bwana. (RICE*'s eyes do not leave* CHARLIE*'s*) De young boys—dey read de books . . . dey go to de city . . . dey tinks dey want be white men in black skins. Without de white man—de jungle close on Africa again. De huts be empty of God and de water turn to dust and de tsetse fly rule de savannah again.

RICE (*A man touched and confirmed*) When you write your articles, Mr. Morris, I trust you will also bear Peter in mind. Thank you, Peter. (*As* PETER *starts off*) Please remember me to your wife.

CHARLIE "—or else!" (RICE *shoots him a look and exits after* PETER. CHARLIE *turns immediately to* MME. NEILS-EN) Madame—

MADAME (*Suddenly seeming very old and fragile*) Mr. Morris, if I were a drinker, I would ask you to fix me a drink.

CHARLIE Madame, I am a drinker, and I will fix myself the stiffest drink I can. (*He starts to*) I wish the Reverend were here.

MADAME So do I, Mr. Morris.

CHARLIE I would very much like to have seen how he would have handled this. What would he have done, Madame?

MADAME Young man, I like you. I enjoy talking to you. I even enjoy listening to you, but—I am tired.

CHARLIE What would he have done, Madame?

MADAME What *could* he do? I don't imagine very much. But I expect that by now he would be sitting with you reflecting on the state of man in the universe and where he has plummeted. I think you would have both enjoyed that. And now I must go to bed.

CHARLIE   Madame, this whole country is about to blow up. The Reverend's words are important now, vital. The world would listen to him.

MADAME (*Sighs*)   He is not here, Mr. Morris.

CHARLIE   But you know his sentiments. Perhaps if I could dispatch some word from him . . . If they'll listen to anybody, they'll listen to Reverend Neilsen.

MADAME   Just what would they listen to him about?

CHARLIE   Why Kumalo, the troops, the whole tragic farce. If you would authorize me to release an appeal to reason from the man who to millions *is* Africa—

MADAME (*She is becoming quite agitated as he keeps pressing*)   He is not *here*, Mr. Morris . . .

CHARLIE   But you are. And you know his sentiments. A statement from him . . .

MADAME   Mr. Morris, I cannot speak for him!

CHARLIE   Why? You know what he would say . . .

MADAME (*Painfully*)   Yes, I believe I do. He would say—he is a minister, not a statesman . . . I really must get some rest.

CHARLIE   Madame, forgive me, but whatever the line between the two, it was erased when Major Rice stood here—giving orders . . .

MADAME   Yes, I agree . . .

CHARLIE   Then a statement from you . . .

MADAME   From *me?* It would be of no consequence . . .

CHARLIE   In your husband's name . . . Madame, there are two billion colored people on this planet who have known nothing but Major Rices. Let them know there is *another* white man! Let them know Reverend Neilsen!

MADAME   I cannot speak for my husband and I really must go to bed . . . (*Calls*) Peter . . .

CHARLIE   But he cares about these people . . .

MADAME   Yes he does. Of course. They are his "children" . . .

CHARLIE   Madame, I don't believe it. Are you suggesting that he would accept this horrible . . .

MADAME (*Desperately*)   I am suggesting nothing. Except that I am very tired . . . (PETER *enters*) Peter . . . (*She reaches out for his hand*) Would you mind . . .
    (TSHEMBE *enters. He is dressed in tie and suit for travel, and there is urgency in his manner*)

TSHEMBE   Excuse me, Madame.

MADAME   Tshembe—

TSHEMBE   I am looking for Major Rice.

MADAME   Major Rice?

TSHEMBE   I must have the Major's permission to see Kumalo in Zatembe. I will need an escort—
>   (MADAME *hesitates helplessly and at last* CHARLIE *moves forward*)

CHARLIE   You're too late, Matoseh.

TSHEMBE   Too late? (*He turns to the old lady*) Madame . . . ?

CHARLIE   Believe me, I'll do everything I can—
>   (TSHEMBE *looks at him blankly*)

MADAME   Tshembe, Kumalo's been arrested.

TSHEMBE   Arrested?!
>   (*He glances swiftly at* PETER—*and gestures in ironic concession to the older man's superior wisdom all along*)

CHARLIE   At the airport . . . Matoseh, I'll do everything. I swear to you . . .

TSHEMBE (*Stares at him, then begins to back slowly away with mocking servility*)   Of course. Of course you will. Thank you, Madame. (*He tips his hand. She stands watching helplessly*) Thank you— (*Half bowing to* CHARLIE *and touching his head*)—Bwana!
>   (*The lights dim out on the American and the old lady, as the African continues backing away, then stoops at the tree stump and comes up with* ERIC's *bottle. And now at last it comes—*TSHEMBE's *laughter, involuntary, almost hysterical, slowly at first—*

then rising to a crescendo. The drums build. TSHEMBE *drinks. Drums to a climax and—abruptly— silence. Above him the* WOMAN *appears, eyes fastened upon him. He stiffens, and turns slowly to face her)*

Blackout

ACT TWO
SCENE 4

In the darkness "message" drums begin at the back of the house and move swiftly towards the stage.

It is about noon, the next day. The hut. ABIOSEH *sits reading his Bible with an apple beside him. Several* AFRICANS *rush across stage and off.* ERIC *is among them. He enters hurriedly and reaches for the shield of old Abioseh.*

ABIOSEH   Eric, I have been waiting for you.

ERIC   Kumalo has been arrested!

ABIOSEH   What are you doing, boy?

ERIC (*Grabbing a spear*)   They need warriors.

ABIOSEH   Sit down, Eric. I want to talk about your future.

ERIC   I am summoned!

ABIOSEH   Ah. "Summoned." And shall I also paint *your* cheeks? Sit down, boy.

ERIC   They want me!
      (TSHEMBE *appears unseen upstage and weaves towards them, quite drunk*)

ABIOSEH   What do you know about any of it?

143

ERIC   I know it is time to drive the invaders into the sea.
And that *I* shall carry the spear and shield of our father.

TSHEMBE (*Enters*)   You are half European. Which part of
yourself will you drive into the sea!

ERIC   I am African enough not to mock when my people
call!

TSHEMBE   And what will you do when your doctor calls,
Eric? It takes more than a spear to make a man.

ERIC   What does it take, Tshembe? You teach me! What
does it take to be a man? A white wife and son?
        (*He starts out.* TSHEMBE *blocks the doorway. The
        boy dances from side to side to escape, but* TSHEMBE
        is the more agile)

TSHEMBE   Put down the things, boy. You're not ready to
be—(ERIC *crashes the length of the spear against*
TSHEMBE*'s chest. He takes it from him in a show of
strength*)—a warrior yet . . . I . . . promise you.
        (*He thrusts the spear into the ground and flings* ERIC
        back)

ERIC   You stink of cheap whiskey.

TSHEMBE   Ah, but it flows from expensive ideals!
        (*He sets the shield back in place.* ERIC *seizes the
        moment to run for it—but* ABIOSEH *trips him and falls
        on him in good sportsfield style*)

ERIC   Let me go! They need me.

TSHEMBE   And that is the most important thing in the world, isn't it?

ERIC   Yes.

ABIOSEH   Important enough to go setting fire to farms and murdering people. Why, Eric? Why should you feel that way?

ERIC   I hate them!

ABIOSEH   Why?

TSHEMBE   I find you stranger than he. Why shouldn't he hate them? Are your eyes so full of God you can't see what's become of your own brother?
(*He sits and bemusedly picks up* ABIOSEH'*s apple*)

ABIOSEH   Eric is coming to St. Cyprian's with me.

TSHEMBE (*Polishing the apple with great concentration*) And I would prefer to take him with me.

ABIOSEH   At St. Cyprian's he will be educated.

TSHEMBE   He might also become a priest.
(*He bites the apple*)

ABIOSEH   And that is a horrible possibility?

TSHEMBE   *Horrible.*

ABIOSEH   To give one's life to God . . .

TSHEMBE   To my knowledge it has never been proved that it is *He* who enjoys the gift! (*Picks up the other's Bible*) Besides, Eric would only run off.

ABIOSEH   They have ways at St. Cyprian's to keep boys from running off.

TSHEMBE (*Thumbing through it*)   Yes, come to think of it, they must.

ABIOSEH   Father Mettinger will make him welcome.

TSHEMBE (*Suggestively*)   No doubt.

ABIOSEH   You would be better off, my brother, if your Christian teachings had been more forceful!

TSHEMBE   I never thought much of Christian forcefulness.

ABIOSEH   That is what you think, but God is raging in you, fighting for you!

TSHEMBE (*Slamming the book shut*)   Why does He always tell you and not me what He is doing!

ABIOSEH   In any case, I will look after Eric. He will return with me.

ERIC   No. I am staying here—where I belong! (*To* TSHEMBE, *pleading*) They call me by the name my mother gave me—

TSHEMBE (*Derisively*)   —Ngedi!

ERIC   Yes. Ngedi. They have asked me to take the oath.

ABIOSEH   "They?"

ERIC   Peter . . .
    (*Knowing suddenly he should not have said it.* ERIC *and* TSHEMBE *exchange glances*)

ABIOSEH   Peter? (ERIC *rushes off*) Ah . . . Peter. (*Slow recognition*) ". . . We do not recruit Europeans . . ." Tshembe, you knew this? But why? He works for them. They trust him . . .

TSHEMBE   Abioseh, you really don't understand any of it, do you?

ABIOSEH   I understand that those like Peter must be stopped by whatever means. Kumalo is a dreamer, Peter a fool! Men do not move from lizard powder to legislatures, from sweeping floors to ruling nations—

TSHEMBE   Here men do not move from sweeping floors to anything . . .

ABIOSEH   It is the Peters who make it impossible for us.

TSHEMBE   "Us"?

ABIOSEH   For responsible men. Practical men who know how to bide their time—who understand there is only one way to power here. Tshembe, when the blood of this hour is past, when order and reason are restored to these hills, the West will compromise because they must. The government at Zatembe will call upon us, because they cannot go on in the old way. And then, my brother, it will be *our* time. Black men will sit beside the settlers. Black magistrates, black ministers, black officers! Responsible leaders—

TSHEMBE (*Turning to him slowly as if for all time and all comprehension*)   You are altogether committed to them, aren't you?

ABIOSEH   I am committed to God, to civilization—and to Africa! Yes, Africa, my brother—

TSHEMBE (*Quietly, the controlled precision of a scalpel*) The American blacks have a name for those like you, Abioseh, but it lacks . . . magnitude! (*He starts away, turns back*) Perhaps among the twelve disciples of your Jesus— a better one might be found!

ABIOSEH   Yes, Tshembe—but it is not *I* who am Judas! It is *you* who have sold yourself to Europe! It is I who chose Africa! Tshembe, Tshembe . . . I have watched you and listened to you and desperately wished that you would share my goals for our people. I have waited and prayed. But you believe in nothing! You act on nothing! You have refashioned God in man's image—but you serve neither God nor man!

(ABIOSEH *turns on his heel and starts out*)

TSHEMBE   Where are you going?

ABIOSEH   I must go.

TSHEMBE   Go!? Go where?

ABIOSEH   I must go.

TSHEMBE   Peter . . . !

ABIOSEH (*Turning to him*)   They are murderers, Tshembe. Murderers!

TSHEMBE   Abioseh, stay out of this. It is not your affair!

ABIOSEH (*Taking hold of him*)   It is both our affair. Tshembe, come with me!

TSHEMBE (*Breaking free*)   They will kill him, Abioseh . . .

ABIOSEH   I must go.
> (ABIOSEH *starts out.* TSHEMBE *grabs him*)

TSHEMBE   No!
> (*They grapple and at last* TSHEMBE *flings him to the ground and grabs up the spear to hold him there*)

ABIOSEH   Then you must *use* the spear!

TSHEMBE   Abioseh, there is butchering on both sides. Peter is not your affair. Stay out of this!

ABIOSEH   Christ leaves me no option.
> (ABIOSEH *rises and stands tall in his righteousness, inviting the blow*)

TSHEMBE   Abioseh! We sat together as children and watched the fire and spoke of what we'd become as men. Look at us now!

ABIOSEH (*Advancing on the spear until it rests against his breast*)   Then use the spear. Because that is the side you have chosen. The side of terror, the side of blood. I *make* you your brother's keeper!
> (*The two brothers stand, facing each other.* ABIOSEH *sweeps past him and exits*)

Blackout

ACT TWO
SCENE 5

Not quite an hour later. The Mission.

   CHARLIE *'s portable is open before him on the veranda. He types rapidly, then rips out and crumples the page.* DEKOVEN *looks up from the drink he is nursing.*

CHARLIE   No cable. No mail. No phones. I wish to God there was something I could do.

DEKOVEN   Mr. Morris, you really must learn to give up. You are sitting there, still harboring the fugitive hope that sooner or later Torvald Neilsen will walk out of that jungle and announce, "I have been to Zatembe to intercede for Kumalo!" Isn't that so?

CHARLIE (*Smiles*)   It was only a thought—
   (TSHEMBE *enters*)

TSHEMBE   Mr. Morris! Dr. DeKoven. Is Peter here?

DEKOVEN   He went cross river early this morning.

TSHEMBE   Then I must wait. Do you mind?

DEKOVEN   Of course not.

CHARLIE (*As* TSHEMBE *turns away*)   Tshembe—

TSHEMBE (*With polite finality*)   Mr. Morris.

(*He sits on a stump at some distance down right.*
CHARLIE *at last turns back to* DEKOVEN)

CHARLIE   You know, I care about this place. Very much.

DEKOVEN   I do not doubt that.

CHARLIE   I've been thinking about something you said the other day. About how coming here had "saved your life." Did you mean that?

DEKOVEN   For whatever little that's worth.

CHARLIE   Well. Obviously a great deal to a good many people.

DEKOVEN   Some other age will have to know that, Mr. Morris. I don't.

CHARLIE   Why *not*, Doctor?

DEKOVEN   Mr. Morris, there is a hospital for Europeans only seventy-five miles from here. Entirely modern. Here things are lashed together with vines from the jungle. Surely you must have wondered why.

CHARLIE   Well, I assumed I knew why—that it was obvious . . .

DEKOVEN   Is it? Electric lines between here and Zatembe could be laid within weeks, a road in three months. The money exists. All over the world people donate to Missions like this. It is not obvious, not obvious at all.

CHARLIE   But I thought the African wouldn't come if it were different. Marta—

DEKOVEN (*With a gentle smile*)   Marta is two things, Mr. Morris: a very competent surgeon and a saint; but she questions nothing very deeply. One of the first things that the new African nations have done is to set up modern hospitals when they can. The Africans go to them so freely that they are severely overcrowded, so something is wrong with Marta's quaint explanation, don't you think?

CHARLIE   Apparently.

DEKOVEN (*With great acuteness and irony*)   Mr. Morris, the struggle here has not been to push the African into the Twentieth Century—but at all costs to keep him *away* from it! We do not look down on the black because we really think he is lazy, we look down on him because he is wise enough to resent working for us. The problem, therefore, has been how *not* to educate him at all and—at the same time—teach him just enough to turn a dial and know which mining lever to raise. It has been as precise as that—and that much a failure. Because, of course, it is impossible! When a man knows that the abstraction *ten* exists—nothing on earth can stop him from looking for the fact of *eleven.* That is part of what is happening here. (*Drinking and looking off*) But only part.

TSHEMBE (*Swinging around and smiling slightly*)   You seem disturbed, Mr. Morris—

CHARLIE   Well, it's simply that—well, it takes a hell of a lot of education to turn a backward people into—How many people in this village can even read?

TSHEMBE   Read *what?* Drums? Everyone. Books? Six, eight, a dozen at most.

CHARLIE (*Sitting back, confirmed*)   Well, then.

DEKOVEN (*Smiling*)   Morris, this Mission has been here forty years. It takes perhaps twenty-five to educate a generation. If you look around you will find not *one* African doctor. (*Shrugs*) Until they govern themselves it will be no different.

CHARLIE (*Nods acquiesence, then*)   And the . . . "other part"? You said there was another part, DeKoven—?

DEKOVEN (*Rising and moving about like a man possessed, reliving the past*)   The other part has to do with the death of a fantasy. I came here twelve years ago believing that I could—it seems so incredible now—help alleviate suffering by participating actively in the very institutions that help sustain it.

CHARLIE   You're not suggesting that lives have not been saved here, Doctor? Why, you alone . . .

DEKOVEN   Oh, I have saved hundreds of lives; all of us here have. I have arrested gangrene, removed tumors, pulled forth babies—and, in so doing, if you will please try to understand, I have helped provide the rationale for genocide.

CHARLIE   Genocide!? You can't really—

DEKOVEN   Mr. Morris, colonial subjects die mainly from a way of life. The incidentals—gangrene, tumors, stillborn babies—are only that: incidentals. Our work—(*He interlocks his fingers*)—reinforces the way of life. But when you come with a faith, an ideal of service, it is impossible to believe that. It was, at first, for me. But I saw my first delegations my first year here.

CHARLIE   Delegations?

DEKOVEN   Yes, at that time they were always sending delegations with a petition of some sort; about the land, grazing rights, taxes. And some of them were always making the trek into Zatembe, you know, to see the governor, the ambassador—*anyone* who could do something. But they always came here first.

TSHEMBE   To get the Reverend's opinion.

DEKOVEN   And he would talk and joke with them and, usually, nothing was done, or, if it was, they were invariably herded onto *less* land, the taxes were raised *higher* —or something. And then one day, seven years ago, they came, led by old Abioseh as usual, with a petition to the Governor General for a new constitution that would permit Africans to sit in the legislature in proportion to their numbers. They were petitioning, of all things, to govern the colony; quite like that. I shall never forget his face—

CHARLIE   The Reverend?

DEKOVEN (*He is standing on the very spot, acutely recalling the moment*)   Yes. He had the most extraordinary expression when he finished reading the petition and he put it down—like this, you know—and he stood up and wiped his glasses and then put them back on, and he smiled at them and they smiled back as they always did, and then he walked among them, his arms outstretched, saying,

"Children, children . . . my dear children . . . go home to your huts! Go home to your huts before you make me angry. *Independence indeed!*" (*A beat. He shakes his head*) No, I shall never forget the old man that day. And the thing is that until that moment, standing here, *I* hadn't understood in the least, not the slightest, any different than he. The fact that it was all over was in the face of the second old man there, Abioseh.

TSHEMBE (*Injecting*)   My father.

DEKOVEN   He did not move, he did not smile, he did not speak. He just stood there with the paper in his hand which they had gone to such pains to draw up, that pitiful piece of paper with its awkward syntax and utterly lucid demands which presumed to do what was and remains impossible: *ask* for freedom!

TSHEMBE (*After a beat*)   He never came back.
      (TSHEMBE *rises and drifts upstage*)

DEKOVEN (*Gesturing around him*)   They will murder us here one day—isn't that so, Tshembe? (TSHEMBE *turns and regards him but says nothing. Drums are heard in the distance*) All of us. And the press of the world will send a shudder through men everywhere. It will seem the crowning triumph of bestial absurdity. We pillars of man's love for man rewarded for our pains: our very throats slit ear to ear by rampaging savages. And whole generations will be born and die without knowing any better. (*He drinks; then*) No, my friend, do not let the drums, the skins and the mumbo jumbo fool you. The sun really *is* starting to rise in the world, so we might just as

well stop pretending it is the middle of the night. *They
are quite prepared to die to be allowed to bring it to
Africa. It is* we *who are not prepared. To allow it* or *to
die.*

(TSHEMBE *exits*)

CHARLIE (*Looking after him*) He must have been quite a
guy, his father.

DEKOVEN (*Remembering*) "Quite a guy. . ."

CHARLIE . . . To bring up the boy—and still maintain a
relationship with the Reverend . . .

DEKOVEN (*Bewildered*) The boy . . . ?

CHARLIE Yes. Eric. Well . . . he *is* his father, isn't he?
Reverend Neilsen—with Abioseh's wife?

DEKOVEN (*Smiles and pours himself a drink and sits.
Then*) Yes . . . It was Abioseh's wife. She died in child-
birth: the Kwi say from shame. But, Morris, it wasn't the
Reverend . . . It was George Rice.

CHARLIE Major Rice—?

DEKOVEN (*Nods*) You see, the man really *is* part of this
country. (PETER *enters*) Peter, Tshembe was looking for
you. He went up the path.

PETER I try to find him. Thank you, Doctor.
(*He starts off but halts at the screech of brakes and
hysterical sirens offstage. At the same moment*
TSHEMBE *reenters down right*)

TSHEMBE Peter—

(He starts towards him, but halts as RICE *and* SOL-
DIERS, *guns at the ready, appear with* ABIOSEH)

RICE   There was a raid at M'nabe. Two hundred blacks.
Reverend Neilsen was among the slaughtered.

CHARLIE   Oh my God!
          *(*DEKOVEN *merely closes his eyes)*

RICE *(As* PETER *starts to leave)*   Peter—*(*PETER *freezes.*
TSHEMBE*'s eyes meet* ABIOSEH*'s)* I think we can all use a
drink. *(*PETER *goes to the bar and starts getting drinks)*
We've brought the body back. Out of delicacy I won't
describe the nature of the mutilation but I would suggest
that the ladies be protected from viewing it. *(*PETER *hands*
RICE *a drink)* Thank you, Peter . . . *(*PETER *offers drinks*
to CHARLIE *and* DEKOVEN, *who refuse them)* Yes, two
hundred blacks and it looks like just the beginning. They
don't stand a chance, of course. At dawn we begin a new
coordinated offensive . . . complete with fresh troops,
helicopters, jets, the whole bloody works . . . *(*PETER *starts*
to leave) Don't go, Peter. *(*PETER *halts and* RICE *motions*
that he'd like another drink) Within three weeks the
mopping up will be over, I can promise you that. *(*PETER
hands him the drink) Thank you—*Ntali . . . !* *(*PETER
drops the tray and runs and, in split-second succession, the
SOLDIERS *and* RICE *open fire. He falls, jerks—and lies dead*
at TSHEMBE*'s feet. The* SOLDIERS *turn their guns on*
TSHEMBE. ABIOSEH *starts to pray.* RICE *crosses to the body*
and puts his gun away) I am taking the liberty, Doctor,
of having a new safety flare system installed. Your friend
here had cut the old one—did you know *that,* DeKoven?

LORRAINE HANSBERRY

Yes, well . . . my condolences to Madame. Are you coming, Abioseh? (*To* TSHEMBE, *indicating the body with his
foot*) Get rid of it.

>   (*He exits, followed by* ABIOSEH *and the* SOLDIERS.
>   CHARLIE *and* DEKOVEN *look on silently as* TSHEMBE
>   *sinks to his knees beside* PETER)

ACT TWO
SCENE 6

*In the darkness the roar and burst of jets explodes over-
head. In the distance the muffled sounds of destruction. Then
silence.*

*It is the following day. A clearing in the jungle in shimmer-
ing light and shadow, near center an* OLD MAN *wrapped in
a blanket. The* OLD MAN *raises one hand for attention. In the
scene that follows, drumbeats punctuate and counterpoint
the action.*

OLD MAN (*Hoary-voiced*) Now people, gather close. In
these troubles we must listen to the warriors.

(*At once* NGAGO *steps out of the shadows—a leader
in the uniform of the Freedom of the Land Army:
crude khaki shorts and shirt, a bit of skin across his
shoulders, a band about his head, long knife at the
waist and rifle in hand. A robust* WARRIOR *behind
him is similarly attired.*

NGAGO *makes a ritualistic sign and then moves with
a dancer's grace, almost hypnotically circling the
stage to fix the audience before a word is spoken. He
is no ordinary leader and this is no ordinary speech
of exhortation. His voice at times rises in traditional
anger; more often it is almost a whisper, a hiss, a*

caress. He is the poet-warrior invoking the soul of his people)

NGAGO (*Raising rifle hand ritualistically*) We must speak swiftly and move on. Brothers! (*His hand sweeps the audience*) Here now are our people flying before the enemy—hunted in the land of our fathers—woman and child and grandsires of the Kwi peoples. See them and understand! See them, people! (*Gesturing directly into the audience*) This young one was making her way from the embers of her village when the soldiers caught her. Five of them! Must I tell you of the crime!? (*Gesturing again*) Rise up, old father! This old man came through the woods with his family and met the troops. (*Screaming*) HE IS WITHOUT FAMILY NOW! (*Pointing*) And look there! And there! And there! (*Drums build to a climax, then silence*) People, first we asked only for more of the bad land they gave us when they took the fine fields of our country—the bad lands on which our cattle already starve . . . For relief from the taxes . . . For safety in the mines. We went without weapons, without hate. We pleaded. We sang. We prayed their Christian prayers. We sent our greatest son to them in peace. And what is the answer they have sent? (*A sweeping powerful gesture*) THIS! They drop lakes of fire from the skies on our villages, drive our women and children fleeing before them, herd our men into the great camps they have built for this hour! And have we not seen the rest of it? Have we not seen the great birds that sweep low to devour our harvest! Have we not seen the hummingbirds of death that sit motionless over the fields where our daughters are running and fire on them like animals! WHAT THEN BUT TO FIGHT? WHAT THEN BUT TO DRIVE THEM OUT!? (*Softly, hypnotically: an incantation to the slowly mounting staccato of the drums*) People, pass this word in the forest until the trees *whisper* it, until the rivers *hum* the message: Send us your sons! Send us warriors! KILL THE INVADER! By spear and by rifle. In the night, in the morning. On the roads. In their homes. In their beds. Let us drown them in the blood they have shed for a thousand seasons—(*His voice hushes almost to a whisper, caressing the words*)—and so make Death *black* for all their generations—(*He kneels and circles his hand over the earth*)—so that in all our land no seed of them—(*He picks up a handful of dust*)—no single scent of what they were—(*Letting it sift away through his fingers*)—remains to afflict our children's children's children! (*Rifle in the air in classic pose*) KILL THE INVADER!

Blackout

ACT TWO
SCENE 7

Late afternoon. The Mission.

The sound of the riverboat whistle is heard several times in the distance. ERIC, *who is waiting on the Mission steps, gets up, picks up* CHARLIE's *typewriter and valises, and exits over the rise up right.*

In the parlor MME. NEILSEN, *in mourning black, sits by the bier on which rests her husband's coffin.* CHARLIE *stands for a moment at the bier, then goes to* MADAME *and places his hand on her shoulder; she covers it with hers. He starts after* ERIC *as across the compound comes* TSHEMBE, *wearing tie and jacket for the visit.*

CHARLIE (*Halting*) Matoseh—

TSHEMBE Yes?

CHARLIE I wanted to tell you, before I left, how sorry I am about—about everything.

TSHEMBE (*With cool disinterest as he moves past*) Thank you.

CHARLIE Matoseh—(TSHEMBE *waits*) I may not see you again.

TSHEMBE Goodbye, Mr. Morris.
(*He turns to go*)

CHARLIE I'd like to look you up in London.

TSHEMBE (*Turning*) Still at it? I should think the past few days would have provided enough local color for your book.

CHARLIE My book—?

TSHEMBE You do plan to write a book about us, don't you, Mr. Morris?

CHARLIE No. No . . . a long time ago I had planned to, but . . .

TSHEMBE Oh, but you must! By all means! The whole world is waiting to hear about the martyred Reverend and this temple in the wasteland that is Africa.

CHARLIE Tshembe—

TSHEMBE As a matter of fact, I will help you. I have a suggestion for the title—"Behind the Color Curtain." (*Lifting his hands as if he can already see the words in print*) "The Story of a Mission: how it tried to lift the benighted black from his native sloth and indolence—and how it was rewarded." Tell them, Mr. Morris. Tell them so that when your readers find out it is American planes Zatembe is flying with American bombs for our villages . . . They can relax with assurance that their moral obligation to humanity is being fulfilled!

CHARLIE Are you quite finished, Matoseh?

TSHEMBE Except for the dedication. Americans excel in dedications—"To brotherhood, to the building of bridges!" Now go, sir, write your book! The whole damned world is waiting!

(*He starts away*)

CHARLIE   Thank you. Thank you, I will try—*Bwana!*

TSHEMBE (*Turns*)   What the hell is that supposed to mean?

CHARLIE   It means get off my back, you hypocrite! What makes you so holy? Listen, a week ago—(*The sound of a helicopter is heard approaching overhead*)—you gave me a song and dance about the white intellectual "plumbing" your "depths." Well, stop presuming on mine! Stop writing my book. Stop telling me which side to come out on because it's so much easier to fill your eyes with me than to look at yourself. Where are you running, man? Back to Europe? To watch the action on your telly? (*A beat. An appeal*) Tshembe, we do what we can. We're on the same side. (TSHEMBE *pointedly looks up and smiles ironically at the chopper, which is now directly overhead.* CHARLIE *shouts over the din*) I didn't put those things up there! I'm me—Charlie Morris—not "the White Man"!

TSHEMBE (*Cupping his ear*)   I'm sorry, Mr. Morris, I cannot *hear* you . . .

CHARLIE (*As the chopper recedes somewhat*)   Then try, Matoseh. Because I've heard you.

> (*A beat.* CHARLIE *holds out his hand.* TSHEMBE *studies him and, at last, takes it. Then: as the chopper circles back again, the African lifts their clasped hands towards the sky*)

TSHEMBE   What does it prove, Morris? What will it solve?
(*Abruptly letting go, he turns and crosses into the
Mission. Behind him the American stands alone confronting the chopper's roar before he slowly turns and
exits*)

ACT TWO
SCENE 8

Immediately following. Sunset. MADAME *sits in the parlor as before;* TSHEMBE *sits cross-legged at her feet, his head resting back gently against her.*

TSHEMBE   You will stay on, then?

MADAME   At my age, one goes home only to die. I am already home.

TSHEMBE   Yes, of course. When you first came here, did you know that you would stay here and die here?

MADAME   Yes, I think so. One knows, doesn't one? When the ship steamed into Bremmer Pool and I saw the African Coast for the first time, I did indeed feel that strange foetal moment when, for some reason or other, we know that our destinies are being marked. (*Laughing a little*) Doesn't always turn out like that, of course. But those are the times we remember, so it seems true enough. Torvald was twenty-seven; resplendent in his helmet and a new pair of boots. Steaming down to Africa! Ah, we were something in our circle in that day. "Going out to Africa," people would say, "Ahhhh, ahhhh . . ." and then wonder if they should give us a coin or two. (*Gentle reflective laughs punctuate all of these allusions*) And then, there we were: Torvald and me, a cello and forty crates of hymnals. I was twenty-eight, had two pairs of culottes made of fine Egyptian linen, shots for malaria and a helmet of my own—and what else might one need for any adversity in life!?

TSHEMBE   What was he like then, Madame?

MADAME   It is not all legend. He was a good man, Tshembe, in many ways. He did some amazing things.

TSHEMBE (*He rises abruptly and crosses away*)   Then why did he let my mother die like that?

MADAME   Because, my child, no man can be more than a man; yet that is what was expected of him. He was a White Man in Darkest Africa—not God, but doing God's work—and to him it was clear: the child was the product of an evil act, a sin against God's order, the natural separation of the races. Its fate was for God to decide. He never forgave me for interfering.

TSHEMBE   I do not think most missionaries' wives would have delivered that child . . .

MADAME   He never spoke of it again after that night—nor, as you know, acknowledged the existence of Eric. (*She sits forward rigidly*) Well, he *couldn't* give in, don't you see, Tshembe? He was helpless. Eric was the living denial of everything he stood for: the testament to three centuries of rape and self-acquittal. He *wanted* the child dead; *wanted* your mother to die! (*She closes her eyes*) Do you—hate us terribly, Tshembe?

TSHEMBE (*Gently, crossing behind her and placing his hands on her shoulders*)   Madame, I have seen your mountains. Europe—in spite of all her crimes—has been a great and glorious star in the night. Other stars shone before it— and will again with it. (*Lightly, smiling at his own imagery*) The heavens, as *you* taught me, are broad and can afford a galaxy.

MADAME   And what of *your* mountains, Tshembe? Your beautiful hills. What will you do now?

TSHEMBE   What will I *do?* Madame, I know what I'd like to do. I'd like to become an expert at diapering my son . . . to sit in Hyde Park with a faded volume of Shakespeare and come home to a dinner of fried bananas with kidney pie and—(*He is fighting the tears now as a terrible anguish rises within him*)—turn the phonograph up loud, loud, until the congo drums throb with unbearable sweetness—and then hold my wife in my arms and bury my face in her hair and hear no more cries in the night except those of my boy because he is cold or hungry or terribly wet. (*He hesitates*) I'd like—I'd like my brothers with me. Eric—and Abioseh. Do you remember when we were boys, Abioseh and I? How many times we . . . (*He cannot go on*) I want to go *home.* It seems your mountains have become mine, Madame.

MADAME   Have they, Tshembe?

TSHEMBE   I think so. I thought so. I no longer know. I am one man, Madame. Whether I go or stay, I cannot break open the prison doors which hold Kumalo. I cannot bring Peter back from the dead. I cannot . . . (*He breaks off*)

I am lying, Madame. To myself. And to you. I *know* what I must do . . .

MADAME   Then do it, Tshembe.

TSHEMBE (*Desperately*)   But when I think of . . . (*He lowers his head to touch the top of hers*) Help me, Madame.

MADAME   You have forgotten your geometry if you are despairing, Tshembe. (*She strains forward and rises*) I once taught you that a line goes on into infinity unless it is bisected. Our country needs *warriors*, Tshembe Matoseh. Africa needs warriors. Like your father.

TSHEMBE (*Staring at her*)   You knew about my father.

MADAME   *Warriors*, Tshembe. Now more than ever. Goodbye, child. Now leave me with my husband.
(*She sits, worn out by the effort.* TSHEMBE *observes and absorbs*)

TSHEMBE   Good night, Madame.
(*He turns on his heel as only very resolute men can do and exits*)

MADAME (*Reaching out and ending the light of one of the candles at the bier*)   Well, now . . . the darkness will do for this hour, will it not?
(*She settles back, both hands on her cane, to keep the vigil and await some final episode*)

Dimout

ACT TWO
SCENE 9

*In the darkness—the laughter of a hyena and the sounds
of night as in the Prologue.*

*It is several hours later. The Mission is bathed in moon-
light. Ceiling lanterns flicker in the parlor, where* MADAME
sits as before. ABIOSEH *stands by the coffin.*

ABIOSEH   Madame, your husband was an extraordinary human being, above race, above all sense of self. I know he
would have approved of what I did. (MADAME *says nothing*) There was no other way to handle the terror.
Madame, don't you agree? (MADAME *says nothing. He
crosses down and sits on the veranda edge*) Well, it will
be over for good now. If men choose violence they will
be met by violence. Am I right, Madame? (MADAME *says
nothing*) Those who live by the sword . . . (*He suddenly
pauses, regarding the night*) What a marvelous light. How
beautiful this day has been. How beautiful the night
. . . Ah, but how I wish you could have seen the sunset!
That was always your favorite time, was it not, Madame?
Today it looked as if the edge of the earth was melting.
God was raining down glory.

MADAME   Glory, Abioseh?

ABIOSEH (*The irony is lost on the man wrapt in his own*

reflections) Do you remember the stories you used to tell us to explain the sunset? (*Smiling with warm remembrance*) I believed those stories with all my heart, Madame. But not Tshembe. No, not Tshembe. (TSHEMBE *enters unseen, wearing the robe his father had last worn to the Mission, and walks slowly to* MADAME) My brother wouldn't have it that the sun was eaten by a giant who rose out of the ocean. Remember? (TSHEMBE places his hand on MADAME's *shoulder and she covers it with hers, but says nothing*) He had to know exactly what happened to the sun when it went down, and where it went. He always —

(*Sensing his brother's presence,* ABIOSEH *looks up, regards* TSHEMBE *for a moment and then, with fateful premonition, begins to back away as* TSHEMBE *advances.* ABIOSEH *turns.* WARRIORS *appear over the rise and at the edges of the stage, rifles in hand. Among them is* ERIC—*who blocks the way down right.*

As ABIOSEH *turns back to him,* TSHEMBE *takes out the pistol he has been concealing in his robe and considers it, not so much seeking courage as thoughtfully, then levels it. For a moment the two brothers stand facing each other, aware of all the universal implications of the act; the one pulls the trigger, the other falls, and with a last effort at control* TSHEMBE *crosses to the body, kneels and gently closes* ABIOSEH's *eyes.*

In the same moment, shouts and shots are heard offstage. A crouching SOLDIER *rushes past, shooting as he goes—the* WARRIORS *open fire and* MADAME *staggers erect, hit.* TSHEMBE *whirls and races to catch* her as ERIC *throws a grenade into the Mission. There is an explosion, the* WARRIORS *run off—and* TSHEMBE *stands alone,* MADAME *in his arms, rocking her back and forth. As flames envelop the Mission, he sinks to the ground, gently sets her body beside that of his brother and, in his anguish, throws back his head and emits an animal-like cry of grief as—*

The curtain falls

POSTSCRIPT

It is one measure of *Les Blancs'* success that on opening night no less than six reviewers found it pertinent to discuss not simply the play, but the state of mind of the audience. An audience so personally involved, so visibly affected that if one closed one's eyes one might have imagined that this was not the Broadway of the seventies—the Broadway of the lethargic listeners—but the impassioned theater of the thirties. Or perhaps the Abbey Theatre of Sean O'Casey. In *The Village Voice*, critic Arthur Sainer described the scene:

> Much feeling at the Longacre Sunday night. . . . A sense of emotional investment throughout the audience—black, white audience—partly a celebration of the spirit of the playwright, partly a response to the nature of the material. Much cheering . . . some scattered heckling, and a disturbance at the back of the house . . . At best, an audience feeling something at stake. . . . [in a play] that manages to speak where the century is discovering it lives.*

---

*"And there is something at stake," continued Sainer, "that talks about the condition of human beings, some of whom are cutting each other to pieces for the sake of other human beings. At its best, the play is a harrowing revelation of what we have brought each other to. A time without answers because the questions have become too urgent." Sainer quarreled with aspects of the script and especially— alone among the critics—the production, which he found much too "high-gloss." Nonetheless, he concluded, "The spirit of a brave woman flashes through the synthetic brilliance. What is best about *Les Blancs* is the intelligence of Lorraine Hansberry, the passion and the courage. The playwright suggests no absolutes, with the execption of a moral imperative which moves like a brushfire through the action—the necessity to become free. This necessity cuts through all other sentiment, is ultimately clear and terrifying."

On the radio, Alvin Klein, bored by "the pervading dullness and didacticism" of the play, pondered an audience that "seemed to be divided into two different clapping camps," while Rex Reed in *The Sunday News* was more direct:

> The opening night audience responded violently. Every time the whites were insulted on stage, the blacks applauded. When Mr. Mitchell finally called Mr. Jones a hypocrite, the whites applauded. One black militant was led from the theatre screaming. . . . *Les Blancs* is, if you'll forgive me, too black and white.

In this context, Richard Watts in the New York *Post* considered that "it must surely be a sign of the author's fairness" that the audience seemed "equally divided" in its charged responses to what was happening on stage, while Lee Silver in the *Daily News* congratulated the producer for his "courage," compared the playwright to "the great Bernard Shaw," and described *Les Blancs* as "a most absorbing drama" that "had last night's audience cheering. . . ."

It remained, however, for a black reviewer, Clayton Riley, *The New York Times'* sometime critic of black theater, to link the reactions of the crowd unabashedly to his own, analyzing, in somewhat different terms, the "camps" to which the others had referred. To Riley, *Les Blancs* was not just "a piece of theater" but an event that had become for him:

> . . . an incredibly moving experience. Or, perhaps, an extended moment in one's life not easily forgotten. . . . in a commercial theatre that takes such pains to protect us from knowing who and what and where we are in 20th-Century America. . . .

"Moving" in *that* fashion. In such a way as to polarize an opening night audience into separate camps, not so much camps of color, of Black and White, although that, too, was part of it. The play divides people into sectors inhabited on the one hand by those who recognize clearly that a struggle exists in the world today that is about the liberation of oppressed peoples, a struggle to be supported at all costs. In the other camp live those who still accept as real the soothing mythology that oppression can be dealt with reasonably—particularly by Black people—if Blacks will just bear in mind the value of polite, calm and continuing use of the democratic process.

. . . Somewhere, past performance, staging and written speech, resides that brilliant, anguished consciousness of Lorraine Hansberry, at work in the long nights of troubled times, struggling to make sense out of an insane situation, aware—way ahead of the rest of us—that there is no compromise with evil, there is only the fight for decency. If even Uncle Sam must die toward that end, *Les Blancs* implies, then send *him* to the wall.

If what Riley surmised was true, then it might help to explain why the reactions of many tended to extremes: John Simon in *New York*:

. . . the result is unmitigated disaster. *Les Blancs* (the very French title in what is clearly a British African colony testifies to the utter confusion) is not only the worst new play on Broadway, of an amateurishness and crudity unrelieved by its sophomoric stabs at wit, it is also, more detestably, a play finished—or finished off—by white liberals that does its utmost to justify the slaughter of whites by blacks. . . . It is a malodorous, unenlightening mess.

Walter Kerr in *The New York Times*:

I urge you to go to see Lorraine Hansberry's . . . ranging, quick-witted, ruefully savage examination of the state of the African mind today. . . . Virtually all of *Les Blancs* is there on the stage, vivid, stinging, intellectually alive, and what is there is mature work, ready to stand without apology alongside the completed work of our best craftsmen. The language in particular is so unmistakably stage language that . . . it achieves an internal pressure, a demand that you listen to it, that is quite rare on our stages today.

Indeed, to read the reviews that week was almost to come away with the feeling that the critics had attended different plays—or, in any event, had come out marching to the sound of quite different (Congo) drummers. And this was the more striking in view of their virtually unanimous acclaim for the performances, the direction and production.* The issue was the play.

Martin Gottfried in *Women's Wear Daily*:

There is no story to the play, really . . . a didactic play, existing for its ideas rather than its theatre. Its characters are stereotypes, created as points of view rather than as people, and its language heavy with information. . . . It is still unfinished because, as a work for the theatre, it was mistakenly begun.

---

*James Earl Jones' performance was hailed by many as the greatest of his career; Lili Darvas' unforgettable Madame won her a Tony nomination; Cameron Mitchell's sensitive Charlie, his first appearance on Broadway since *Death of a Salesman*, moved many and was cited by Richard Watts as "brilliant"; Earle Hyman, Harold Scott and Humbert Allen Astredo, among others in the large cast, were singled out by many for special praise. Designer Peter Larkin won the Variety Poll of New York Drama Critics for best set design of the year.

Lee Silver in the *Daily News*:

Les Blancs depends upon interesting characters that talk to each other and who move you one way or another because of what they are, what they have to say and what they become. . . . Miss Hansberry, like the great Bernard Shaw, knew how to make provocative characters become real people on stage . . . representing a variety of viewpoints on a subject of overriding importance. . . . A drama of conflicting ideas salted with some action, but never so concerned about action in itself as to interfere with the steady development of character and story to its inevitable explosive conclusion.

Haskel Frankel in *The National Observer*:

. . . the African setting is no more African than those walking symbols are really stage people. . . . the play is strictly yesterday. . . . The uncommitted man caught between two cultures is a man *passé*, at least insofar as the theatre is concerned. . . .

Richard Watts in *The New York Post*:

. . . things move so rapidly in black Africa that conditions have altered there in many ways since the coming of independence. Yet her final drama . . . remains a timely and powerful work and one of the most important we've had this season. . . . I think the quality that stays with you is its compassionate fair-mindedness. She was not out to get "whitey" but to understand him. . . . It is not a drama of heroes and villains but of worried and completely believable human beings. . . . I happen to be very fond of Africa and have never felt rejected by it, and I know *Les Blancs* is truthful as well as deeply haunting.

Hobe Morrison in *Variety*:

It is an absorbing show that offers little of the entertainment quality necessary for popular appeal . . . and its conclusion seems to boil down to . . . revolution and the ghetto slogan, *"kill whitey."*

Emory Lewis in *The Record*:

The heart of the matter is that Miss Hansberry is a major U.S. writer, in the grand tradition. The most penetrating, passionate and liberating of all her glorious works, it is also a compassionate exploration in depth of the making of a black revolutionary. . . . She shows us not a mass stereotype, but a gallery of . . . varied, profoundly complicated, and engrossing persons. It is easily the best play of the season.

In short, it would not be amiss to conclude of *Les Blancs*, in the year of its premiere production, that Broadway's tastemakers were somewhat less than unanimous. Neither vituperation nor the use of superlatives is new in the theater, of course. But where the disparity is this great, it would appear—at least in some cases—that quite apart from questions of taste and standards of dramaturgy, something else was operating. In an unsigned report on the "erupting" black-theater movement, *Playboy* summarized what was evidently uppermost in some minds: "A number of critics generally sympathetic to black-theatre aims were . . . appalled by Miss Hansberry's *Les Blancs*, produced posthumously on Broadway, which advocated *genocide of non-blacks as a solution to the race problem.*" (Emphasis my own—R.N.)

It was in response to such interpretations that the noted director Harold Clurman, long one of the deans of theater

criticism, took the unusual step in his *Nation* column of
actually questioning motives:

> At a time when rave reviews are reserved for plays like *Sleuth*
> and *Conduct Unbecoming*, I am tempted to speak of *Les
> Blancs* in superlatives.
>
> I suspect, too, that resistance to the play on the ground
> of its simplistic argument is a rationalization for social em-
> barrassment. *Les Blancs* is not propaganda, as has been in-
> ferred; it is a forceful and intelligent statement of the tragic
> impasse of black and white relations all over the world.
> . . . it clarifies, but does not seek to resolve, the historical and
> human problems involved. It does not provide an Answer. It
> is an honest play in which thought-provoking matter is given
> arrestingly theatrical body.

And the following week Mr. Clurman, himself caught in the
cross-fire, returned to the subject:

> Friends have taken me to task for having reacted favorably
> to a play they thought a set of declamations, "propaganda"
> on behalf of blacks opposed to whites.
>
> The play is no such thing; it is a dramatic statement of the
> tragedy in history. . . .

Mr. Clurman concluded:

> What [the ending]signifies is that mankind has always
> made its progress through a mess of bloody injustices and
> inevitable cruelty. There can be no "nice" war, however
> "justified" it may be. Thus only the saintly can be wholly
> neutral or extricate themselves from the ruthless machine
> which is history.
>
> . . . To wave aside *Les Blancs* . . . is an evasion which I

am inclined to ascribe to bad faith, especially in view of what certain folk call "good theatre."

But Clurman was not the only critic to return to *Les Blancs* in the weeks following. About a dozen times that season, as the play struggled for survival (and even long afterward), Richard Watts came back to extol the qualities of the production, the "power" and "fair-mindedness" of the playwright, and the fact that, in his view, it was "too meagre praise to describe it as the one first-rate new American play of the New York season." Others followed suit. And Howard Lord devoted several columns in the *Long Island Catholic* to the plight of *Les Blancs* as symptomatic of a larger problem:

> If the theatre reflects the times, these are times when no one says what's really on his mind. We speak in veiled allusions, and the forthright person who takes a stand is immediately ostracized.
>
> Lorraine Hansberry took a stand in *Les Blancs.* . . .
>
> How can the last play of one of America's great Playwrights fail to attract large audiences? . . . especially when she's in top form as a dramatist.
>
> The answer is in the play—fear—fear of blacks, fear of the race problem, fear of facing it, fear of ourselves.
>
> But we all know the truth: a disease, ignored, doesn't disappear; it just becomes more virulent. The problem must be faced. . . .
>
> *Les Blancs* shows us an image of our fears, but it charges that ultimate image with so much humanity—so much goodness, suffering, love and fear—that we leave the theatre unafraid. At least, we are no longer afraid of ourselves. And we feel we are moving in light, not darkness. We understand. . . .

The play moves inevitably to a tragic end. But James Earl Jones' howl at the end is the howl in the head of every viewer. We weep for him and for ourselves. We have learned that racism is not an abstraction out there, but an anguish in here. . . .

Les Blancs is the finest drama of the season so far. . . . I think you ought to see it, especially if you think you won't like it. You will see humanity at its best—and worst—struggling desperately against history, the facts of the past.

Yet Lord's searching analysis of why such a play could fail to attract large audiences dealt with only one (although, in terms of our society, the most important) aspect. It ignored considerations rooted in the general crisis of the theater itself which arise from its commercial nature: the fact, for instance, that given the skyrocketing costs of production and operation, and the resultant exhorbitant price of tickets which makes theatergoing a luxury, the number of plays that most people can afford to see is severely limited—and the number of *serious* plays (as distinct from musicals and comedies) even more so. Within this context, a very simple factor operates which most critics tend to pass over inasmuch as it touches on the efficacy of their own positions, yet nine times out of ten one need not look beyond it to determine whether a production will live or die. One might call it Sulzberger's Law, after the publisher of *The New York Times*: the fact that, given the situation described, no *serious* play can withstand a cool review from the daily reviewer of *The New York Times*.* For no matter how enthusiastic his colleagues may be, it is to the *Times* that the brokers,

*Which is not the same thing at all, it should be noted, as saying that a *good* review can assure success.

the businesses, the large commercial and organizational accounts who together make up the major slice of Broadway box-office—and for whom a "prestige" ticket is but commerce in another form—turn first. And by the time the *Times'* Sunday man may follow up two weeks later with a perhaps contrary review, the die is already cast. In the past decade, it is difficult to think of a single exception to Sulzberger's Law. Now this, it should be emphasized, is a power the *Times'* reviewers never sought; it is simply the reality within which they—and the theater—operate. And as it happens, the paper's current critic, Clive Barnes, did not like *Les Blancs*, although he acknowledged "many moving moments." "The major fault of the play," he wrote,

> . . . is the shallowness of the confrontations. The arguments have all been heard before . . . and the people in the play are debased to labeled puppets mouthing thoughts, hopes and fears that lack the surprise and vitality of life. No one, throughout the play, says anything unexpected. . . .
>
> I wonder how much Miss Hansberry knew or Mr. Nemiroff really knows about Africa? . . . It is obvious that they are trying to tell us something about America—and I think they would have done better to have told it to us straight.

All the more heartening and unusual, therefore, when some weeks later, in Mr. Barnes' roundup of the season, the following appeared:

> What else is new? We have the late Lorraine Hansberry's play, *Les Blancs*, in a realization by her former husband, Robert Nemiroff, which has enlivened the theatre scene with a great deal of discussion. Personally I feel that its treatment of European racism and African nationalism is

oversimplified and distilled into a cliché. But some very good people think otherwise, and I concede that James Earl Jones is giving an absolutely great performance in the play. I hope it succeeds. It is a flawed play, but if you have any sensitivity to our times I think you will appreciate it. At times a flawed play on a vital subject is more valuable than a flawless variation on inconsequentiality.

It was the kind of gesture that does not surprise from Mr. Barnes—the mark of a man who cares more about the theater than he does about proving himself right.

Encouraged by it—and the magnificent reviews of Walter Kerr and Clayton Riley in the Sunday *Times*—we even hoped for a time to reverse the tide and struggle through the disastrous pre-Christmas slump that inevitably engulfs Broadway. For the word-of-mouth was catching and, as appears by now to be the case with virtually everything Lorraine Hansberry has written, something was being generated in the world beyond Broadway which brought forth volunteers on every hand who cared enough about the play to fight for it. In the very first days, for example, when it had just opened and was about to close, the late Whitney Young, Jr., of the National Urban League had called to offer an unsolicited statement:

James Earl Jones is chilling in this overpowering drama of a modern black man caught betwixt worlds and war in Africa. *Les Blancs* represents a rare moment in American theatre where history, rage and drama meet. No simple platitudes will do. This play must be seen.

That same week meetings were held with Dr. C. Eric Lincoln and Julia Prettyman, president and executive secretary of the Black Academy of Arts and Letters, to arrange a reception for United Nations delegates. Producer Matthaei, with the support of a number of his backers, undertook to meet personally the heavy losses of keeping the show alive while others swung into action: Jocelyn Cooper of the Human Resources Administration of the City of New York;* trade unionists from District 65 of the Retail, Wholesale and Distributive Workers, from Local 1199 of the Drug and Hospital Workers, the Fur and Leather Workers Joint Board, the Social Service Employees and the State, County and Municipal Employees unions; ministers called together by Reverend Wyatt Tee Walker, formerly executive director of the Southern Christian Leadership Conference; members of the Harlem Writers Guild, Headstart Mothers, Operation Breadbasket, the Urban Coalition, parents' and teachers' groups. In an incredible, virtually round-the-clock three-day push, almost $10,000 in commitments for tickets for youth and low-income groups—to be matched by a like amount from the Theatre Development Fund—was raised as a temporary finger in the box-office dike.

Thus, for a time it almost seemed as if the miracle of 1964—the miracle that had saved *The Sign in Sidney Brustein's Window* and ultimately secured it a lasting place in our theater—was about to be repeated. But miracles are, I am afraid, just that: they only prove the rule. On Broadway they may give struggling artists the momentary lift to go on against the heartbreaking odds of commerce—but don't

*One of the permanent offshoots of *Les Blancs* was the formation of the Lorraine Hansberry People's Theatre Foundation to foster community theater throughout the city under the leadership of Mrs. Cooper and Commissioner Major Owens.

count on them. And in this case, a "miracle" of another kind was about to strike: the New York taxi strike of December 1971—which in one stroke knocked the props out from under every Broadway box-office that did not have a heavy advance.

Les Blancs, with its large cast and handsome settings, cost more than $35,000 a week just to operate. The result was inevitable: After forty-seven performances, we closed.

Yet, of course, the story doesn't end there.

In succeeding weeks—indeed for months afterward—occasional comments would appear in reviewers' columns expressing the hope that the play might be revived off-Broadway.*

On January 17, 1971, an extraordinary review appeared in the Detroit *Sunday News* in which critic Jay Carr, who had seen *Les Blancs* just before its closing, expressed what was in the minds of many:

> NEW YORK—Only one play of any reach or importance has opened on Broadway so far this season. It was Lorraine Hansberry's *Les Blancs*. . . . I am convinced *Les Blancs* will resurface, and repeatedly. It is too strong a play to meekly shuffle off into oblivion.
>
> The play is a collision course between the races . . . and

*And indeed it did seem—briefly—as if that might happen. If the opening night audience of *Les Blancs* had recalled the theater of the thirties, it was in precisely that spirit—that passion, that solidarity—that the cast now rallied around the inspired, committed figure of director John Berry, himself a product of those times as a young actor in Orson Welles' Mercury Theatre, who offered to restage and redirect *Les Blancs* gratis anywhere that we could move it. And, by contrast, I personally shall never forget the image of Lili Darvas, for two generations one of the authentic great ladies of world theater, widow of the reknowned Hungarian dramatist Ferenc Molnar, announcing that it didn't matter where, she would perform *Les Blancs* in churches, lofts, in the streets of Harlem, without sets or costumes, for union minimum—because this was a play that the world must see!

Miss Hansberry's plotting of that course is wise, sure, ironic, clear-eyed, and electrifying in the drive and finality of its tragedy.

. . .

Again and again I was impressed by the craftsmanship and daring in the writing, and by the thoroughly developed assessment of the impasse between the races. Miss Hansberry was too honest an intellect to take any detours into mere shrillness. The insistence and urgency in *Les Blancs* stem from breadth of vision and masterly technique. The largeness of gesture in *Les Blancs* is exhilarating in a theatre that has all but abdicated to zombies, novelty-chasers, and infant drool.

Had I not known that the play was left unfinished by Miss Hansberry at her death . . . I don't think I'd have suspected it. The play seemed not only finished, but possessed of the sort of unrelenting power that only a very few playwrights are capable of in any one generation.

And in May 1971 six of the New York Drama Critics voted for *Les Blancs* as first, second or third choice for the Best American Play of the Year.

It is now almost eleven years since the day when Lorraine looked up from the typewriter to announce, as was her way, that she had a bit of "a surprise" for me: the first working draft of "a play about Africa." Today it will surprise no one that my own, hardly unprejudiced view is that Mr. Carr is right, that *Les Blancs* will resurface "repeatedly." But fortunately that is out of my hands now. With the publication of this first Random House edition, its future is for others to decide.

Robert Nemiroff

The Drinking Gourd

A CRITICAL BACKGROUND

> My mother first took us south to visit her
> Tennesee birthplace one summer when I was
> seven or eight. I woke up on the back seat of
> the car while we were still driving through
> some place called Kentucky and my mother
> was pointing out to the beautiful hills and tell-
> ing my brothers about how her father had run
> away and hidden from his master in those very
> hills when he was a little boy. She said that his
> mother had wandered among the wooded
> slopes in the moonlight and left food for him
> in secret places. They were very beautiful hills
> and I looked out at them for miles and miles
> after that wondering who and what a "master"
> might be.
>
> —LORRAINE HANSBERRY,
> *To Be Young, Gifted and Black*

The Drinking Gourd was the first play ever written for
national television that attempted seriously and without sentiment to explore "what a master might be." It was commissioned for NBC by producer-director Dore Schary to initiate
a series of ninety-minute television dramas commemorating
the Centennial of the Civil War. It was commissioned in

1960, the year of the first student sit-in against segregation in the South, the year before the formation of SNCC and the wave of nonviolent protest that filled the South's jails with modern-day counterparts of Hannibal and Sarah, and the nation's TV screens with real scenes of cattleprods and firehoses, dynamite and bullets. It was a time when the essential patterns of this country's black-white relations—and the accompanying myth of the "contented" black—had not changed much in half a century. A time before the "freedom rides," the Birmingham riot, the "Mississippi Summer" voter registration campaigns, James Meredith at Ole Miss, the Marches on Washington and Selma—and, of course, before the new mood of mingled despair and militancy, revolution and separation that rose from the flames of Watts and the bullet-punctured bodies of Malcolm X and Martin Luther King. A time, in short, when the tenor of the country was perhaps best summed up in the statement to Congress of President-elect John F. Kennedy that, while he favored Civil Rights legislation, it was not a "priority" part of the New Frontier.

It was in such a year that NBC proposed to celebrate the Centennial of the Civil War with a series of "five special shows" which, according to the announcements, "promise to be one of the most important events of coming TV seasons"—a series which, apart from its unusual content, was to be written by prominent playwrights whose participation was, among other things, intended to mark the return of serious drama to the airwaves. Lorraine Hansberry's *The Drinking Gourd* was to open the series. It was the only script actually completed. Its subject was slavery, its subtitle "The Peculiar Institution," and unlike most writers on the subject, its author brought to it some quite private and intimate insights of her own. Insights which could be traced back as far as a child's trip South and her first "startled" view of her grandmother:

> All my life I had heard that she was a great beauty and no one had ever remarked that they had meant a half century before! The woman that I met was as wrinkled as a prune ... and always seemed to be thinking of other times. But she could still rock and talk and even make wonderful cupcakes which were like cornbread, only sweet ... She died the next summer and that is all that I remember about her, except that she was born in slavery and had memories of it and they didn't sound anything like *Gone with the Wind*. . . .

The Drinking Gourd did not sound anything like *Gone with the Wind* either. And that fact cannot be separated from what happened to it.

In a symposium on the "Negro Writer in America," a freewheeling discussion recorded by radio station WBAI at the start of the Centennial Year, January 1, 1961, with James Baldwin, Langston Hughes, Alfred Kazin, Lorraine Hansberry, Nat Hentoff and Emile Capouya as the participants, Lorraine Hansberry told a little of the story:

> ... They asked me for it. They paid me for it—and if I may say so, in contradiction of everything that we have said, Langston, rather *well*—and then I read in the newspaper that some studio official—a vice president ... had attached a notation to it saying, moreover, that they thought it was "superb" ... *and then they put it away in a drawer*. . . .

What happened to *The Drinking Gourd* was not, of course, unique. On one level it can be viewed as simply one more in the long and, by now, traditional line of casualties of the Great Wasteland. Yet on another, there is more to the story. For the drawer that closed on *The Drinking Gourd* also managed to slam shut on every other publicly announced network plan to seriously commemorate the single most important event of our national life in the second half of the nineteenth century—the war that freed four million Americans, cost the lives of several million others, opened the floodgates to our economic transformation into the nation we have become, and dominated our politics directly for a generation and, indirectly, ever since.

In that light, the fate of *The Drinking Gourd* was and is relevant for reasons that are worth examining.

In the symposium cited earlier, Lorraine Hansberry took the occasion to amplify why she had agreed to write the play in the first place:

> ... You said, I thought rather beautifully, a number of times how this question—the Negro question—does tend to go to the heart of various and assorted American agonies, the Negro question does, beginning with Slavery itself. And I am so profoundly interested to realize that in these 100 years since the Civil War very few of our countrymen have really *believed* that their Federal Union and the defeat of the slavocracy and the negation of slavery as an institution is an admirable fact of American life. So that it is now possible to get enormous books on the Civil War and to go through the back of them and not find the word "slavery," let alone "Negro."
>
> We've been trying very hard—this is what Jimmy and I mean when we speak of guilt—we've been trying very hard

in America to pretend that this greatest conflict didn't even
have at its base the only thing it had at its base: where person
after person will write a book today and insist that *slavery*
was not the issue! You know, they tell you it was the "economy"—as if that economy was not based on slavery. It's
become a great semantic game to try and get this particular
blot out of our minds, and people spend volumes discussing
the *battles* of the Civil War, and which army was crossing
which river at five minutes to two, and how their swords were
hanging, but the slavery issue we have tried to get rid of. To
a point that while it has been perfectly popular, admirable,
the thing to do—all my life since *Gone with the Wind*—to
write anything you wanted about the slave system with
beautiful ladies in big, fat dresses screaming as their houses
burned down from the terrible, nasty, awful Yankees . . . this
has been such a perfectly acceptable part of our culture that
the first time that I know of that someone came to *me* and
asked me to write ninety minutes of television drama on
slavery—which, if you will accept my own estimate, was not
a propaganda piece in either direction but, I hope, a serious
treatment of family relationships by a slave-owning family
and their slaves—*this* is controversial. This had never been
done. . . .

Yet one man, at least, believed it *could* be done. And so
Dore Schary, long one of the more socially committed pro-
ducers in Hollywood and on Broadway, had asked Lorraine
to a meeting and assured her that, controversy or no, she
would have full freedom to confront the historical truth.
The series, he explained, was to be an honest, objective
dramatization of the issues underlying the war. It was to
begin with (1) her portrait of slavery, and follow with works
based on (2) the confrontation of pro- and anti-slavery forces

in the U. S. Senate in the decade preceding secession; (3) the origins of the Confederacy; (4) the mobilization of the Union; and (5) the drawing of first blood. How frank could it be? "As frank as it needs to be," said Schary.*

It was with this understanding that Lorraine set to work. And with this understanding that Schary informed NBC that he had engaged as his first writer the young black winner of the previous year's Drama Critics' Circle Award for the best play on Broadway. The announcement was made to a roomful of top network brass. Schary recounts their response thusly:

> "There was a long moment of silence. And then the question was asked: 'What's her point of view about it—slavery?'
>
> "I thought they were pulling my leg, and so I answered presently, gravely: 'She's against it.'
>
> "Nobody laughed—and from that moment I knew we were dead."

Schary, however, refused to give in and so he said nothing to Lorraine, preferring not to burden her as long as a fighting chance remained. In the months that followed, down to the very day that "death" became official and his own contract with NBC was quietly dropped, he never once suggested in any way that the playwright's vision be compromised.

Meanwhile, Lorraine began work in the Main Reading

---

*"I want no part of this nonsense," Schary later told a reporter in commenting upon "television's timidity about letting its audience in on the final result of the Civil War. . . . They want to call it the War Between the States. I would rather call it the War of the Rebellion. . . . The slaves were subjects of an evil. They wanted freedom."

Room of the Forty-second Street Library, the Schoemburg Collection in Harlem, and at home, poring over her own rather extensive collection of works on the slavery era. She consulted transcripts of the pre-War *Congressional Record* sent up from Washington, studied sermons and speeches, diaries and journals and newspaper accounts of slave insurrections, pondered auction notices and "wanted" posters for runaway slaves and bills of sale for men and women, and inevitably thought of her grandmother as slowly the arguments and abstractions of a century before began to come alive. For her ultimate goal was to write not history but drama:

> What I think a dramatist has to do is to thoroughly inundate himself or herself in an awareness of the realities of the historical period and then dismiss it. And then become absolutely dedicated to the idea that what you are going to do is to create human beings whom you know in your own time, you see. So that all of us sitting out in the audience feel that, "Oh yes, we know him." No matter what period . . . we must feel, "I have had this experience, I have known this person." So that once you know the realities of the time, you use them really as residue at the back of the head. So that, you know, you don't have them go out and get into an automobile, but where the human emotion is universal in the *time* sense as well as the world sense.*

The essential view of "the realities of the time," of slavery, that Lorraine Hansberry brought to *The Drinking Gourd*—the "residue at the back of the head"—this is

*From an interview with film director Frank Perry on the N.E.T. program *Playwright at Work*.

nowhere better summarized than in a letter she wrote some years later to the *Village Voice*. Dated January 11, 1964,* it is a letter so pertinent to the themes and characters explored in the play that it is worth quoting extensively. Its point of departure was the *Voice*'s review of another work, James Weldon Johnson's *Trumpets of the Lord:*

To the Editor:

I have not yet seen "Trumpets of the Lord" and know nothing of the production save that it is in the hands of some extraordinarily gifted and capable people, Mr. Donald McKayle and Miss Vinnette Carroll.

But the show apart, I was amazed, and amused, to learn from Mr. Michael Smith's review that *he* is amazed at the utilization of Hebraic history and myth in the folk materials of American Negroes! That he suspects the present production of having used "Israeli-Egyptian" relations to promote the "integration" aspirations of what he takes to be the "recent" militancy of Negroes.

He must first be told that anyone would be hard pressed to put together such a program that *was* devoid of either protest or biblical content. There are excellent and rather glaring reasons why this is so and I am afraid that suspicions to the contrary are a confession of ignorance of the nature of American slavery. But I have long since learned that it is difficult for the American mind to adjust to the realization that the Rhetts and Scarletts were as much monsters as the keepers of Buchenwald—they just dressed more attractively and their accents are softer. (I *know* I switched tenses.)

The slavocracy was neither gentle nor vague; it was a system of absolutism: he who stood up and preached "dis-

*But to my knowledge, never completed or mailed.

196

content" *directly* had his courageous head chopped off; his militant back flogged to shreds; the four points of his limbs fastened down to saplings—or his eyes gouged out. . . . Learning to read or write was variously corporally and capitally punishable; and, of course, from the beginning of the slave trade all expressions of what might have been a unifying force among the New World Blacks, African cultural survivals, were conscientiously and relentlessly destroyed.

Consequently, it should not be difficult to understand how the slaves used, and ingeniously used, the only cultural tools permitted them: the English language and the Bible. (Think of "Go Down Moses!" in that light and you will swiftly discover why what must be the mightiest musical phrase in the entire musical literature of a great musical culture was assigned by my forebears to the only people they had ever heard of who "got away"—and that proudly—from bondage, the ancient Israelites.)

Interestingly, *The Drinking Gourd* took its title from a spiritual, a song of the Underground Railroad which derived, in turn, from the old slave metaphor for the Big Dipper which points to the North Star, the symbol and beacon to freedom for many an escaped slave seeking his way North in the Southern night. (Frederick Douglass similarly named his abolitionist journal *The North Star.*) Songs like "Follow the Drinking Gourd" and "Steal Away to Jesus" (also used in the play), were ingenious examples of the "signal" songs employed by the slaves to pass on secret messages and double meanings encloistered in "innocent" imagery. Folklorist Irwin Silber's *Songs of the Civil War* provides revealing commentaries on these two songs, which I have included as an addendum to the play. It was to such uses of "the only cultural tools permitted them" that Lorraine's letter referred. It continues:

> The simple fact is, black sedition in the United States was defined by the reality that surrounded it, which was the armed white camp which was the slave-south: less than a million big slave owners who had thoughtfully [enlisted the support] of the impoverished poor white in the maintenance of his "property."
>
> Negro protest and revolt is not new. It is as old as the slave trade. Negroes came here fighting back. They mutinied on the high seas; they organized hundreds of insurrections which were ruthlessly and predictably put down; they indulged in sabotage, mutilation, murder and flight, and fled into the quite unfriendly ranks of the Union armies by the tens of thousands to return as largely unpaid, hardly uniformed and equipped fighting soldiers and spies and service personnel of the reluctant "freedom" armies. . . .
>
> Why then did it [black revolt] fail? Black folk constituted four million unarmed and illiterate people circumscribed by twice their number of hostile elements including, above all, to the genius of the slaveholding South, those six or seven million poor whites who, pathetically, regarded themselves as the interested protectors of the system that impoverished them. For the return of fugitives there was money and a reassurance that his miserable life was better than a black man's. And very little else. But it worked. The Negro and his culture came up under encirclement. . . .

It was out of this reality—and this strong sense of the continuity of black oppression past and present—that *The Drinking Gourd* emerged.

To Dore Schary, former studio head of Metro-Goldwyn-Mayer and himself the author of *Sunrise at Campobello*, the play Lorraine handed him was, as he looks back on it now, "a powerful, marvelous script that might have been—with the cast we had in mind and a little luck—one of the great things we've seen on television." Within days of receiving it, he called to say that Henry Fonda had agreed to play the Soldier, and a comparable cast was in the making; he was passing it on to NBC.

Their response was not long in coming. On August 30, 1960, Lorraine learned of it in the morning paper—neatly summarized by *New York Herald-Tribune* TV columunist Marte Torre under the headline "Dore Schary Tells Why TV Shies From Civil War." The column began with a quoted news release so classic that one can only suppose it was NBC's press agent who later wrote the releases for President Johnson on Vietnam:

> NEWS ITEM: "NBC has solved the problem of producing a Civil War series without offending the South. It will pit brother against brother so that both sides will have their innings in the projected series, 'The Canfield Brothers,' formerly known as 'The Blue and the Gray.'"

"And what about the 'projected' Civil War series," wondered Miss Torre, that cannot be "altered to conform to the 'safe, bland, inoffensive' canons" of television?

After two years, she informed the reader—"during which time Mr. Schary turned in one script and four outlines ('all excellent,' in NBC's words)"—his contract had expired and would not be renewed. "I would say that my failing," Schary told her, "was that I could not turn the series into 'a Wagon

Train' of the Civil War . . . the slavery issue . . . is a very sensitive area. . . ." Mr. Schary was returning to the theater. Moreover, the column concluded, all other Civil War network projects, including one announced "during a bold brave moment" by ABC and another to have been supervised for CBS by Pulitzer Prize historian Bruce Catton, were being shelved.

Yet, interestingly enough, the story did not end quite there. For months thereafter occasional calls would come from friends on the fringes of the industry or simply with tomorrow's TV column in hand, to report that perhaps the project was being revived. A story by *New York Post* columnist Bob Williams (10/5/60) is typical:

> NBC's long-projected 90-minute exploration of the institution of slavery may yet be emancipated from a desk drawer in the program department. . . .
>
> For the slavery project . . . NBC programming vice president David Levy still cherishes some hope. Attached to the script is a memo from his pad which says: "This is superb."
>
> To us, he said:
>
> "I want it on the air. I believe it should go on. It's a program that says something about the peculiar institution of slavery."

Yet even if, in off-guard moments, one indulges a fantasy —that television might somehow have been induced to preserve a relatively realistic portrayal of slavery—I realize as I look back upon it now that there were two things that irretrievably and immutably doomed *The Drinking Gourd.*

The first had to do with Lorraine Hansberry's view of history and its effect upon people, which was inseparable from her essential nature as a dramatist. What interested her in *The Drinking Gourd,* as to one degree or another in all her works, was the dissection of personality in interaction with society. Not personality viewed in the abstract, as some universal, unchanging "human nature," but as human nature manifesting itself under the impact of a particular society, set of conditions, way of life. Her object was not to pose black against white, to create black heroes and white villains, but to locate the sources of human behavior, of both heroism and villainy, *within* the slave society.

What was so troubling, so damning about *The Drinking Gourd* was not, I believe, its frankness but, oddly enough, its *fairness:* the objectivity of its approach to character and the nature of the indictment that resulted. It was not even the horrors she showed—the fact that the young black hero was to be shown on perhaps fifty million American home screens being blinded for the statutory crime of learning to read—but the fact that she insisted upon empathizing as well with the *white* forced to blind him! In a medium not noted for the avoidance of horror, an industry whose stock-in-trade is violence, one might suppose that this image could be tolerated. But the approach to Zeb Dudley and Hiram Sweet was something else again.

For it is one thing for the black writer to view the *black* as victim, but to also view the *white* as victim is to step entirely outside the racial categories upon which the society stands. That is an act of effrontery far more disquieting because, in the very act of extending a hand to whites, it strips them of their claim to uniqueness, and presupposes on the black playwright's part a degree of liberation, an absolute equality to treat both black and white as if they are exactly alike: that is, in the profoundest sense as human beings, linked victims of a society that victimized both (which is not the same thing at all as suggesting that our suffering or degree of responsibility for that society is equal).

Moreover, if only the black is viewed as victim, the impact may touch the conscience of the viewer, but at the same time, to white America, it is vaguely reassuring: the failure to deal with the complexity of "our" motivations—the fact that we "suffer" too—confirms the sense of apartness. ("You see! They can't understand us any more than we can understand them. We are different species.") If this view is powerfully and dramatically rendered, it may arouse guilt— but guilt too removed to require anything more than a surface commitment to kindness, amelioration, reform— that "we" treat "them" better than "we" have *within the system*. But *The Drinking Gourd* goes for the gut: it takes on the system itself, requires that we examine ourselves, and what it implies is revolution. Revolution within and without. Not guilt but action. It shatters the myth that the Civil War was anything other than a tragic *necessity*, a revolution that *had to be* fought not out of some doubtful benevolence to the slaves but for the good of the whole nation. And it suggests, in whatever degree art can ever affect attitudes, the appropriateness if need be of means perhaps equally drastic, if we are ever to complete the revolution that was left unfinished a hundred years ago and thereby free us all.

In order to achieve this, *The Drinking Gourd* depicted, as never before in a television script, the crimes of American slavery. But the purpose was not merely to set the record straight, or to condemn the whites who perpetrated, profited from, or by their silence acquiesced in the crimes. Far more important, it was to focus on the system that *required* the crimes, the culture that shaped the Southern white personality in its countless variations, maimed it, distorted it, turned ego into a monstrous and all-devouring thing. In the process, the facts of white villainy could not be ignored. The extremes of white behavior in the slave South—the cruelties, the brutalities—had to be shown; they were integral to the system for essential reasons, not of color but of economics and psychology, reasons that were set forth concisely and brilliantly in passages like the following from W. E. B. Du Bois's *Black Reconstruction*, which the playwright marked and often cited:

> The Southern planter suffered not simply from his economic mistakes—the psychological effect of slavery upon him was fatal. The mere fact that a man could be, under the law, the actual master of the mind and body of human beings had to have disastrous effects. It tended to inflate the ego of most planters beyond all reason; they became arrogant, strutting, quarrelsome kinglets; they issued commands; they made laws; they shouted their orders; they expected deference and self-abasement. Their "honor" became a vast and awful thing, requiring wide and insistent deference. Such of them as were inherently weak and inefficient were all the more easily angered, jealous, resentful, while the few who were superior, physically or mentally, conceived no bounds to their power and personal prestige. As the world had long learned, nothing is so calculated to ruin human nature as absolute power over human beings.

But that was precisely the point: to show the extremes that the system produced not as aberrations but in their relation to the culture, to suggest how and why they grew logically and inevitably out of the "peculiar institution."

And that is why in conceiving *The Drinking Gourd*, Lorraine chose not to concentrate on the system's "monsters" —the "Rhetts and Scarletts" described in her letter or their equivalent, young Everett Sweet—but on quite a different cut of human being. As her central white character she chose Hiram Sweet: a good man, a sympathetic hero, a man who epitomized the best virtues the society claimed for itself. And a man, moreover, who understood the evils of the system and consciously tried to impose his will upon it, tried to live by the code of benevolent paternalism the South professed but could not maintain.

Hiram Sweet is defeated because he *had to be.* The system demanded it, and demanded it for very sound and practical reasons; reasons which form the core of his conflict with Everett, his son, and Macon Bullett, the aristocrat, over hours of work, the use of overseers and the conditions under which his slaves shall labor. For the simple fact of the matter was that by the mid-nineteenth century, when the play takes place, slavery itself, as an economic system, had become outmoded and, increasingly, not viable. In competition with the advanced industrial economy of the North, the planter found himself facing curious difficulties inherent in the system of production. He could not avail himself of higher wages as a means of inducing better work or a larger labor supply. He could not allow his labor to become overly trained, skilled or educated, because education might well be turned against the master himself. And psychologically, he *required* ignorance as the proof of his own superiority. He could not hire or fire at will and had to bear the burden of the old and the sick and inefficient whom he could not simply destroy or allow to starve to death en masse if he expected even a modicum of cooperation from their mothers, brothers and children in the fields. And, finally, with the one- or two-crop system mass slave labor required, he could not even maintain the fertility of the land. Slavery was its own worst enemy, and by the 1850's "King Cotton" had "burned out" the land to such a degree that the system could survive only by (1) shifting its emphasis from the production of crops to the production of slaves (as happened in the Old aristocratic South which found itself transformed, slowly but surely, into a primarily slave-breeding region—in the last decade of slavery fully 50,000 to 80,000 slaves were shipped from the border states alone to the lower South); (2) acquiring new lands to the West and South, Mexico and the Caribbean and even, as some Confederate military plans envisioned, through the conquest of Brazil (it was this desperate need for expansion that perhaps more than any other factor precipitated the collision course with the North over Kansas, the West and the ordering of national priorities); and (3) in any event, ever more intensive and brutal exploitation of the slave—that is, greater and greater "excesses" of the sort that defeat Hiram Sweet and ultimately bring about his death. For the individual planter, no matter what his wishes, the choice was clear: either adopt the methods of Everett or go under.

HIRAM

I—I wanted to tell you, Rissa—I wanted to tell you and ask you to believe me, that I had nothing to do with this. I— some things do seem to be out of the power of my hands after all . . . Other men's rules are a part of my life . . .

RISSA

Why? Ain't you *Marster?* How can a man be marster of some men and not at all of others—

It is in this very real, not merely metaphorical, sense that, as I suggested at the beginning, *The Drinking Gourd* examines "what a master might be." It is a study of the limits of individual freedom within an evil system. And it is because of this that it acquires, within the limitations of the condensed and abbreviated ninety-minute form, some of the elements, and above all the sense of inevitability, of classical tragedy, in which the hero smashes himself against the walls of immutable circumstance, the victim of his own tragic flaw—which is, in this case, his humanity, the absolute contradiction between the human being and his society that makes it impossible to preserve the humanity of the one within the context of the other.

The second consideration that, I would suggest, doomed *The Drinking Gourd* has to do with the character Rissa and the inviolability of a cherished American myth.

In the essay "The New Paternalists," Lorraine Hansberry wrote:

> America long ago fell in love with an image. It is a sacred image, fashioned over centuries of time: this image of the unharried, unconcerned, glandulatory, simple, rhythmical, amoral, dark creature who was, above all else, a *miracle of sensuality*. It was created, and it persists, to provide a personified pressure valve for fanciful longings in American dreams, literature, and life, and it has an extremely important role to play in the present situation of our national sense of decency.
>
> I think, for example, of that reviewer writing in a Connecticut newspaper about *A Raisin in the Sun*, which had opened for the first time in New Haven the night before, and

marvelling, in the rush of a quite genuine enthusiasm, that
the play proved again that there was a quaint loveliness in
how our "dusky brethren" can come up with a song and hum
their troubles away. It did not seem to disturb him one whit
that there is no single allusion to that particular mythical gift
in the entire play. He did not need it there; it was in his head.

And she went on in the essay to discuss why this was so. The
myth was "necessary because":

> . . . in almost paradoxical fashion, it disturbs the soul of
> man to *truly* understand what he invariably senses: that
> *nobody* really finds oppression and/or poverty tolerable.
>
> Guilt would come to bear too swiftly and too painfully if
> white America were really obliged quite suddenly to think of
> the Negro quite as he is, that is, simply as a human being.
> That would raise havoc . . . White America has to believe
> not only that the oppression of the Negro is unfortunate
> (because most of white America does believe that), but
> something *else*, to keep its sense of the unfortunate from
> turning to a sense of outrage . . . White America has to
> believe the Blacks are different—and not only so, but that,
> by the mystique of this difference, they actually profit in
> certain charming ways which escape the rest of us with all
> our engrossing complexities.

Now, the myth of which she is speaking has many variations. But there is one that is particularly sacred, one that
has provided a special solace and reassurance to the white
conscience from the earliest days of slavery to our own time,
and that is the image of the Black Mammy: the Black
Mother figure, patient, long-suffering, devoted and indomi-
table, heroic if need be, but above all *loving*. And forgiving.

A kind of black superwoman, repository of all the sins that the whites have visited upon the blacks, who by her very existence confirms that blacks are not human in the sense that we are: who receives evil and returns good, however sternly or cantankerously, and thereby proves, out of her soulful eyes and warming heart and healing laughter and all-encompassing bosom, that somehow everything comes out all right in the end. It is this legendary figure, persisting in song and story, popular fiction and the most serious art, that has endlessly provided the Hattie MacDaniels to our Vivian Leighs, the Louise Beavers to our Claudette Colberts, but also the Nancys and Dilseys in William Faulkner ("brave, courageous, generous, gentle and honest . . . much more brave and honest and generous than me," as Faulkner said in an interview) and the Berenices in Carson McCullers.

In the Centennial symposium referred to earlier, Lorraine and James Baldwin discussed the scene in *Member of the Wedding* that occurs when the young black nephew of Berenice is being chased by a lynch mob, and Berenice takes the young white boy who is her charge, whom she has reared from childhood, and in that moment her preoccupation is with the child; her concern is with the white boy, not the black man about to be lynched. "Now the point," for Lorraine, was not to disparage the play (which, she said, "I happen to think was a lovely play") or the talent of the author, but to demonstrate that writers like McCullers and Faulkner were prisoners of a myth which made it impossible for them to reflect fully and adequately the realities of such a moment because:

... the intimacy of knowledge which the Negro may culturally have of white Americans does not exist in the reverse. So that William Faulkner has never in his life sat in on a discussion in a Negro home where there were all Negroes. It is physically impossible. He has never heard the nuances of hatred, of total contempt from his most devoted servant and his most beloved friend—who means every word when she is telling it to him and who expresses to him profoundly intimate thoughts—but he has never heard the truth of it. It is physically impossible. So that I am saying that for you* this scene is a fulfilling image . . . because *you haven't either.*

And Baldwin carried the point a step further:

It's an absolutely incredible moment, as Lorraine points out . . . Now this doesn't say anything about the truth of Negro life, but it reveals a great deal about the state of mind of the white Southern woman who wrote it . . . Southerners have an illusion and they cling to it desperately—not only Southerners, the whole American republic does—and these characters come out of a compulsion. And Dilsey . . . is Faulkner's proof that the Negroes who . . . have been worked and worked and worked and worked for nothing, and who have been lynched and burned and stolen, etc., for generations have forgiven him. The reasons the walls in the South cannot come down—the reason that the panic is so great—is because when the walls come down the truth will come out . . .

It is in relation to this psychic need—this compulsion to cling to illusion—that Rissa in *The Drinking Gourd* makes an impermissible breach in the walls. She literally reverses

*A white panelist

the image. And the thing that is so troubling about her, so subversive of everything we have told ourselves, is that she seems at first to be the *same woman*, cut from the same cloth, as that other archetypal Black Mother: she is devoted to Hiram, Christian to the core, bound to the system, embodying all the virtues we have come to expect—"more brave and honest and generous than me." Only with one profound difference: She is the same woman *observed not from the white consciousness but the black*. And therefore, as Lorraine Hansberry wrote of her counterpart, Lena Younger in *A Raisin in the Sun*, she may be:

> . . . wrong, ignorant, bound over to superstitions which yet lash down the wings of the human spirit and yet, at the same time, apparently she is . . . an affirmation. She is the only possible recollection of a prototype whose celebration in the mythos of the culture of the American Negro began long before the author was born. Lena Younger, the mother, is the black matriarch incarnate, the bulwark of the Negro family since slavery, the embodiment of the Negro will to transcendance. It is she, who in the mind of the black poet scrubs the floors of a nation in order to create black diplomats and university professors. It is she, while seeming to cling to traditional restraints, who drives the young on into the fire hoses. And one day simply refuses to move to the back of the bus in Montgomery. Or goes out and buys a house in an all-white neighborhood where her children may possibly be killed by bricks thrown through the windows by a shrieking racist mob.

But whereas it might have been possible in the case of *A Raisin in the Sun* for America to deceive itself about this other—more outspoken and militant—side of Lena, not so with Rissa in *The Drinking Gourd.* In *Raisin,* as the example of that New Haven critic so wondrously illustrates, it was possible to ignore the play and what it was saying in the rush to embrace Mama.*

But what is merely implicit in Mama becomes explicit in *The Drinking Gourd.* For Rissa unmistakably completes the journey that Lena had started on—and thereby reverses the sacred image. In *Member of the Wedding* the Black Mother ministers to her white surrogate son while the black man is murdered. In *The Drinking Gourd* she ministers to her *own* son and lets the white man—the *good* white man who has cared for and treated her *almost* as an equal—die pleading for her help. In effect, she murders him—and, what is more, steals his guns and places them in the black hands of her children; and in that moment the universe itself—the entire mythos on which stands four hundred years of black-white relations in this country—comes unhinged.

It is a simple act. A simple, human, motherly act of vengeance for a son wronged which, in any other context but America's, should have been anticipated as entirely natural and inevitable. And yet here it is cosmic, too frightening in its implications to contemplate, because it says: *We are human and if you misjudge that fact you will live to pay the consequences.*

---

*In effect, as Ossie Davis observed in a most trenchant piece, white America "captured" Lena, turned her into what she was not, made this ghetto domestic— wife of a porter, mother of a chauffeur—into the "middle class" (!) Mama that suited us. We shut out the fact that the quest of her whole being had been toward "freedom" and "a pinch of dignity too," and comforted ourselves, above all, with what we insisted was the play's "happy ending"—rather than facing the idea of the confrontation with racist mobs into which Mama is surely leading her embattled brood as the curtain comes down.

It was an act which could not, in any circumstance, be tolerated on television.

At midnight, December 31, 1961, C.Y.W. (the Centennial Year that Wasn't), "all right, title and interest in and to *The Drinking Gourd*" reverted to the playwright. And in 1965, after her death, I decided the time might be ripe to try again. After all, not a few things had happened in the intervening years: civil rights was now the law of the land, Martin Luther King had come out of jail to win a Nobel Prize, television was proclaiming a new image, "serious" drama was about to come back, and an occasional black face could even be seen in the commercials. Accordingly, a letter and a copy of the script to Florence Eldridge and Frederic March—and a prompt response: Mr. and Mrs. March would be happy to portray the Sweets, Hiram and Maria, if a production could be arranged. Claudia McNeil expressed similar interest in Rissa, and with that—the assurance that a truly distinguished cast could be assembled—the wheels went into motion.

I need not have bothered.

To the executive producer of Hallmark Playhouse *The Drinking Gourd* was "a beautiful script . . . but frankly . . . not the sort of thing the sponsor is looking for. Hallmark is a *family* show and—well, you know . . ." To CBS Playhouse it was not "contemporary" enough. To NBC's Experimental Theatre it was not "experimental" enough. And to assorted executives at all three networks there was a new wrinkle now: *The Drinking Gourd* had become "offensive." "Well, that is, times have changed. Negroes are into their own thing now. They don't want to be reminded that they once were slaves . . ."

Not until 1967 did even a portion of *The Drinking Gourd* reach the airwaves, and then hardly in the manner anticipated. That was when, to commemorate the second anniversary of the playwright's death, WBAI, a small noncommercial radio station, broadcast the two-part program "Lorraine Hansberry in Her Own Words," taped by sixty-one of the country's leading actors. The program included two scenes from *The Drinking Gourd*, with James Earl Jones as Hannibal, Cicely Tyson as Sarah, Rip Torn as Everett and Will Geer as the Preacher. One of these scenes was later used in the biographical play *To Be Young, Gifted and Black*, and it has been gratifying to find it consistently one of the most commented-upon moments in the play, both in the New York reviews and across the country. In 1972, this scene was at last seen on television as a part of the NET motion picture of the same title—but in one decade of trying that is the closest *The Drinking Gourd* has gotten to the medium for which it was conceived.

James Baldwin has written, in "Letter to My Nephew on the One Hundredth Anniversary of the Emancipation," that Americans

> . . . are, in effect, still trapped in a history which they do not understand; and until they understand it, they cannot be released from it. They have had to believe for many years, and for innumerable reasons, that black men are inferior to white men. Many of them, indeed, know better, but, as you will discover, people find it very difficult to act on what they know. To act is to be committed, and to be committed is to be in danger.

The Drinking Gourd was one small key to unlocking that history. "They put it away in a drawer" and it remains in a drawer where, from time to time, as the impact of who Lorraine Hansberry was and what she was trying so urgently to tell us continues to grow in the country and among the young especially, I shall be tempted to withdraw it for another submission. But I am not hopeful of the results. I am gratified, of course, that the present edition will at last enable a number of those who could not *see* it to read the script; students will now have access to it, it will find its way into anthologies, be commented upon in doctoral theses, and no doubt a certain number of letters will arrive each year asking, *Can't something be done about getting it on?* But as to the audience for whom it was written and the medium for which the work was conceived—the *only* one in which its full power and artistry can be realized*—I am afraid the time is not yet.

And not likely until there is a much deeper commitment than at present, on the part of whites as well as blacks, to release us from history, complete the revolution, and once and for all confront the challenge posed in the final lines of *The Drinking Gourd:*

*In reading *The Drinking Gourd,* the fullness of treatment in some areas makes it easy to forget sometimes that it is a work for a very special medium: not the printed page or even the theater but an art form that is above all filmic—in which dialogue is only one, and often not the primary, means of exploring character and relationships. An art form in which the juxtaposition of a face against the Big Dipper, for example, the panning shot of a line of slaves, or the agitated flicking of a riding crop on a boot—the close-up of Zeb Dudley's clenching hands or the eyes of Hannibal or the tightened lips of Rissa—can say more of character, its recesses and potentials, than a thousand words. As they appear, then, on the printed page, the men and women of the Sweet plantation are conceived as essences only, outlines for the camera to fill. For the language of film is the image not the word—and they must await the physical reality of the actors, the environs and the selective camera eye that will give them life.

SOLDIER

. . . it is possible that slavery might destroy itself—but it is more possible that it would destroy these United States first. That it would cost us our political and economic future. *(He puts on his cap and picks up his rifle)* It has already cost us, as a nation, too much of our soul.

Robert Nemiroff

THE DRINKING GOURD
An Original Drama
for Television

"Our new government is founded upon the great truth that the Negro is not equal to the white man—that slavery is his natural and normal condition."

—Alexander H. Stephens,
Vice President of the Confederacy

CAST OF CHARACTERS
(*In order of appearance*)

THE SOLDIER
SLAVES—MEN, WOMEN, CHILDREN
RISSA
SARAH
JOSHUA
HANNIBAL
HIRAM SWEET
MARIA SWEET
TWO MALE HOUSE SERVANTS
EVERETT SWEET
TOMMY
DR. MACON BULLETT
ZEB DUDLEY
ELIZABETH DUDLEY
TWO DUDLEY CHILDREN
THE PREACHER
COFFIN
A DRIVER

FOLLOWING PRELIMINARY PRODUCTION TI-
TLES: Introduce stark, spirited banjo themes.

MAIN PLAY TITLES AND CREDITS

FADE IN: UNDER TITLES

EXTERIOR. TWO SHOT: HANNIBAL, TOMMY—
BRIGHT DAY.

HANNIBAL *is a young slave of about nineteen or twenty.*
TOMMY, *about ten, is his master's son. It is* HANNIBAL *who*
is playing the banjo, the neck of which intrudes into close
opening shot frame.

CAMERA MOVES BACK TO WIDER ANGLE to
show that TOMMY *is vigorously keeping time by clapping his*
hands to the beat of the music. They are seated in a tiny
wooded enclosure. Sunlight and leaf shadow play on their
faces, the expressions of which are animated and happy.

If workable, they sing, from top.

At completion of titles:

Fade out

ACT ONE

FADE IN:
EXTERIOR. HIGH-ANGLED PANNING SHOT:
AMERICAN EAST COAST—DUSK.

PAN down a great length of coast until a definitive mood is established. Presently the lone figure of a man emerges from the distance. He is tall and narrow-hipped, suggesting a certain idealized American generality. He is not Lincoln, but perhaps Lincolnesque. He wears the side whiskers of the nineteenth century and his hair is long at the neck after the manner of New England or Southern farmers of the period. He is dressed in dark military trousers and boots which are in no way recognizable as to rank or particular army. His shirt is open at the collar and rolled at the sleeves and he carries his dark tunic across his shoulders. He is not battle-scarred or dirty or in any other way suggestive of the disorder of war; but his gait is that of troubled and reflective meditation. When he speaks his voice is markedly free of identifiable regionalism. His imposed generality is to be a symbolic American specificity. He is the narrator. We come down close in his face as he turns to the sea and speaks.

SOLDIER

This is the Atlantic Ocean. (*He gestures easily when he needs to*) Over there, somewhere, is

Europe. And over there, down that way, I guess, is Africa. (*Turning and facing inland*) And all of this, for thousands and thousands of miles in all directions, is the New World.

He bends down and empties a pile of dirt from his handkerchief onto the sand.

And this—this is soil. Southern soil. (*Opening his fist*) And this is cotton seed. Europe, Africa, the New World and Cotton. They have all gotten mixed up together to make the trouble.

He begins to walk inland, a wandering gait, full of pauses and gestures.

You see, this seed and this earth—(*Gesturing now to the land around him*) only have meaning—potency—if you add a third force. That third force is labor.

The landscape turns to the Southern countryside. In the distance, shadowed under the incredibly beautiful willows and magnolias, is a large, magnificently columned, white manor house. As he moves close to it, the soft, indescribably sweet sound of the massed voices of the unseen slaves wafts up in one of the most plaintive of the spirituals.

VOICES

"Steal away, steal away,
Steal away to Jesus.
Steal away, steal away home—
I ain't got long to stay here.

My Lord he calls me,
He calls me by the thunder.
The trumpet sounds

within-a my soul—
I ain't got long to stay here.

Steal away, steal away,
Steal away to Jesus.
Steal away, steal away home—
I ain't got long to stay here."

Beyond the manor house—cotton fields, rows and rows of cotton fields. And, finally, as the narrator walks on, rows of little white-painted cabins, the slave quarters.

The quarters are, at the moment, starkly deserted as though he has come upon this place in a dream only. He wanders in to what appears to be the center of the quarters with an easy familiarity at being there.

This plantation, like the matters he is going to tell us about, has no secrets from him. He knows everything we are going to see; he knows how most of us will react to what we see and how we will decide at the end of the play. Therefore, in manner and words he will try to persuade *us of nothing; he will only tell us facts and stand aside and let us see for ourselves. Thus, he almost leisurely refreshes himself with a drink from a pail hanging on a nail on one of the cabins. He wanders to the community outdoor fireplace at center and lounges against it and goes on with his telling.*

SOLDIER

Labor so plentiful that, for a while, it might be
cheaper to work a man to death and buy another
one than to work the first one less harshly.

The gentle slave hymn ends, and with its end comes the arbitrarily imposed abrupt darkness of true night. Somewhere in the distance a driver's voice calls: "Quittin' time! Quittin'

*time!" in accompaniment to a gong or a bell. Silent indica-
tions of life begin to stir around the narrator. We become
aware of points of light in some of the cabins and a great fire
has begun to roar silently in the fireplace where he leans.
Numbers of slaves begin to file, also silently, into the quarters;
some of them immediately drop to the ground and just sit or
lie perfectly still, on their backs, staring into space. Others
slowly form a silent line in front of the fireplace, holding
makeshift eating utensils. The narrator moves to make room
for them when it is necessary and occasionally glances from
them out to us, as if to see if we are truly seeing.*

*There is, about all of these people, a grim air of fatigue and
exhaustion, reflecting the twelve to fourteen hours of almost
unrelieved labor they have just completed. The men are
dressed in the main in rough trousers of haphazard lengths
and coarse shirts. Some have hats. The women wear single-
piece shifts, some of them without sleeves or collars. Some
wear their hair bound in the traditional bandana of the black
slave women of the Americas; others wear or carry the wide
straw hats of the cotton fields.*

These people are slaves. They did not come here
willingly. Their ancestors were captured, for the
most part, on the West Coast of Africa by men
who made such enterprise their business.

*We come in for extreme close-ups of the faces of the people
as he talks, moving from men to women to children with
lingering intimacy.*

Few of them could speak to each other. They
came from many different peoples and cultures.
The slavers were careful about that. Insurrection

is very difficult when you cannot even speak to your fellow prisoner.

All of them did not survive the voyage. Some simply died of suffocation; others of disease and still others of suicide. Others were murdered when they mutinied. And when the trade was finally suppressed—sometimes they were just dumped overboard when a British Man-o'-War got after a slave ship. To destroy the evidence.

That trade went on for three centuries. How many were stolen from their homeland? Some scholars say fifteen million. Others fifty million. No one will ever really know.

In any case, today some planters will tell you with pride that the cost of maintaining one of these human beings need not exceed seven dollars and fifty cents—a year. You see, among other things there is no education to pay for—in fact, some of the harshest laws in the slave code are designed to keep the slave from being educated. The penalties are maiming or mutilation—or death. Usually for he who is taught; but very often also for he who might dare to teach—including white men.

There are of course no minimum work hours and no guaranteed minimum wages. No trade unions. And, above all, no wages at all.

As he talks a murmur of low conversation begins among the people and there is a more conspicuous stir of life among them as the narrator now prepares, picking up his tunic and putting it across his shoulder once again, to walk out of the scene.

Please do not forget that this is the nineteenth century. It is a time when we still allow little children—white children—to labor twelve and thirteen hours in the factories and mines of America. We do not yet believe that women are equal citizens who should have the right to vote. It is a time when we still punish the insane for their madness. It is a time, therefore, when some men can believe and proclaim to the world that this system is the—(*Enunciating carefully but without passion*)—highest form of civilization in the world.

He turns away from us and faces the now-living scene in the background.

This system:

The CAMERA immediately comes in to exclude him and down to a close-up of a large skillet suspended over the roaring fire which now crackles with live sound. Pieces of bacon and corn pone sizzle on it. A meager portion of both is lifted up and onto a plate by Rissa, the cook. She is a woman of late years with an expression of indifference that has already passed resignation. The slave receiving his ration from her casts a slightly hopeful glance at the balance but is waved away by the cook. He gives up easily and moves away and retires and eats his food with relish. A second and a third are similarly served.

The fourth person in line is a young girl of about nineteen. She is SARAH. *She holds out her plate for service but bends as she does so, in spite of her own weariness, to play with a small boy of about seven or eight,* JOSHUA, *who has been lingering about the cook, clutching at her skirts and getting as much in her way as he can manage.*

SARAH

Hello, there, Joshua!

JOSHUA

I got a stomick ache.

RISSA

(*Busy with her serving*) You ain't got nothing but the devil ache.

SARAH

(*To the child, with mock and heavily applied sympathy*) Awww, poor little thing! Show Sarah* where it hurt you, honey.

He points his finger to a random place on his abdomen; clearly delighted to have even insincere attention.

Here?

She pokes him—ostensibly to determine the place where the pain is, but in reality only to make him laugh, which they both seem to know.

Or here? Oh, I know—right here!

She pokes him very hard with one finger, and he collapses in her arms in a fit of giggling.

RISSA

If y'all don't quit that foolin' 'round behind me while I got all this here to do—you better!

*Invariably pronounced "Say-rah."

She swings vaguely behind her with the spatula.
Stop it, I say now! Sarah, you worse than he is.

SARAH

(*A little surreptitiously—to Joshua*) Where's your
Uncle Hannibal?
The child shrugs indifferently.

RISSA

(*Who overhears everything that is ever spoken on
the plantation*) Uh-hunh. I knew we'd get 'round
to Mr. Hannibal soon enough.

SARAH

(*To Rissa*) Do you know where he is?

RISSA

How I know where that wild boy of mine is? If he
ain't got sense enough to come for his supper, it
ain't no care of mine. He's grown now. Move on
out the way now. Step up here, Ben!

SARAH

(*Moving around to the other side and standing
close*) He was out the fields again this afternoon,
Aunt Rissa.

RISSA

(*Softly, suddenly—but without breaking her working rhythm or changing facial expression*) Coffin
know?

SARAH

Coffin know everything. Say he goin' to tell Marster Sweet first thing in the mornin'.

SARAH

(*Decision*) See if you can find that boy of mine,
child.

SARAH *pushes the last of her food in her mouth and starts off.*
RISSA *halts her and hands her a small bundle which has been
lying in readiness.*

His supper.

CUT TO:
EXTERIOR. MOONLIT WOODS.

*Sarah emerges from the woods into a tiny clearing, bundle in
hand.*

SARAH

(*Calling softly*) Hannibal—

*The camera pans to a little hillock in deep grass where a lean,
vital young man lies, arms folded under his head, staring up
at the stars with bright commanding eyes. At the sound of
SARAH's voice off-camera we come down in his eyes. He
comes alert. She calls again.*

Hannibal—

He smiles and hides as she approaches.

Hannibal—

*She whirls about fearfully at the snap of a twig, then reas-
sured crosses in front of his hiding place, searching.*

Hannibal—

*He touches her ankle—she screams. Laughing, he reaches for
her. With a sigh of exasperation she throws him his food.*

HANNIBAL

(*Romantically, wistfully—playing the poet-fool*)
And when she come to me, it were the moonrise

231

. . . (*He holds out his hand*) And when she touch
my hand, it were the true stars fallin'.
*He takes her hand and pulls her down in the grass and kisses
her. She pulls away with the urgency of her news.*

SARAH

Coffin noticed you was gone first thing!

HANNIBAL

Well, that old driver finally gettin' to be almost
smart as a jackass.

SARAH

Say he gona tell Marster Sweet in the mornin'!
You gona catch you another whippin', boy. . . !
(*In a mood to ignore peril, Hannibal goes on eating
his food*) Hannibal, why you have to run off like
that all the time?

HANNIBAL

(*Teasing*) Don't run off *all* the time.

SARAH

Oh, Hannibal!

HANNIBAL

(*Finishing the meager supper and reaching out for
her playfully*) "Oh, Hannibal. Oh, Hannibal!"
Come here. (*He takes hold of her and kisses her
once sweetly and lightly*) H'you this evenin', Miss
Sarah Mae?

SARAH

You don't know how mad old Coffin was today, boy, or you wouldn't be so smart. He's gona get you in trouble with Marster again.

HANNIBAL

Me and you was *born* in trouble with Marster. (*Suddenly looking up at the sky and pointing to distract her*) Hey, lookathere!—

SARAH

(*Noting him and also looking up*) What—

HANNIBAL

(*Drawing her close*) Lookit that big, old, fat star shinin' away up yonder there!

SARAH

(*Automatically dropping her voice and looking about a bit*) Shhh. Hannibal!

HANNIBAL

(*With his hand, as though he is personally touching the stars*) One, two three, four—they makes up the dipper. That's the Big Dipper, Sarah. The old Drinkin' Gourd pointin' straight to the North Star!

SARAH

(*Knowingly*) Everybody knows that's the Big Dipper and you better hush your mouth for sure now, boy. Trees on this plantation got more ears than leaves!

HANNIBAL

(*Ignoring the caution*) That's the old Drinkin'
Gourd herself!

*Releasing the girl's arms and settling down, a little wistfully
now.*

HANNIBAL

Sure is bright tonight. Sure would make good
travelin' light tonight . . .

SARAH

(*With terror, clapping her hand over his mouth*)
Stop it!

HANNIBAL

(*Moving her hand*)—up there jes pointin' away
. . . *due North!*

SARAH

(*Regarding him sadly*) You're sure like your brother, boy. Just like him.

HANNIBAL *ignores her and leans back in the grass in the
position of the opening shot of the scene, with his arms
tucked under his head. He sings softly to himself:*

HANNIBAL

"For the old man is a-waitin'
For to carry you to freedom
If you follow the Drinking Gourd.
Follow—follow—follow . . .
If you follow the Drinking Gourd . . ."

SARAH

(*Over the song*)—look like him . . . talk like him

. . . and God knows, you sure think like him. (*Pause*) In time, I reckon—(*Very sadly*)—you be gone like him.

HANNIBAL

(*Sitting bolt upright suddenly and peering into the woods about them*) You think Isaiah got all the way to Canada, Sarah? Mama says it's powerful far. Farther than Ohio! (*This last with true wonder*) Sure he did! I bet you old Isaiah is up there and got hisself a job and is livin' fine. I bet you that! Bet he works in a lumberyard or something and got hisself a wife and maybe even a house and—

SARAH

(*Quietly*) You mean if he's alive, Hannibal.

HANNIBAL

Oh, he's alive, all right! Catchers ain't never caught my brother. (*He whistles through his teeth*) That boy lit out of here in a way somebody go who don't mean to never be caught by nothin'! (*He waits. Then, having assured himself within*) Wherever he is, he's alive. And he's free.

SARAH

I can't see how his runnin' off like that did you much good. Or your mama. Almost broke her heart, that's what. And worst of all, leavin' his poor little baby. Leavin' poor little Joshua who don't have no mother of his own as it is. Seem like your brother just went out his head when Marster sold Joshua's mother. I guess everybody on this plantation knew he wasn't gona be here long then. Even Marster must of known.

HANNIBAL

But Marster couldn't keep him here then! Not all Marster's dogs and drivers and guns. Nothin'. (*He looks to the woods, remembering*) I met him here that night to bring him the food and a extry pair of shoes. He was standin' right over there, right over there, with the moonlight streamin' down on him and he was breathin' hard—Lord, that boy was breathin' so's you could almost hear him on the other side of the woods. (*A sudden pause and then a rush in the telling*) He didn't say nothin' to me, nothin' at all. But his eyes look like somebody lit a fire in 'em, they was shinin' so in the dark. I jes hand him the parcel and he put it in his shirt and give me a kind of push on the shoulder . . . (*He touches the place, remembering keenly*) . . . Here. And then he turned and lit out through them woods like lightnin'. He was *bound* out this place!

He is entirely quiet behind the completion of the narrative. SARAH *is deeply affected by the implications of what she has heard and suddenly puts her arms around his neck and clings very tightly to him. Then she holds him back from her and looks at him for the truth.*

SARAH

You aim to go, don't you, Hannibal?
He does not answer and it is clear because of it that he intends to run off.

H'you know it's so much better to run off? (*A little desperately, near tears, thinking of the terrors involved*) Even if you make it—h'you know what's up there, what it be like to go wanderin' 'round by yourself in this world?

HANNIBAL

I don't know. Jes know what it is to be a slave!

SARAH

Where would you go—?

HANNIBAL

Jes North, that's all I know. (*Kind of shrugging*) Try to find Isaiah maybe. How I know what I do? (*Throwing up his hands at the difficult question*) There's people up there what helps runaways.

SARAH

You mean them aba—aba-litchinists? I heard Marster Sweet say once that they catches runaways and makes soap out of them.

HANNIBAL

(*Suddenly older and wiser*) That's slave-owner talk, Sarah. Whatever you hear Marster say 'bout slavery—you always believe the opposite. There ain't nothin' hurt slave marster so much— (*Savoring the notion*)—as when his property walk away from him. Guess that's the worst blow of all. Way I look at it, ever' slave ought to run off 'fore he die.

SARAH

(*Looking up suddenly, absorbing the sense of what he has just said*) Oh, Hannibal—*I* couldn't go!

2 3 7

(*She starts to shake all over*) I'm too delicate. My breath wouldn't hold out from here to the river . . .

HANNIBAL

(*Starting to laugh at her*) No, not you—skeerified as you is! (*He looks at her and pulls her to him*) But don't you worry, little Sarah. I'll come back. (*He smoothes her hair and comforts her*) I'll come back and buy you. Mama too, if she's still livin'. *The girl quivers in his arms and he holds her a little more tightly, looking up once again to his stars.*

I surely do that thing!

CUT TO:
INTERIOR. THE DINING ROOM OF THE "BIG HOUSE."

HIRAM SWEET *and his wife,* MARIA, *sit at either end of a well-laden table, attended by two male servants. The youngest son,* TOMMY, *about ten, sits near his father and across from his older brother,* EVERETT, *who is approaching thirty. A fifth person, a dinner guest, is seated on* EVERETT's *left. He is* DR. MACON BULLETT. *The meal has just ended, but an animated conversation which characterized it lingers actively.*

EVERETT

—by Heaven, I'll tell you we don't have to take any more of it! (*He hits the table with his fist for emphasis*) I say we can have 600,000 men in the field without even feeling it. The whole thing

wouldn't have to last more than six months, Papa.
Why can't you see that?

HIRAM

(*A man in his mid-sixties, with an overgenerous physique and a kind, if somewhat overindulged, face*) I see it fine! I see that it's the river of stupidity the South will eventually drown itself in.

BULLETT

(*A man of a slightly quieter temperament than the other two men; with an air of deeply ingrained "refinement"*) I don't see that we have much choice, however you look at it, Hiram. They've pushed our backs against the wall. Suddenly every blubber-fronted Yankee industrialist in New England has begun to imagine himself the deliverer of the blacks—at least in public speeches.

At the epithet, HIRAM *looks down at his own stomach and then back at his friend with some annoyance.*

The infernal hypocrites! Since all they want is the control of Congress, they ought to call a snake by its name.

EVERETT

Hear, hear, sir!

HIRAM

(*Eating something*) The only thing is—it doesn't make sense to fight a war you know you can't win.

EVERETT *is so exasperated by the remark that he jumps up from the table. His mother laughs.*

EVERETT

(*With genuine irritation*) Whatever are you laughing about, Mother?

MARIA

Forgive me, darling. It's just that it always amuses me to see how serious you have become now-a-day. (*To* BULLETT) He was so boyish and playful for so long. (*Innocently*) Right up until his twenty-first birthday he used to love to have me come to him and—

EVERETT

Mother, please. Papa, how can you constantly talk about our *not* winning when—(*On his fingers*)— we have the finest generals in the country and a labor force of four million who can just go on working undisturbed. Why, don't you see—if we had to, we could put every white man in the South in uniform! Will the North ever be able to boast that? (*Smiling at* BULLETT) What will happen to that great rising industrial center—if its men go off to war? (*He bends close to* BULLETT *so they can laugh together*) Who will run the machines then? New England schoolmarms?

They laugh heartily together. HIRAM *watches them and folds his hands on his stomach.*

HIRAM

And may I ask something of you, my son? When *you* and the rest of the white men of the South go off to fight your half of the war, who is going

to stay home and guard your slaves? Or are they
simply going to stop running away because then,
for the first time in history, running away will be
so easy?

EVERETT's *mouth is a little ajar from the question, though it
is far from the first time he has heard it. He and* BULLETT *are
merely exasperated to hear it asked again. They begin to
smile at one another as though a child had once again asked
a famous and tiresome riddle.*

(*Waving his hands at absurdity*) Hiram, you know
perfectly well that that is not a real consideration.
Abolitionist nonsense that any slaveholder should
know better than worry about!

I see. Tell me something, Macon. How many
slaves did you lose off your plantation last year?

Why—two. Prime hands, too, blast them!

Two. And Robley hit the jackpot with his new
overseer: he lost five. And one from the Davis
place. And I lost one. Let's see . . . two, seven,
eight, nine—from this immediate district . . . in
spite of every single precaution that we know how
to take . . .

Oh, come on now, Sweet, everyone knows that

the ones who run away are the troublemakers, the malcontents. Usually bad workers . . .

HIRAM

Mmm-hmm. Of course. Then why are there reward posters up on every other tree in this county? Come, man, you're not talking to a starry-eyed Yankee fool! You're talking to a slaveholder!

BULLETT

I don't follow your point.

HIRAM

You follow my point! We all follow my point! Or else will somebody here stop laughing long enough to tell me why you and me and Robley and all the others waste all that money on armed guards and patrols and rewards and dogs? And, above all, why you and me and every other planter in the cotton South *and* the Border States tried to move heaven and earth to get the fugitive slave laws passed? Was it to try and guarantee the return of property that you are sitting there calmly and happily telling me doesn't run off in the first place!

EVERETT

Well, Papa, of course a few—

HIRAM

A few, my eyelashes! What's the matter with you two! I believe in slavery! But I also understand it! I understand it well enough not to laugh at the very question that might decide this war that you are just dying to start.

EVERETT

You forget, Papa, it's not going to be much of a war. And if it is, then we can always arm the *blacks!*

HIRAM *puts down his cup with astonishment and even* MACON *looks at* EVERETT *askance for his naïve remark.*

HIRAM

(*With undiluted sarcasm*) I have to admit that my boy here is as logical as the rest of the leaders of our cause. For what could be more logical than the idea that you can give somebody a gun and make him fight *for* what he's trying like blazes to run away *from* in the first place. (*Dryly*) I salute you, Everett. You belong in Washington—immediately—among your peers.

MARIA

Now, Hiram—

EVERETT

You don't have to be insulting, Papa.

HIRAM

I'll be what I please in this house and you'll mind your manners to me in the face of it!

EVERETT *looks to his mother in outrage for support.*

MARIA

Well, dear, you shouldn't sass your father.

EVERETT

Mother, I am not Tommy! I am a grown man. Who, incidentally, any place but this would be running his father's plantation at my age.

HIRAM

You'll run it when I can depend on you to run it in my tradition. And not before.

EVERETT

Your "tradition" is running it to ruin!

MARIA

(*Upset*) Everett, I'll not have it at the table. I simply won't have it at the table. (*To the younger boy to get him away from the argument*) You may excuse yourself and go to your room if you are through, Tommy. Say good night to Dr. Bullett.

TOMMY

Good night, sir.
            (*He exits*)

HIRAM

(*Immediately*) So I am running it to ruin, am I! You hear that, Macon! This polished little pepper is now one of the new experts of the South. Knows everything. Even how to run a plantation. Studied it in Paris cafés!

BULLETT

At this point, Hiram, I hear only that you must quiet yourself. (*Looking at his watch*) In fact, let's get upstairs and get it over.

HIRAM

I don't feel like going upstairs and I don't feel like being poked all over with your little sticks and tubes.

BULLETT

I came over this evening to examine you, Hiram, and I am going to examine you if we have to do it right here at the table.
> *(He rises and gets his black bag and* MARIA *sits nodding her appreciation of his forcefulness with the difficult man)*

MARIA

He's been eating salt again, too, Macon. I declare I can't do a thing with him.

HIRAM

(*To his wife*) Yahhhhhh.

EVERETT

(*Watching his father's antics*) Stubbornness, backwardness, disorder, contempt for new ways. It's the curse of the past and it is strangling us.

HIRAM

All I can say is that if you are the spirit of the Future, it sure is going to be talkative.

MARIA

Can't you ever talk nicely to him, Hiram?

EVERETT

I don't want him to talk "nice" to me. For the eighty-thousandth time, I am not a little boy!

HIRAM

(*To* MACON) Isn't there something you are always quoting to me from your Shakespeare about people protesting too much? (*To* EVERETT) Seems to me, son, that I haven't done too badly with what you seem to think are my backward ways. You can testify to that, can't you, Macon? Came into this country with four slaves and fifty dollars. Four slaves and fifty dollars! (*He becomes mellow and a little grand whenever he recalls this for the world*) I planted the first seed myself and supervised my own baling. That was thirty-five years ago and I made this one of the finest—though I am the first to admit, not one of the biggest— plantations in this district. So I must know a little something about how to run it.

EVERETT

Maybe you *knew* about running it.

HIRAM

I *know* about running it!

BULLETT

Calm down now, Hiram.

HIRAM

(*To* MACON) You know what HIS idea is of running this place? It's simple. It's the "modern" way. It's what everybody does. You put the whole thing in the hands of overseers! That's all! Then you take off for Saratoga or Paris. Those aren't planters who do that—those are parasites! I'm a cotton grower, and I'll manage my own plantation until I'm put under. And that I promise God!

EVERETT

Papa, can I ask you a simple unemotional question —when is the last time our yield came anywhere near ten bales to the hand? When, Papa? You tell me.

HIRAM

Well, the land is just about finished. Five bales to the hand is pretty good for our land at this point.

EVERETT

(*Looking triumphantly from his father to the other*) And when are we going to buy new land?

HIRAM

(*Troubled in spite of himself*) Next year, if the crop is good.

EVERETT

And if the crop is poor? Listen close to this circular conversation, Macon.
> (*He waves his hand to point up the absurdity*)

HIRAM

Well, we'll borrow.

247

EVERETT

Yes—and then what?

HIRAM

We'll buy more land.

EVERETT

And who will work the extra land? You going to buy new slaves too?

HIRAM

(*Rubbing his ear*) Well, if those Virginia breeders weren't such bandits we could take on one or two more prime hands—

EVERETT

But they *are* bandits, and until such time as we can get some decent legislation in this country to reopen the African slave trade we have to meet their prices. So now what?

HIRAM

Don't goad me!

EVERETT

Don't goad you! What do you expect me to do, sit around and watch you let this place go bankrupt! You don't seem to understand, Papa, we don't have much choice. We have got to up our yield or go under. It's as simple as that. (*To the doctor*) You know what this place is, Macon? A resort for slaves! You know what they put in the fields here? I am ashamed to tell you. Nine and one half hours!

HIRAM

Nine and a half hours is plenty of labor for a hand!

EVERETT

(*Almost shouting*) Not on that cotton-burned land it isn't! (*Then fighting to hold himself in check*) Sure, I know—there was a time when the land was pure and fertile as a dream. You hardly had to do anything but just poke something in it and it grew. But that is over with. It has to be coaxed now, and you have to keep your labor in the fields a decent length of time. Nine and one half hours! Why the drivers stroll around out there as though it were all a game. (*Looking at his father*) And the high-water mark gets higher and higher and higher. But he doesn't care! This is his little farm, run in his little way, by his dear old friends out there who understand him and love him: Fa-la-la-la-la!

MARIA

I think that will do, son.

EVERETT

Yes, that will do! That will do—!
    (*He jumps up as if to leave the room*)

HIRAM

Where are you going?

EVERETT

I am going to find John Robley and his brother and—

HIRAM

—drink and gamble the night away! Is that the
way you would be master here! Sit down!

EVERETT *halts with his mouth open to speak to his father in
outrage.* MACON *interrupts with a deliberately quiet note.*

BULLETT

(*To* MARIA) Get him to take these four times a
day, if you can, Maria. (*To* HIRAM) Not three
times and not five times—*four.*

MARIA

(*Taking the bottle and going out with it*) I will try,
Macon, I will try. (*To* EVERETT *as she passes
him*) Do try not to upset your father so, darling.
                    (*She kisses him lightly and pats his cheek
                    and exits with the bottle*)

EVERETT *moves to a window and stands looking out at the
darkness in irritation.* BULLETT *clearly waits for* MARIA*'s distance and then looks at his patient as he starts to put his
things away.*

BULLETT

Well, Hiram—it's all over.

From the finality of his tone, EVERETT *turns slowly to listen
and stare at them and* HIRAM, *who also understands the
opening remark, at once also winds up for a great and loud
protest.*

No, I mean it. There's nothing left to joke about
and no more trusting to luck. It's that bad.

HIRAM *stares hard at him and the protest starts to fall away
as the gravity of his friend penetrates.*

As much as you hate reading, you have got to buy all the books you can and spend the rest of your life doing very little else. That's all. I absolutely insist that you stay out of the fields.

HIRAM

Well, now, just a minute, Macon—

BULLETT

I'm sorry, Hiram—

HIRAM

Well, your being sorry doesn't help me one bit!

EVERETT

Papa!

BULLETT

That's all right, son.

HIRAM

What do you expect me to do with my plantation? Turn it over to *him* so he can turn it over to a pack of overseers?

BULLETT

Well, I hadn't intended to get into that, Hiram, but since you ask me, I think it would be the best thing that could happen to the Sweet plantation. (*Seeing that the remark has cut the man deeply, he tries to amplify in the most impartial and reasonable tone*) You and I have to face the fact that this is a new era, Hiram. Cotton is a big business in a way it never was before. If you treat it any other way, you're lost. You just have to adjust to that, Hiram. For the good of yourself and for the good of the South.

HIRAM

(*Bitterly*) That's easy talk for a blue blood, Macon! We all know that you came from a long line of lace-hankied Bordeaux wine-sniffers, but I think you forget that I don't.

EVERETT

(*Hating most of all that he should raise the question*) Papa, please!

BULLETT

(*Coolly*) I cannot imagine what makes you think I have forgotten. Certainly not your manners.

EVERETT

(*Obligatory*) Sir, I must remind you this is my father's house.

HIRAM

(*To* EVERETT) Don't you ever hush? I'm sorry, Macon, I was a little insulting and a little—

EVERETT

(*Almost to himself, involuntarily*)—common.
This is clearly EVERETT*'s anguish. All three men suffer a moment of extreme discomfort and* MACON *stirs himself for departure.*

BULLETT

Well, that was an extraordinary meal as usual. That Rissa of yours is an eternal wonder.

HIRAM

Macon, tell me something. Don't you have the
gray hours, too?

BULLETT

The what?

HIRAM

The gray hours—you know what I mean, don't sit
there looking dumb. I call them the gray hours,
you probably call them something else. That doesn't matter. I know perfectly well you have them,
whatever you call them. I think every man that
draws breath on this earth has those hours when—
well—when, by God, he wonders why the stars
hang out there and this planet turns and rivers
run—and what he's here for.

BULLETT

Yes, I suppose we all do.

HIRAM

Then what happens, Macon, if it's all a lie—the
way we live, the things we tell ourselves?

BULLETT

Oh, come now, Hiram . . .

HIRAM

No, I mean it—what happens if there really is
some old geezer sitting up there, white beard and
all—

BULLETT

I don't think I'm so unready to meet my Maker, Hiram. I haven't been the worst of men on this earth—

HIRAM

Macon—*you own slaves.*

BULLETT

Well, that's not a sin. It was meant to be that way. That's why He made men different colors.

HIRAM

Is it? I hope so, Macon, I truly hope so.

BULLETT

(*Rising*) Hiram, I really must get on. No, don't call Maria. Harry can see me out. Good night, Everett.

EVERETT

Good night, sir.

BULLETT

(*Touching his friend on his shoulder as he exits*) Books and long afternoon naps. Good night, Hiram.

HIRAM

(*Having become strangely quiet*) Good night, Macon.

>   (*The doctor exits.*)

EVERETT

(*Turning on him savagely as soon as the man is out of sight*) Papa, why must you insist upon eternally bringing up your "humble beginnings"—

HIRAM

(*Sighing*) Good night, son. I want to be alone. I am tired.

EVERETT

(*Concerned*) Are—you all right?

Hiram

Yes. Good night.

EVERETT *does not say another word and exits quietly from the room as the planter sits on. Presently a stir in the shadows behind him makes him turn his head.*

That you, Rissa? You there.

RISSA

(*Coming out of the shadows as all of the servants seem to do when they are called or needed*) Yessah.

HIRAM

(*Himself*) There wasn't enough salt in the greens.

RISSA

There was all you gona get from now on.

HIRAM

Now, Rissa—

RISSA

If you aimin' on killin' yourself, Marster Hiram, don't be askin' Riss' to hep you none 'cause she ain't gona do it.

HIRAM

One thing about always listening to other people's conversations, Rissa, is that you hear a lot of blasted nonsense.

RISSA

I don't have to listen to no other folks' conversations to see h'you ailin'. You sittin' there now, white as cotton, sweatin' like you seen the horseman comin'. (*She stands behind him and forces him to sit back in the chair with comforting gestures*) Lord, you one stubborn man. I 'spect you was allus the most stubborn man I ever come across.

HIRAM

Took a stubborn man to do the things I had to. To come into the wilderness and make a plantation. Came here with four slaves and fifty dollars and made one of the finest plantations in this district.

RISSA

(*Attending to him, gently, patiently, mopping his brow as she stands behind his chair*) Yessah. Jes you and me and old Ezra and Zekial who run off and poor old Leo who died last year.

HIRAM

(*Shaking his head*) You ever expect that Ezekial would run off from me after all those years?

RISSA

Sprise me just as much as you. Reckon I don't know what gets into some folks.

HIRAM

(*Suddenly breaking into laughter*) Remember that time when we were building the old barn and Zeke fell from the loft straight into that vat of molasses you had put in there to cool the day before? By God, he was a sticky boy that day!
(He roars and she does also)

RISSA

—Come flyin' to me in the kitchen screamin'; "Rissa, Rissa, I'se kilt, I'se kilt!" Me and Ezra had to tie him down to wash him he was so scared. (*A new surge of laughter*) Finally had to shave his head like a egg, 'member?

HIRAM

And the time the wild hogs went after the corn in the south fields and I had to go after them with the gun and Farmer Burns thought I was shooting at him!

RISSA

Do I remember?—Why we had po'k 'round here for months after that!

LORRAINE HANSBERRY

HIRAM

(*Feeling festive*) Fetch the gun, Rissa, go ahead
let's have a look at it—

RISSA

(*Fussing good-naturedly as she obeys, reaching for
a key hanging among a dozen or so keys on her
belt*) I knew it! Every time you get to thinkin'
'bout them days I have to get out that old gun so's
you kin look at it.

*She opens a long drawer and pulls the old weapon out. It is
wrapped in a cloth and has been kept in excellent repair.*

HIRAM

(*Reaching out for it eagerly as she brings it to
him*) Ah! . . . And still shoots true as an arrow
. . . (*He caresses it a little*) My father gave me this
gun and I remember feeling—I was fourteen—I
remember feeling, "I'm a man now. A true man.
I shall go into the wilderness and not seek my
fortune—but *make* it!" Hah! What a cocky boy
I was! . . .

(*Hiram is smiling happily*)

RISSA

(*Clearly getting ready to remind him of something.
Placing both fists on her hips*) Speakin' of boys,
Marster Sweet, ain't you forgot about a certain
promise in the last couple of months?

HIRAM

(*Frowning like a boy being reprimanded*) Oh,
Rissa, Maria says she won't have it. She put up a
terrible fuss about it . . .

RISSA

(*Just as childishly—they are, in fact, very much alike*) Marster, a promise is a promise! And you promise me when that boy was born that he wasn't never gona have to be no field hand . . .

HIRAM

But we need all the hands in the fields we've got and Maria says there is absolutely nothing for another house servant to do around here.

As he is saying this, MARIA *has reentered with a single pill and a glass of water. She stands where she is and watches the two of them.*

RISSA

He kin do a little bit of everything. He kin hep me in the kitchen and Harry some in the house. He's gettin' so unruly, Marster Hiram. And you promised me—

HIRAM

All right, for God's sake! Anything for peace in this house! Soon as pickin's over, Hannibal is a house servant—

RISSA *sees* MARIA *and becomes quite still.* HIRAM *follows her eyes and turns to see* MARIA *as she advances toward him with the medicine and water, her face set in silent anger.* HIRAM *shouts at her suddenly.*

Because I say so, that's why! Because I am master of this plantation and every soul on it. I am master of those fields out there and I am master of this house as well. (*She is silent*) There are some men born into this world who make their own destiny.

Men who do not tolerate the rules of other men
or other forces.

*He is angry at his illness and goes into a mounting rage as
the camera pans away from him to the slightly nodding* RISSA
*who is cut of the same cloth in her individualism; to his wife
who feels in the moment only clear despair for her husband;
across the floor through the open door where* EVERETT *stands
listening in half-shadow*

I will not die curled up with some book! When the
Maker wants me, let him come for me in the place
where He should know better than all I can be
found . . .

EVERETT *'s face turns intently as if for the first time he is
hearing the essence of his father.*

I have asked no man's permission for the life I
have lived—and I will not start now!

Fade out
End of Act One

ACT TWO

FADE IN:
INTERIOR. EVERETT'S BEDROOM—
AFTERNOON.

He is sitting dejectedly alone. Drinking. The door bursts open and his mother stands there with urgency in her face.

MARIA

You had better come, son!

EVERETT

(*With concern*) An attack?

MARIA

Yes, I've sent for Macon.
He rushes to her and steadies her.

EVERETT

It's all right, Mother. It's going to be all right.

CUT TO:
INTERIOR. HIRAM'S BEDROOM.

The shades have been pulled and HIRAM *lies stretched out on his back, fully dressed. A male house servant is trying to gently remove his clothes.* EVERETT *and* MARIA *enter and go directly to his bedside.*

MARIA

Hiram, Macon is on his way. Everything is going
to be all right.

HIRAM

Saw him that time . . . old horseman . . . riding
out the swamps . . . He was smiling at me.

MARIA

(*Taking over from the servant in an effort to make
him comfortable*) Just lie still. Don't talk. Macon
will be here in a little while and everything will be
all right.

EVERETT

(*Aside, to the servant*) When did it happen?

SERVANT

Jes a little while ago, suh. They found him
stretched out yonder in the fields. Eben and Jed
carried him up here and me and Missus got him
on the bed fust thing. I think he's powaful sick
this time, suh.

HIRAM

Fifty dollars and four slaves . . . Planted the first
seed myself . . .

MARIA *looks at her husband intently in his pain and then rises
with a new air of determination and signals for her son to
follow her out of the room. He obeys—a little quizzically.*

MARIA

(*To the servant as they go out*) We'll be right here,
Harry.

SERVANT

Yes, ma'am.

MARIA

(*In the hall, in half tones and with a more precise spirit than her son has ever seen before*) Do you propose to wait any longer now, son?

EVERETT

(*Confused*) For what—?

MARIA

To become master here.

EVERETT

Oh, Mother . . .

MARIA

Everett, your father is perfectly capable of killing himself. We must become perfectly capable of stopping him from doing it.

EVERETT

You heard him last week—"Some men make their destiny"—Well—

MARIA

(*Sharply*) I am not interested in your bitterness at this moment, Everett. You must take over the running of the plantation—no, listen to me—and you must make him believe you have done no such thing. Every night, if necessary, you must sit with pencil and pad and let him tell you everything he wishes. And then—well, do as you please. You will be master then. But he will think that he is still, which is terribly important.

(With that, she turns to the door)

EVERETT

You would deceive him like that?

MARIA

(*Only half-turning to reply*) Under the circumstances, Everett, I consider that to be the question of a weak boy, when I have clearly asked you to be a very strong man. (*Looking at him*)Which is the only kind I have ever been able to truly love.

(She turns and goes and the camera lingers with Everett's face)

DISSOLVE TO:
EXTERIOR. A SMALL FARM.

A lean farmer stands in a cornfield between rows of feeble burnt-out looking corn. A bushel basket sits at his feet. He reaches out and twists an ear off a stalk, pulls back the green shuck and looks at the ear with anger and despair and throws it roughly into the basket, where other ears like it are collected. He picks up the basket and strides angrily toward his cabin.

CUT TO:
INTERIOR. THE CABIN.

His wife is working at the stove. ZEB DUDLEY, *the farmer, kicks the door open roughly with his foot and walks in and slams the basket down with fury. The woman watches him.*

ZEB

That ain't corn. That's sticks!

(ELIZABETH *wipes her hands and comes to inspect the corn.
She picks up a piece or two and drops them sadly back into
the basket*)

ZEB

Ain't nobody going to buy that! Can't hardly get
a decent price when it's good. Who's going to buy
that?

ELIZABETH

Well, take it in anyhow. We have to try at least,
Zeb.

*Two small children stand in a corner watching them, looking
as if they might welcome the corn at the moment, no matter
what its condition.*

ZEB

Well then—you try!

*He strides across the floor and gets a jug down from the shelf
and uncorks it and drinks deeply from it.*

ELIZABETH

We ain't got no choice, Zeb.

ZEB

I said all right, you try! (*More quietly*) How's
Timmy?

ELIZABETH

(*Looking into the crib in a corner of the room*) He
ain't been cryin' at least.

The man walks over to his baby's crib and then turns away

and takes another drink from the jug, only to discover that it is now empty. He looks at it and suddenly smashes it on the floor. An old man has appeared at the door which ZEB *has left open.*

PREACHER

H'dy do.
He surprises both of them a little.

ELIZABETH

Oh, hello, Preacher, come on in.

PREACHER

Thought I'd pay my respects to the Dudleys and mebbe find out why they ain't made it to meetin' in the last month of Sundays. Reckon I could stand a cup of lemonade too, if you got it handy, 'Lizabeth.
He signals the two older children without interrupting his remarks and gives them each a candy.

Zeb, you look like a stallion somebody been whip-pin' with a bullwhip.
ZEB *strides out of the cabin and makes splashing sounds from a basin outside the door.* ELIZABETH *puts a glass of lemonade before the Preacher.*

What's the matter with Timmy, there?

ELIZABETH

Got the croup all week.
Her husband comes back in, stripped to the waist, water dripping from his head. She pours lemonade for him also.

PREACHER

Now, that's better. Nothin' to bring temper down off a man like a little coolin' water.

ZEB

I'm clearin', Preacher.

PREACHER

Clearin' where, son?

ZEB

Don't know. The West, mebbe.

PREACHER

Oh, the West?

ZEB

(*Defensively*) Well, a lotta folks been pullin' out goin' West lately.

PREACHER

Lookin' for the Frontier again? I kin remember when this was the Frontier.

ZEB

(*Quickly*)   That was a long time ago.

PREACHER

A long time. Before the big plantations started gobblin' up the land and floodin' the country with slaves.

ZEB

I heard me some good things 'bout the West. That if a man got a little get up in him, he still got a chance. Hear there's plenty of land still. Good land.

PREACHER

Seems to be three things the South sends out more than anything else. A steady stream of cotton, runaway slaves and poor white folks. I guess the last two is pretty much lookin' for the same thing and they both runnin' from the first.

ZEB

Not me—! No sir! I ain't runnin' from cotton! I'm lookin' for some place where I kin plant me some, that's what! I know 'bout plantin' and I know how to drive slaves!

PREACHER

And you figger you kin get to be somebody, eh? Like the Sweets, mebbe?

ZEB

If I ever got my chance, I make that Sweet plantation look like a shanty! . . . Why you laughin' like that?

PREACHER

Allus been a laughin' man, allus loved a good joke.

ZEB

Well, I ain't told none.

PREACHER

Yep, it's a hard life.

ZEB

It's a hard life if you ain't got slaves.

PREACHER

That what you think, Zeb?

ZEB

That's what I know.

PREACHER

Your Pa managed to be a pretty good farmer without slaves, Zeb.

ZEB

My Pa was a fool.

PREACHER

Sure hate to hear good men called fools. He was
honest and he worked hard. Didn't call anybody
Master and caused none to call him Master. He
was a farmer and a good one.

ZEB

And he died eatin' dirt.
There is a sound of reining-up outside the cabin. ELIZABETH
goes to look out.

ELIZABETH

Why it's Everett Sweet, Zeb!

ZEB

Who—
*He rises from the table with a quizzical expression and goes
to the door and looks out to where* EVERETT *is sitting astride
his horse.*

EVERETT

(*Abruptly*) I'm looking for a good overseer, Zeb Dudley.

ZEB

(*Feeling his way*) Well, what you come here for?

EVERETT

I heard you had some experience driving slaves.

PREACHER

(*Coming and standing behind* ZEB *in the doorway, while* ELIZABETH *looks on with interest in the background*) Well, you musta heard wrong. This boy ain't cut from what makes overseers. He's a farmer.

ZEB

(*Scanning* EVERETT *with his eyes, interested*) I helped out once on the Robley place. I can handle blacks if I have to. But how come you interested? You Pa don't 'low no overseer on his place.

EVERETT

My father is ill in bed. I'm master at our place now and I intend to grow cotton there—a *lot* of cotton, and I want and need an overseer.

PREACHER

(*To* ZEB) Tell him you don't know nobody 'round here for that kind of work, Zeb.

ZEB

(*Shrugging the* PREACHER*'s hand off his shoul-*

der) Leave me be, Preacher. (*To* EVERETT) How much you figger to pay?

EVERETT

I'll go as high as fifteen hundred if your work is good. And if you up my yield at the end of the year, I'll give you a bonus.

ZEB

Your word on that, sir?

EVERETT

You heard. But I want cotton.

ZEB

(*Vigorously*) For two thousand dollars—I'll get them slaves of yourn to grow cotton 'tween the rows!

EVERETT

You're on. Be at our place early tomorrow.

ZEB

You got yourself an overseer!

EVERETT *touches his hat to them and rides off.* ZEB *gives a yell and wheels and picks up his wife and whirls her around happily. She too is very happy. The* PREACHER *watches their celebration and sits down in his defeat.*

Two thousand dollars! (*He tousles the hair of his kids and gets to the* PREACHER *at the table*) You a book-learned man, Preacher, help me figger that. Fertilizer, tools on credit, so's mebbe I could put the whole two thousand t'ward two prime hands—

PREACHER

(*Looking at him sadly*) So that's what it's come to 'round here. Man either have to go into slavery some kind of way or pull out the South, eh?

ZEB

Aw, come on, Preacher—

PREACHER

You think a man's hands was made to drive slaves?

ZEB

If they have to, Preacher, if they have to . . . Or mebbe you think they was made to sit idle while he watches his babies turn the color of death?

PREACHER

Zeb, I seen your daddy the day he come ridin' into this here country. Perched up on his pony with a sack of flour and some seed. And he done all right with them two hands of his. He dug in the earth with 'em and he made things grow with 'em. (*He takes* ZEB'*s hands*) Your hands is the same kind, boy.

ZEB

Leave me be, Preacher.

PREACHER

They wasn't meant to crack no whip on no plantation. That ain't fit thing for a man to have to do, Zeb. (*Pointing after* EVERETT) Them people hate our kind. Ain't I heard 'em laughin' and talkin' 'mongst themselves when they see some poor cracker walkin' down the road—about how the ne-gras was clearly put here to serve their betters but how God must of run clear out of ideas when He got to the poor white! Me and you is farmers, Zeb. Cotton and slavery has almost ruined our land. 'N' some of us got to try and hold out 'ginst it. Not go runnin' off to do their biddin' every time they need one of us. Them fields and swamps and pastures yonder was give to us by Him what giveth all gifts—to do right by. And we can't just give it all up to folks what hates the very sight of us—

ZEB

(*Frightened inside by the sense of the speech*) You talk for yourself, Preacher! You go on bein' and thinkin' what you want, but don't be 'cludin' me in on it. 'Cause I ain't *never* found nothin' fine and noble 'bout bein' no dirt-eater. I don't aim to end up no redneck cracker the rest of my life, out there scrapin' on that near-gravel trying to get a little corn to grow. Allus watchin' somebody else's plantation gettin' closer and closer to my land! (*A cry of anguish and a vow: his only claim, his only hope for something better, the one thing he can cling to in this life:*) *I'm a white man, Preacher!* And I'm goin' to drive slaves for Everett Sweet and he's goin' to pay me for it and this time next year, Zeb Dudley aims to own himself some slaves and be a man—you hear!

LORRAINE HANSBERRY

PREACHER

Yes . . . I hear. And I reckon I understand. And
all I kin say is—God have mercy on all of
us . . .

CUT TO:
INTERIOR. RISSA'S CABIN—LATE.

Within, a collection of slaves have formed a play circle
around which various individual members of the group sing
and perform "Raise a Ruckus."

ALL

"Come along, little children, come along!
Come where the moon is shining bright!
Get along, little children, get along—
We gona raise a ruckus tonight!"
Outside the cabin, HANNIBAL and SARAH linger a moment
before going in.

SARAH

(With a sense of conspiracy) I seen you this morning, Hannibal.

HANNIBAL

(Who is tuning his banjo) Where—?

SARAH

You know where! Boy, you must be crazy!
HANNIBAL looks frightened. Then waves it away and smiles
at her and takes her by the arm and leads her in to join the
others. HANNIBAL begins to accompany on his banjo. Joshua
is in the center of the singing circle, rendering the verse.

274

JOSHUA

"My old marster promise me
Mmm Mmm Mmm
That when he died he gona set me free
Mmm Mmm Mmm
Well, he live so long 'til his head got bald
Mmm Mmm Mmm
Then he gave up the notion of dying at all!"

ALL

"Come along, little children, come along!
Come where the moon is shining bright!
Get on board, little children, get on board—
We're gona raise a ruckus tonight!"

SARAH

"My old mistress promise me
Mmm Mmm Mmm
        (Mimicking)
"Say-rah! When I die I'm going to set you free!"
Mmm Mmm Mmm
But a dose of poison kinda helped her along
Mmm Mmm Mmm
And may the devil sing her funeral song!"

SARAH *pantomimes gleefully helping "Mistress" along to her grave with a shoving motion of her hand. The chorus of the song is repeated by all. A man is now pushed out to the center. He gets the first line out—*

MAN

"Well, the folks in the Big
House all promise me—"

His eyes suddenly grow wide as the camera pans to a slave who has just entered the cabin. It is COFFIN, *the driver. The others follow his gaze and the song dwindles down and goes out completely, and the people start to file out of the cabin with disappointment.*

COFFIN

(*Looking about at them in outrage*) Jes keep it up! That's all I got to say—jes keep on! Oughta be shamed of yourselves. Good as Marster is to y'all, can't trust none of you nary a minute what you ain't 'round singing them songs he done 'spressly f'bid on this here plantation.

When the last of the guests are gone, including SARAH, HANNIBAL *settles in a corner on the floor, and* COFFIN *turns his attention to* RISSA, *who has been sitting apart from the festivity, mending by the light of the fire.*

RISSA

'Spect you better get yourself to bed, Joshua. H'you this evenin', Brother Coffin?

COFFIN

There ain't supposed to be no singin' of them kind of songs and you knows it good as me!

RISSA

H'I'm supposed to stop folks from openin' and closin' they mouths, man?

COFFIN

This here your cabin.

RISSA

But it's they mouths. Joshua-lee, I told you to get
yourself in the bed. Don't let me have to tell you
again.

COFFIN

(*To* HANNIBAL *who has been sitting watching both
of them with his own amusement*) Wanna see you,
boy.

HANNIBAL

I'm here.

COFFIN

Yes, and it's the only place you been all day where
you was *supposed* to be, too.

HANNIBAL *Looks uncomfortably to his mother, but she stud-
iedly does not look up from her mending.*

Jes who you think pick your cotton ever'time you
decides to run off?

HANNIBAL

Reckon I don't worry 'bout it gettin' picked.

COFFIN

(*To* RISSA) Why don't you do something 'bout this
here boy! I tries to be a good driver for Marster
and he the kind what makes it hard for me.

HANNIBAL

And what gon' happen when you show Marster
what a good, good driver you is? Marster gon'
make you overseer? Maybe you think he'll jes
make Coffin marster here—

COFFIN

You betta stop that sassy lip of yours with me boy
or—

HANNIBAL

Or what, Coffin—?

COFFIN

You jes betta quit, thas all. I'm—

HANNIBAL

"—one of Marster Sweet's drivers"—

COFFIN

And thas a fact!

HANNIBAL

Get out this cabin 'fore you get smacked upside
your head.

RISSA

(*Looking up from her sewing*) I 'spect that'll be
enough from you, Mr. Hannibal.

HANNIBAL

I say what I please to a driver, which, as everybody
know, next to a overseer be 'bout the lowest form
of life known.

COFFIN

Why? 'Cause I give Marster a day's work fair and
square and don't fool 'round. Like you, f'instant,
with all your carryin' ons. Draggin' along in the
fields like you was dead; pretendin' you sick half
the time. Act like you drop dead if you pick your

full quota one of these days. I knows your tricks.
You ain't nothin'!

HANNIBAL

Coffin, how you get so mixed up in your head?
Them ain't my fields yonder, man! Ain't none of
it my cotton what'll rot if I leaves it half-picked.
They ain't my tools what I drops and breaks and
loses every time I gets a chance. None of it *mine*.

COFFIN

(*To* RISSA, *shaking his head ruefully*) Them was
some wild boys you birthed, woman. You gona pay
for it one of these days, too.

RISSA

(*Putting down her sewing finally*) What was I
supposed to do—send 'em back to the Lord? You
better get on back to your cabin now, Coffin.

COFFIN *exchanges various glances of hostility with them and
leaves. As soon as he is gone the mother turns on the son.*

RISSA

Where you run off to all the time, son?

HANNIBAL

That's Hannibal's business.

RISSA

(*With quiet and deadly implications*) Who you
think you sassin' now?

HANNIBAL

(*Intimidated by her*) I jes go off sometimes,
Mama.

279

She crosses the cabin to his pallet and gets a cloth-wrapped package from under it and returns with it in her hands. She unwraps it as she advances on him: it is a Bible.

RISSA

Is that when you does your stealin'?
He sees that the matter is exposed and is silent.
What you think the Lord think of somebody who would steal the holy book itself?

HANNIBAL

If he's a just Lord—he'll think more of me than them I stole it from who don't seem to pay nothin' it says no mind.

RISSA

H'long you think Marster Hiram have you 'round his house if he thinks you a thief?

HANNIBAL

He ain't got me 'round his house and I ain't aimin' to be 'round his house!

RISSA

Well, he's aimin' for you to. Said last night that from now on you was to work in the Big House.

HANNIBAL

(*In fury*) You asked him for that, didn't you?

RISSA

He promised me ever since you was a baby that you wouldn't have to work in the fields.

HANNIBAL

And ever since I could talk I done told you I ain't
never goin' be no house servant, no matter what!
To no master. I ain't, Mama, I ain't!

RISSA

What's the matter with you, Hannibal? The one
thing I allus planned on was that you and Isaiah
would work in the Big House where you kin get
decent food and nice things to wear and learn nice
mannas like a real genamun. (*Pleadingly*) Why,
right now young Marse' got the most beautiful red
broadcloth jacket that I heard him say he was tired
of already—and he ain't hardly been in it. (*Touching his shoulders to persuade*) Fit you everywhere
'cept maybe a little in the shoulder on account you
a little broader there—

HANNIBAL

(*Almost screaming*) I don't want Marster Everett's bright red jacket and I don't want Marster
Sweet's scraps. I don't want nothin' in this whole
world but to get off this plantation!

RISSA

(*Standing with arms still outstretched to where his
shoulders were*) How come mine all come here
this way, Lord? (*She sits, wearily*) I done tol' you
so many times, that you a slave, right or not, you
a slave. 'N' you alive—you ain't dead like maybe
Isaiah is—

HANNIBAL

Isaiah ain't dead!

RISSA

Things jes ain't that bad here. Lord, child, I been
in some places (*Closing her eyes at the thought of
it*) when I was a young girl which was made up by
the devil. I known marsters in my time what come
from hell.

HANNIBAL

All marsters come from hell.

RISSA

No, Hannibal, you seen what I seen—you thank
the good Lord for Marster Sweet. Much trouble
as you been and he ain't hardly never put the whip
to you more than a few times.

HANNIBAL

Why he do it at all? Who he to beat me?

RISSA

(*Looking only at her sewing*) He's your marster,
and long as he is he got the right, I reckon.

HANNIBAL

Who give it to him?

RISSA

I'm jes tryin' to tell you that life tend to be what
a body make it. Some things is the way they is and
that's all there is to it. You do your work and do
like you tol' and you be all right.

HANNIBAL

And I tell you like I tell Coffin—I am the only kind of slave I could stand to be—a *bad* one! Every day that come and hour that pass that I got sense to make a half step do for a whole—every day that I can pretend sickness 'stead of health, to be stupid 'stead of smart, lazy 'stead of quick—I aims to do it. And the more pain it give *your* marster and the more it cost him—the more Hannibal be a man!

RISSA

(*Very quietly from her chair*) I done spoke on the matter, Hannibal. You will work in the Big House.
There is total quiet for a while. HANNIBAL *having calmed a little, speaks gently to his mother.*

HANNIBAL

All right, Mama. (*Another pause*) Mama, you ain't even asked me what I aimed to do with that Bible. (*Smiling at her, wanting to cheer her up*) What you think I could do with a Bible, Mama?

RISSA

(*Sighing*) Sell it like everything else you gets your hands on, to them white-trash peddlers comes through here all the time.

HANNIBAL

(*Gently laughing*) No—I had it a long time. I didn't take it to sell it. (*He waits, then*) Mama, I kin read it.
RISSA *lifts her head slowly and just looks at him.*

I kin. I kin read, Mama. I wasn't goin' tell you yet.

RISSA *is speechless as he gets the book and takes her hand and leads her close to a place in front of the fireplace, opening the Bible.*

Listen—(*Placing one finger on the page and reading painfully because of the poor light and the newness of the ability*) "The—Book of—Jeremiah."

He halts and looks in her face for the wonder which is waiting there. With the wonder, water has joined the expression in her eyes, and the tears come.

RISSA

(*Softly, with incredulity*) You makin' light of your old Mama. You can't make them marks out for real—? You done memorized from prayer meetin'—

HANNIBAL

(*Laughing gently*) No, Mama— (*Finding another page*) "And I said . . . (*With longing: the words reflect his own aspiration*) "Oh, that I . . . had wings like . . . a dove . . . then would I . . . fly away . . . and . . . be at rest . . . "

(*He closes the book and looks at her*)

RISSA

Lord, Father, bless thy holy name I seen my boy read the words of the Scripture!

She stares at him in joy, and then suddenly the joy and the wonder are transformed to stark fear in her eyes and she snatches the book from him and hurriedly buries it and runs

to the cabin door and looks about. She comes back to him,
possessed by terror.
How you come to know this readin'?

HANNIBAL
(*Smiling still*) It ain't no miracle, Mama. I learned
it. It took me a long time and hard work, but I
learned.

RISSA
That's where you go all the time—Somebody
been learnin' you—
He hangs his head in the face of the deduction.
Who—?

HANNIBAL
Mama, that's one of two things I can't tell nobody
. . . I'm learnin' to letter too. Jes started but I kin
write a good number of words already.

RISSA
(*Dropping to her knees before him almost involun-*
tarily in profound fear) Don't you know what they
do to you if they finds out? I seen young Marster
Everett once tie a man 'tween two saplin's for
that. And they run the white man what taught
him out the county . . .

HANNIBAL
(*Angrily*) I took all that into account, Mama.

RISSA
You got to stop. Whoever teachin' you got to stop.

285

HANNIBAL

(*Tearing free of her*) I thought you would be proud. But it's too late for you, Mama. You ain't fit for nothin' but slavery thinkin' no more.
(*He heads for the door*)

RISSA

Where you going?

HANNIBAL

With all my heart I wish I could tell you, Mama. I wish to God I could believe you that much on my side!

He steps quickly into the night and the camera comes down on RISSA's *deeply troubled face.*

DISSOLVE TO:
EXTERIOR. THE FIELDS—MORNING.

Close-up of a pistol in a holster slung about a mounted man's hips. We move back to see that it is ZEB *astride his horse in the fields, surrounded by the drivers. A work song surrounds the dialogue.*

ZEB

(*Shouting a little because he is out of doors and topping the singing*) . . . the hands are to be in the fields an hour and a half before regular time and we're cuttin' the noon break in half and we'll hold 'em an hour and a half longer than the usual night quittin' time.

The drivers look at each other with consternation.
What's the matter?

DRIVER

Jes that these here people ain't used to them kinda hours, suh. Thas a powaful long set. 'Specially when you figger to cut the midday break like that, suh. The sun bad at midday, suh. They kin get to grumblin' pretty bad, suh, and makin' all kinds of trouble breakin' the tools and all.

ZEB

You gonna be surprised to find out how fast these people kin learn to change their ways. And any hand who don't learn fast enough will learn it fast enough when I get through with 'em.

COFFIN

Yessuh! They sho' will, suh! They got inta some bad habits, though, on accounta the way this here place been run. We got some hands, suh, that jes takes advantage of po' Marster Sweet. Breakin' his tools and runnin' off all the time—

ZEB

(*With incredulity*) Running off—? Who runs off?

COFFIN

Oh, Lord, suh! You don't know the carryin' ons what goes on 'round this here place. Some of these here folks done got so uppity they think Marster Sweet should be out there hoein' for them, that's what. (*Pointing out* HANNIBAL *in a nearby row*) There's one there, suh. Lord, that one! You'll see what I mean soon, suh. Once a week he jes pick hisself up and run off somewhere, big as he please.

I done told Marster and told him and it don't do a bit of good.

ZEB

Ain't he been flogged?

COFFIN

Hmmmph. Floggin' such as Marster 'low don't mount to much. That one there, shucks, he jes take his floggin' and go on off next time like befo'. He's a bad one, suh.

ZEB

(*Looking to* HANNIBAL *and calling to him*) Come here, boy.

HANNIBAL

(*Straightening up and looking around as if he is not certain who is being summoned*) Who?

ZEB

WHO?—YOU, that's who! Get yourself over here!

HANNIBAL *puts down his bag with a simmering sullenness and comes to the overseer.*

What's the matter with your cap there?

HANNIBAL *draws off his cap, keeping his eyes cast down to the ground. The other slaves sense trouble and slow down to watch.* ZEB *notices them.*

Who called a holiday around here? Get to work!

They stir with exaggerated activity for a few minutes and gradually slow down, more interested in the incident.

Raise your eyes up there, boy!

HANNIBAL *raises his eyes and looks in the other man's eyes.*
What's his name?

COFFIN

This be Rissa's boy, Hannibal. He got a brother
who's a runaway.

HANNIBAL *looks at* COFFIN *with overt hostility.*

ZEB

(*Getting down from his horse, with his whip*)
Well, now, is that so? Well, what you doin' still
hangin' 'round here? Ain't your brother never
come back and bought you and your mama and
carried you off to Paradise yet?

One or two of the drivers giggle.

Maybe you jus' plannin' to go on off and join him
some day?

He reaches up and with the butt end of his whip turns
HANNIBAL*'s face from side to side to inspect his eyes.*

You carry trouble in your eyes like a flag, boy.

He brings the whip up with power and lands it across HANNI-
BAL*'s face. An involuntary murmur rises from the watching
slaves. To them all.*

That's right, for *nothin'!*

HANNIBAL *is doubled up before him, holding his face.*

I hope y'all understand it plain! From now on this
here is a plantation where we plant and pick cotton! There ain't goin' to be no more foolin', no
more sassin' and no more tool breakin'! This is
what kin happen to you when you misbehave.
Now, everybody get to work! And let's have a song
there!—make noise, I say!

LORRAINE HANSBERRY

Singing comes up. He turns to the drivers.

> Keep 'em at a good pace till the break, and for
> God's sake keep 'em singin'! Keeps down the
> grumblin'! (*Noticing* HANNIBAL *still clutching at
> his face*) And that's enough of your playactin'
> there, boy. Get on back to your work in the rows.

HANNIBAL *obeys and goes to his row. We come down for a
medium-close shot of* ZEB *remounted, one hand poised on
his hip, surveying the fields before him, gun at his hip, whip
still in his fingers, watching the land that is not his.*

DISSOLVE TO:
EXTERIOR. THE VERANDA.

EVERETT *is lounging in a porch chair, sipping a drink.* ZEB
stands before him with his field hat in his hand.

EVERETT

All the same, it would have been better to have
picked another boy. His mother is one of my father's favorite house slaves, and they have a way
of getting him to know about everything that goes
on in the fields.

ZEB

(*Hotly*) I reckon there's some things have to be
left up to me if you want this here plantation run
proper, Mister Sweet.

EVERETT

(*Slowly turning his eyes on the man and moving
them up the length of his body in inspection which
overtly announces his disgust at the sight of him*)

And, as you say, "I reckon" you had better reckon
on knowing who is master here and who is merely
overseer. Let us be very clear. You are only an
instrument. Neither more nor less than that. This
is my plantation. I alone am responsible, for I
alone am master. Is that clear?

ZEB

(*Looking back at his employer with hatred in
kind*) Yes, sir, I reckon that's pretty clear.
They are interrupted by COFFIN *coming onto the veranda at
a run.*

COFFIN

'Scuse me, suhs, 'scuse me, but I got somethin'
most pressin' to tell you, Marster.

ZEB

Now what?

COFFIN

He's gone agin, suh. He's out in the fields like I
told you he do all the time!

ZEB

HANNIBAL!

COFFIN

Yessuh! Even with what you showed him an' all
the other day, he done run off from the fields again
to'day. But I fix him t'day, suh! Old Coffin
knowed it was time for him to pull something like
this again. I followed him, suh, yessuh. Coffin
know whar he be—

ZEB

Well, don't stand there like a dumb ape. Fetch
him and put him in the shed and strip him and—
(*Looking with triumph at his employer*)—I'll attend to him there. (*To* EVERETT, *bitterly again*)
That is, with your permission, *sir*.

COFFIN

(*Truly agitated*) You don't understand. He's with
young Marster, suh!

EVERETT

(*Sitting up with interest for the first time*) He is
with *whom*?

COFFIN

Young Marster Tom, suh!

EVERETT

(*With incredulity*) My brother?

COFFIN

Yessuh!

ZEB

Let's go!

EVERETT

(*Rising abruptly*) I'm coming with you.

CUT TO:

HANNIBAL's *clearing in the woods as per opening frame before
titles. Simultaneously with a close-up shot of his head framed
with a banjo neck are introduced stark, spirited banjo*

rhythms. Now the camera moves back to show the books and papers lying about where HANNIBAL *and* TOMMY *sit. He finishes playing with a flourish and hands the instrument to the child, who puts it awkwardly in his lap and carefully begins to finger it in the quite uncertain manner of one who is learning to play. He plucks a few chords as his teacher frowns.*

HANNIBAL

Aw, come on now, Marse Tommy, get yourself a little air under this finger here. You see, if the fat of your finger touch the string, then the sound come out all flat like this.

He makes an unpleasant sound on the instrument to demonstrate and to make the boy laugh, which he does.

Okay, now try again.

TOMMY *tries again and the slave nods at the minor improvement.*

That's better. (*Comically cheating*) That's all now, time for *my* lessons.

TOMMY

Play me another tune first, please, Hannibal?

HANNIBAL

(*Boy to boy*) Aw, now, that ain't fair, Marse Tom. Our 'rangement allus been strictly one lesson for one lesson. Ain't that right?

The child nods grudgingly.

And ain't a genamum supposed to keep to his 'rangement? No matter how bad he wants to do something else?

TOMMY

Oh, all right. (*Holding out his hand*) Did you do the composition like I told you?

HANNIBAL

(*With great animation, reaching into his shirt and bringing up a grimy piece of paper*) Here. I wrote me a story like you said, suh!

TOMMY

(*Unfolding it and reading with enormous difficulty the very crude printing*) "The—Drinking—Gourd."

(*He looks at his pupil indifferently*)

HANNIBAL

(*A very proud man*) Yessuh. Go on—read out loud, please.

TOMMY

Why? Don't you know what it says?

HANNIBAL

Yessuh. But I think it make me feel good inside to hear somebody else read it. T'know somebody else kin actually make sense outside of something I wrote and that I made up out my own head.

TOMMY

(*Sighing*) All right—"The Drinking Gourd. When I was a boy I first come to notice"—All you have to say is *came*, Hannibal—"the Drinking Gourd. I thought"—There is a *u* and a *g* in *thought*—"it was the most beautiful thing in the heavens. I do not know why, but when a man lie on his back and see the stars, there is something that can happen to a man inside that be"—*Is,* Hannibal—"bigger than whatever a man is." (TOMMY *frowns for the sense of the last*) "Something that makes every man feel like King Jesus on his milk-white horse racing through the world telling me to stand up in the glory which is called— freedom.

HANNIBAL *sits enraptured, listening to his words.*

"That is what happens to me when I lie on my back and look up at the Drinking Gourd." Well— *that's* not a story, Hannibal . . .

HANNIBAL

(*Genuinely, but less raptured because of the remark*) Nosuh?

TOMMY

No, something has to *happen* in a story. There has to be a beginning and an end—

He stops midsentence seeing the legs of three male figures suddenly standing behind HANNIBAL. HANNIBAL *looks into his eyes and leaps to his feet in immediate terror.*

EVERETT

(*In an almost inexpressible rage*) Get back to the house, Tommy.

TOMMY

(*Reaching for the banjo*) Everett, you wanna hear how I can play already? I was going to surprise

you! Hannibal said we should keep it a secret so
I could surprise you!

EVERETT

Get home, at once!
*The child looks quizzically at all the adults and gathers up
his books and goes off.* HANNIBAL *backs off almost involuntarily from the men.* EVERETT *turns to* HANNIBAL.
So you told him it would be your little secret.

HANNIBAL

I was jes teachin' him some songs he been after me
to learn him, suh! (*Desperately*) He beg me so.

EVERETT

(*Holding the composition*) Did you write this—?

HANNIBAL

What's that, suh?

EVERETT

(*Hauling off and slapping him with all his strength.*
ZEB *smiles a little to himself, watching*) THIS!
. . . Don't stand there and try to deceive me, you
monkey-faced idiot! Did you write this?

HANNIBAL

Nosuh, I don't know how to write! I swear to you
I don't know how to write! Marse Tommy wrote
it . . .

EVERETT

Tommy could print better than this when he

was seven! You've had him teach you, haven't you . . .

HANNIBAL

Jes a few letters, suh. I figger I could be of more use to Marster if I could maybe read my letters and write, suh.

EVERETT

(*Truly outraged*) You have used your master's own son to commit a crime against your master. How long has this been going on? Who else have you taught, boy? Even my father wouldn't like this, Hannibal.

A close-up shot as EVERETT*'s hand reaches out and takes* HANNIBAL*'s cheeks between his fingers and turns his face from side to side to inspect his eyes.*

There is only one thing I have ever heard of that was proper for an "educated" slave. It is like anything else; when a part is corrupted by disease—

Suddenly with all his energy HANNIBAL *breaks for it.*

ZEB

Get him, Coffin!

The driver tackles HANNIBAL *and throws him to the ground, and* ZEB *comes over to help subdue him, while* EVERETT *stands immobile, slapping his leg with his riding crop.*

EVERETT

. . . when a part is corrupted by disease—one cuts out the disease. The ability to read in a slave is a disease—

HANNIBAL
(*Screaming at him, at the height of defiance in the face of hopelessness*) You can't do nothing to me to get out my head what I done learned . . . I kin read! And I kin write! You kin beat me and beat me . . . but I kin read . . . (*To* ZEB) I kin read and *you* can't—

ZEB *wheels in fury and raises his whip.* EVERETT *restrains his arm.*

EVERETT
He has told the truth. (*To Zeb, coldly*) As long as he can see, he can read . . .

ZEB *arrests his arm slowly and slowly frowns, looking at* EVERETT *with disbelief.*

You understand me perfectly. Do it now.
Astonished and horrified, ZEB *looks from the master to the slave.* EVERETT *nods at him to proceed and the man opens his mouth to protest.*

Proceed.
ZEB *looks at the master one more time, takes the butt end of his whip and advances slowly toward the slave, who comprehends what is to be done to him.* EVERETT *turns on his heel away from the scene, and with a traveling shot, we follow his face, as he strides through the woods and as, presently, the tortured screams of an agonized human being surround him . . .*

Fade out
End of Act Two

ACT THREE

FADE IN:
EXTERIOR. PLANTATION GROUNDS—
LATE NIGHT.

The shadow of a man ingeniously strung by all four limbs between two saplings, each of which is bent to the ground away from the other. Two male shadows loom near and a voice says: "All right, guess we might as well cut him down now . . . gangrene must've set in."

DISSOLVE TO:
INTERIOR. HIRAM SWEET'S BEDROOM.

He is in bed and conducting a violent tirade. A medicine bottle smashes against the fireplace and we move across to his bed where he is in the midst of an angry denunciation of ZEB *and* EVERETT, *who both stand in the center of the floor affecting various moods of defiance, fear and impatience.* MARIA *stands near her husband's bedside, wringing her hands for fear of what the mood will do to a cardiac.* EVERETT *reaches out in a restraining gesture toward his father.*

HIRAM
Don't you put your murderous hands on me!

EVERETT
(*To his mother quietly*) Who in the name of God told him about it?

MARIA

(*Shrugging*) One of them, of course.
They look at the one lone house servant in the room, who
casts his eyes quickly away.

HIRAM

None of your business who told me! Should have
been told before of your doings. Should have been
told when you hired this—this—GET THIS
CREATURE OUT OF MY SIGHT AND OFF
MY LAND BEFORE I SHOOT HIM!

ZEB

All I got to say is that I done as I was told, sir. I
was just following instructions . . .

SWEET

Get him out of here!

MARIA

Please leave, Zeb.

ZEB

Yes ma'am—but you got to tell him I just done
as I was told.

EVERETT

Oh, get out.
(ZEB *exits*)

MARIA

Now, darling, just calm yourself—

HIRAM

(*To his son*) So this is the way you took over the plantation.

SERVANT

Dr. Bullett, suh.

MACON BULLETT *enters in a jubilant mood, with a newspaper.*

BULLETT

Have you all heard the news—?

MARIA

Why, Macon, wherever are your manners to-day—?

BULLETT

I'm so sorry, Maria, my dear.

He bows to her a little and greets the two men, and then resumes his excitement.

Have you heard the news?

EVERETT

What news—

BULLETT

Why, my dear friends, the conflict has come to life! Gentlemen, ma'am, we fired on Sumter two days ago. The South is at war!

There is total silence for a second, and then EVERETT *and* MACON *whoop with joy, and* EVERETT *climbs up and pulls a scabbarded sword from above the mantelpiece and begins to wave it about, alternately embracing* MACON.

MARIA

Son, will you have to go?

EVERETT

Oh, Mother, of course, if I am offered a commission!

MARIA

(*Handkerchief to her eyes*) Oh, my little darling.
Then, slowly, all notice HIRAM, *who has been stricken quiet and sober by the news.*

HIRAM

(*With great sadness*) You fools . . . you amazing
fools . . .

MARIA

Now, Hiram—

HIRAM

The South is lost, and you two are jumping around
like butterflies in your happiness.

EVERETT

Lost! The South is going to assert itself, Papa. It
is going to become a nation among nations of the
world—

HIRAM

Don't you know that whoever that idiot was who
fired on Sumter set the slaves free? Well, get out
the liquor, gentlemen, it's all over. (*Pause*) A way
of life is over. The end is here and we might as well
drink to what it was.

BULLETT

Now, look here, Hiram—

HIRAM

Look where? What do you want me to see? You look. You step to the window there and look at all those people that you and your kind have just set free.

EVERETT

Oh, Papa, what is all this nonsense?

HIRAM

(*Slowly pulling on his robe*) I give you my word that they already know about it in the quarters. (*Sadly*) They do not know who or how or why this army is coming. They do not know if it is *for* them or indifferent to them. But they will be with it. They will pour out of the South by the thousands —dirty, ignorant and uncertain what the whole matter is about. But they will be against *us*. And when those Yankee maniacs up there get up one fine morning feeling heady with abolitionist zeal and military necessity and decide to arm any and every black who comes ambling across the Confederate lines—and they will—because they will have to—because you will put on your uniforms and fight like fiends for our lost cause . . . But when the Yankees give them guns and blue uniforms, gentlemen, it will all be over.

MARIA

Hiram, what are you doing? Where do you think you are going?

HIRAM

(*Pulling himself fully out of the bed*) I am going out to see Rissa.

BULLETT

As your physician, Hiram, I expressly forbid you to leave that bed.

HIRAM

Macon, shut up. My time is over. I don't think I want to see that which is coming. I believed in slavery. But I understood it; it never fooled me. It's just as well that we die together. Get out of my way now.

BULLETT *stands back and he exits slowly.*

CUT TO:
EXTERIOR. RISSA'S CABIN.

HIRAM *stands outside a moment. Somewhere in the distance, a slave sings plaintively.* He goes into the cabin.* RISSA *is at the fire, boiling something in a pot.* HANNIBAL *lies flat on a bed, his eyes covered by a cloth. One or two slaves file out wordlessly as the master enters. Occasionally* HANNIBAL *cries out softly.* RISSA *methodically tastes an extract she is preparing. She then dips a fresh white cloth in a second pot and*

*Perhaps "Lord, How Come Me Here?," "Motherless Child," "I'm Gonna Tell God All of My Troubles."

*wrings it out lightly and starts toward her son. Her eyes
discover the master standing clutching at the collar of his
robe, himself in panting pain. He is looking down at Hannibal. She looks at the master with uncompromising indictment
and he returns her gaze with one of supplication, and drops
his hands in a gesture of futility. She ignores him then and
goes to the boy and removes the old cover and replaces it
with a fresh one. The song continues.*

HIRAM

I'll send for Dr. Bullett.

RISSA

I doctorin' him.

HIRAM

But fever—

RISSA

I makin' quinine. Be ready soon.

HIRAM

I—are you sure . . . ? I think I should get Bullett.

RISSA

(*Without looking up*) He put his eyes back?
Silence.

HIRAM

I—I wanted to tell you, Rissa—I wanted to tell
you and ask you to believe me, that I had nothing
to do with this. I—some things do seem to be out
of the power of my hands after all . . . Other men's
rules are a part of my life . . .

RISSA

(*For the first time looking up at him*) Why? Ain't you *Marster*? How can a man be marster of some men and not at all of others—

HIRAM

(*The question penetrates too deeply and he looks at her with sudden harshness*) You go too far—

RISSA

(*With her own deadly precision*) Oh—? What will you have done to me? Will your overseer gouge out my eyes too? (*Shrugging*) I don't 'spect blindness would matter to me. I done seen all there was worth seein' in this world—and it didn't 'mount to much. (*Turning from him abruptly*) I think this talkin' disturb my boy.

HIRAM *looks at the face which will not turn to him or comfort him in any way and slowly rises. He starts out and we follow him into the darkness several feet, a dejected, defeated figure, which suddenly collapses. He cries out for help and one by one the lights of the cabins go out and doors close. He crawls a little on the grass, trying to get back to* RISSA's *cabin. Inside, we see her at the table again, preparing another cloth for* HANNIBAL. *She lifts her eyes and looks out of the window to see the figure of the man she can distinctly hear crying for help. She lowers her lids without expression and wrings the cloth and returns to* HANNIBAL's *bedside and places it over his eyes and sits back in her chair with her hands folded in her lap. We come down on her face as she starts to rock back and forth as* HIRAM's *cries completely cease.*
FADE OUT.

FADE IN:
EXTERIOR. THE VERANDA—EVENING.

MARIA *sits, dressed completely in black, not moving and not looking where she stares.* EVERETT *comes up the steps; he wears a Confederate Officer's uniform and a mourning band.*

EVERETT

Mother . . .
His manner with her is that of someone seeking very hard to distract another from grief.
What would you think if I got the carriage and took you for a nice long ride in the cool, out near the pines—?

MARIA

No, thank you, son.

EVERETT

Oh do—it would be so refreshing and cooling for you, and tomorrow I think you should treat yourself to a nice social call on the Robleys—

MARIA

(*Pulling her shawl about her a bit*) Thank you, Everett, but I find it chilly right here tonight. And your father never cared for the Robleys.
He starts to argue a little, but looks at her and changes his mind and relaxes back in his chair and lets his eyes scan the darkness in front of him, where his plantation lies stretched out, as a gentle hymn rises up from the quarters, the same one as in the introduction—"Steal Away to Jesus."

EVERETT

Yes—you're right. Let's just sit here in the peace and the quiet. The singing is pretty tonight, isn't it?

MARIA

(*Looking dead ahead*) Peaceful? Do you really find it peaceful here, Everett?

EVERETT

Sure it is, Mother. (*Enthusiastically*) Things are going to go well now. Zeb is beginning to understand how I want this place run; the crops are coming along as well as can be expected, and the slaves have settled down nicely into the new routine of the schedule. Everything is very orderly and disciplined. (*Touching her hand gently*) Above all, there is nothing for you to worry about. This thing will all be over soon and I'll be home before you know it and everything will be back to normal. Only better, Mama, only better . . .

The camera starts to pan away from them and moves down the veranda in through the front door, into the foyer and across to the darkened dining room, where it discovers, at low angles which do not show her face, RISSA's *figure in the darkness standing before the gun cabinet, which she opens with the key which hangs at her waist. She removes the gun with stealth and closes the cabinet carefully and turns as we follow her skirts and rapidly moving bare feet across the dining room into the dark kitchen and out the back way. Waiting in the darkness outside is the boy,* JOSHUA. *Still unseen above her waist, she takes him by the hand and they go at a half-run towards and into the woods. We stay with them until they come to* HANNIBAL*'s clearing where* SARAH *stands, poised for traveling, and trembling mightily. Just beyond her is the figure of a man, seated, waiting patiently— the blind* HANNIBAL. RISSA *locks the other woman's hand about the child's, thrusts the gun into* SARAH*'s other hand, and moves with them to* HANNIBAL, *who rises. There is a swift embrace and the woman and the child and the blind man turn and disappear into the woods.* RISSA *watches after them and the singing of "The Drinking Gourd" goes on as we pan away from her to the quarters where the narrator last left us. Only now, his musket leans against the fireplace. Once again the slaves are gone. He walks into the scene with his coat on now—buttoning it with an air of decided preparation. He looks at us as he completes the attire of a private of the Grand Army of the Republic.*

SOLDIER

Slavery is beginning to cost this nation a lot. It has become a drag on the great industrial nation we are determined to become; it lags a full century behind the great American notion of one strong federal union which our eighteenth-century founders knew was the only way we could eventually become one of the powerful nations of this world. And, now, in the nineteenth century, we are determined to hold on to that dream. (*Sucking in his breath with simple determination and matter-of-factness*) And so—

Distinct military treatment of "Battle Cry of Freedom" of the period begins under.

—we must fight. There is no alternative. It is possible that slavery might destroy itself—but it is more possible that it would destroy these United States first. That it would cost us our political and economic future. (*He puts on his cap and picks up his rifle*) It has already cost us, as a nation, too much of our soul.

Fade out
The End

NOTES ON TWO SONGS:
"FOLLOW THE DRINKING GOURD"
and "STEAL AWAY"*

FOLLOW THE DRINKING GOURD.   The most effective weapon employed by the Negro slaves in the war of attrition against their white masters was escape. Each year, hundreds of thousands of dollars in valuable slave property vanished from the South—borne mysteriously on the midnight trains of the Underground Railroad. This highly secret Abolitionist organization earned its name through the extra-legal activities of thousands of Negro and white Americans who maintained a continuous line of way-stations and hiding places for fleeing Negroes. The Fugitive Slave Law came into existence in a vain effort to stem this annual floodtide of escape.

This song is based on the activities of an Underground Railroad "conductor" by the name of "Peg Leg Joe." Joe was a white sailor who wore a wooden peg in place of his right foot which had been lost in some seafaring mishap.

Peg Leg Joe would travel from plantation to plantation in the South, offering to hire out as a painter or carpenter or

*From *Songs of the Civil War*, edited by Irwin Silber, Bonanza Books, a division of Crown Publishers, by arrangement with Columbia University Press, 1960.

handyman. Once hired, Joe would quickly strike up an ac-
quaintance with many of the young Negro men on the
plantation and, in a relatively short period of time, the sailor
and the slaves would be singing this strange, seemingly
meaningless song. After a few weeks, Joe would hobble on
and the same scene would be enacted at another plantation.
Once the sailor had departed, he was never heard of again.

But the following spring, when "the sun come back and
the first quail calls," scores of young Negro men from every
plantation where Peg Leg Joe had stopped would disappear
into the woods. Once away from the hounds and the posses,
the escaping slaves would follow a carefully blazed trail—a
trail marked by the symbol of a human left foot and a round
spot in place of the right foot.

Traveling only at night, the fleeing man would "follow
the drinking gourd," the long handle of the Big Dipper in
the sky pointing steadfastly to the North Star—and freedom. Following the river bank, which "makes a mighty good
road," the slave would eventually come to the place "where
the great big river meets the little river"—the Ohio River.
There, "the old man was a-waiting"—and Peg Leg Joe or
some other agent of the Underground Railroad was ready to
speed the escapee on his way to Canada.

A good story, perhaps, or is it just an old folk legend? H.
B. Parks of San Antonio, Texas, one-time chief of the Division of Agriculture in the State Research Laboratory, writes:

> One of my great-uncles, who was connected with the (under-
> ground) railroad movement, remembered that in the records
> of the Anti-Slavery Society there was a story of a peg-legged
> sailor, known as Peg Leg Joe, who made a number of trips

through the South and induced young Negroes to run away
and escape. . . . The main scene of his activities was in the
country immediately north of Mobile, and the trail described
in the song followed northward to the head waters of the
Tombigee River, thence over the divide and down the
Tennessee River to the Ohio.

Parks' uncle went on to confirm the story of the sailor's use
of the song as a guide to the escaping slaves.

STEAL AWAY.   It is hard to think of a melody in any music
more plaintive, more fragile, less militant in spirit and tempo
than this, one of the most beautiful of the old spirituals. And
yet, history shows that "Steal Away" was one of the most
widely used "signal" songs employed by the slaves when
they wanted to hold a secret conclave somewhere off in the
woods.

And on closer examination, the song is seen to abound
with the subterfuge and double-meaning imagery which a
secret message would require. The "green trees bending"
and the "tombstones bursting" certainly might refer to spe-
cific meeting places, and it takes little imagination to visual-
ize the lightning-struck hollow tree or abandoned barn
meant by the singer as he sang out, "He calls me by the
lightning."

One researcher believes that the song was written by Nat
Turner, leader and organizer of one of the most famous of
the early nineteenth-century slave revolts. In any event, the
song has lasted as a memory of secret, clandestine revolt, and
as a musical testament to the creative capacity of the people
whose heritage it is.

What Use
Are Flowers?

A CRITICAL BACKGROUND

Despair? Did someone say despair was a question in the world? Well then, listen to the sons of those who have known little else if you wish to know the resilliency of this thing you would so quickly resign to mythhood, this thing called the human spirit. . . .

—LORRAINE HANSBERRY,
To Be Young, Gifted and Black

In a 1962 letter to Mme. Chen Jui-Lan of the Department of Western Languages and Literature, Peking University, Peking, China, Lorraine Hansberry referred to a work "in draft"

. . .which treats of an old hermit who comes out of the forest after we have all gone and blown up the world, and comes upon a group of children. . . . The action of the play hangs upon his effort to impart to them his knowledge of the remnants of civilization which once . . . he had renounced. . . . He does not entirely succeed and we are left at the end, hopefully, with some appreciation of the fact of the cumulative processes which created modern man and his greatness and how we ought not go around blowing it up.

She called it "a bit of a fantasy thing . . . a play about war and peace."

What Use Are Flowers? was conceived, in late 1961, as a fantasy for television. Its inspiration was not William Golding's *Lord of the Flies,* to whose setting it bears such striking resemblance—Lorraine read that novel a year after completing it—but Samuel Beckett's *Waiting for Godot,* which had deeply affected and provoked her. Originally titled *Who Knows Where?* (from a line in Bertolt Brecht's *Mother Courage*) the play was in effect her answer to the questions of life and death, survival and absurdity which Beckett had posed in such novel, compelling terms.

Yet *Godot* was only one of the more striking expressions of the prevailing attitudes of a generation that had come to maturity under the shadow of the Bomb, to which the young black playwright brought a quite different point of view. In her first public address as a writer, to a conference of black artists and intellectuals, she affirmed the need for black writers to devote themselves to *all* aspects of the freedom struggle, including that which opposed the forces of despair, destruction and war in the world. And in conclusion she struck a personal note, recalling a conversation she had had with a friend who was "by way of description, an ex-Communist, a scholar and a serious student of philosophy and literature." Together, she told the audience, they had "wandered . . . into the realm of discussion . . . which haunts the days of humankind everywhere—the destruction or survival of the human race":

"Why," he said to me, "are you so sure the human race should go on? *You* do not believe in a prior arrangement of

life on this planet. You know perfectly well that the reason
for survival does not exist in nature!" . . .

I answered him the only way I could. I argued on his own
terms, which are also mine: that man is unique in the universe, the only creature who has in fact the power to trans-
form the universe. Therefore it did not seem unthinkable to
me that man might just do what the apes never will—*impose*
the reason for life on life. That is what I said to my friend—I
wish to live because life has within it that which is good, that
which is beautiful and that which is love. Therefore, since
I have known all of these things, I have found them to be
reason enough and—I wish to live. Moreover, because this
is so, I wish others to live for generations and generations and
generations and generations.

In order, however, that there be no possible confusion or
misconception about the sources of a "wish" so unfashiona-
bly and unabashedly affirmative—nor about the assumptions on which it was based—Lorraine went on immediately
to define the particular life experience out of which her
assessment came. She described the life of a child "born on
the Southside of Chicago . . . black and a female . . . in a
depression" between two world wars. While she was still in
her teens, she told the audience, "the first atom bombs were
dropped on human beings." She recalled a physical attack
upon her person that had been "the offspring of racial and
political hysteria." She spoke of the loss of friends and relations "through cancer, lynching and war . . . drug addiction
and alcoholism and mental illness," and pictured a period
spent working at New York's Federation for the Hand-
icapped with victims of "congenital diseases that we have
not yet conquered, because we spend our time and ingenuity

in far less purposeful wars." She described "street gangs, prostitutes and beggars" and the "thousand . . . indescribable displays of man's very real inhumanity to man," to which she— "like all of you"—had been witness. And then she concluded:

> . . . I have given you this account so that you know that what I write is not based on the assumption of idyllic possibilities or innocent assessments of the true nature of life. But rather, my own personal view that, posing one against the other, I think that the human race does command its own destiny and that destiny can eventually embrace the stars.

Coming two years after these words were spoken, *What Use Are Flowers?* was, in more fanciful terms, the playwright's answer to Beckett and to her young friend: an entry in the continuing dialogue of our time on the value and purpose of life, which, in one form or another, was to constitute the core of her writing until her own death at thirty-four.

What Use Are Flowers? was never submitted in its original form to television. The experience of *The Drinking Gourd* led the playwright, before completing it, to recast it tentatively for the stage. But the transition between the two media was not fully realized to her satisfaction when, early in 1962, she set it temporarily aside. It would, for example, take an extraordinary director to achieve on the stage the sustained performances from the "wild" children that could easily—and marvelously—be evoked on film. In thinking about the problem, Lorraine had hypothesized as one possible solution a new form: a fantasy on two levels that would juxtapose the old man's soliloquies against modern dancers portraying the children. The idea intrigued her and she always planned to return to the play to try it. But it was to remain an idea only.

In 1967, three scenes from *Flowers* were recorded by Melvyn Douglas, Morris Carnovsky and Lee J. Cobb for the radio program "Lorraine Hansberry in Her Own Words," and one of these, as enacted by John Beal, was featured in the play *To Be Young, Gifted and Black.* The experience of working with these actors (and others like Moses Gunn, who took over the role) suggested minor modifications, cuts and a few outstanding touches that have been incorporated into the final text.

Robert Nemiroff

WHAT USE ARE FLOWERS?
A Fable in One Act

"Lullaby baby
What's rustling there?
Neighbor's child's in Poland
Mine's who knows where"

—Bertolt Brecht
from
Mother Courage

CHARACTERS

An elderly and scholarly hermit.

A party of children of about nine or ten years old.

The scene is a vast rocky plain at the edge

of a great forest.

SCENE 1

A plain somewhere in the world; darkness and wind. The HERMIT *appears from left—an old and bearded man in the residue of manufactured garb and animal skin—he walks with a stick and carries his life's possessions in a bundle. He surveys the area as best he can in the half-light, shuffles to an outcropping of rock at right and crawls up into a crevice and goes to sleep. As he sleeps, the light comes up slowly and the* CHILDREN *appear, on their knees, in stark silence. They are stalking a small creature. The most arresting thing about them, aside from their appearance, which is that of naked beasts with very long hair, is their utter silence—for not one of them is beyond the age of ten. The old man sleeps on. The light is that of dawn.*

Presently, the CHILDREN *pause, as instinctively still as their quarry. One of them rises with a rock in hand and lets it fly; then, as one, the* CHILDREN *rise and run screaming to the animal which has been successfully stoned, and violently fall to fighting over it. They really fight one another; there is nothing to suggest the mere games of children. And, moreover, those who are strongest triumph.*

Among the more savage of the group is a little girl who is wiry and tough and skillful in the fighting. She achieves her share as do one or two of the others, while the remaining children glower and whimper like unfed puppies watching

them consume the raw meat; those who are most frail or slow
are also, noticeably, the thinnest.

At the sound of their noise the old man is roused and sits
up rubbing his mouth and his beard and his eyes. He shifts
his position to see out the cave. He does this while the
CHILDREN *are still actively fighting. He cannot altogether*
make out what they are fighting about. That is, he cannot see
that they eat *it.*

HERMIT (*Dryly but loudly*)

Well, I see you haven't changed, to say the least. *Animals!*
Down unto the fourth and fifth generation of you, that's
what.

   (*Grumbling*)

Well, what did I expect? What, indeed, did I expect?

   (*The* CHILDREN *freeze in astonishment at the sound*
   of his voice.

   He feels gingerly about for a foothold, shifting bun-
   dle and stick, and starts down from the rocks—which
   were easier ascended, even in the dark, than descend-
   ed at his age.

   At the first move, one of the boys stoops, appre-
   hensively, for a rock. The others are taut—ready for
   flight)

Why the devil don't you give an elderly gentleman assistance? I see that your manners haven't changed either.
Well, no matter: the only thing you ever did with manners was hide your greater crimes. How very, very significant, how significant indeed, that the very first thing I
should see upon my return is the sight of little hooligans

abusing a creature of nature! With the blessings of your elders, I am sure, I am sure!

(*He halts and gestures for assistance to the closest youngster*)

You—I am talking to *you*, my little open-mouthed friend—

(*The* CHILDREN *merely continue to stare. He shakes his stick*)

Ah, you don't like that, do you!

(*He gives a surprisingly sprightly jump, for his years, and clears the incline neatly—but then totters a second for balance*)

There we are! What do you think of that!

(*Breathing heavily from the exertion*)

And now if you undisciplined little monsters will be kind enough to give me directions to the city, I shall make myself absent from your admirable company.

(*They stare*)

You there—with the eyeballs! Which way to the city?

(*Holding the courtesy deliberately*)

Please. I should like with your cooperation to reach some outpost of, if you will forgive the reference, "civilization" by nightfall. What is the nearest town? I no longer recall these points, apparently, and have got myself utterly lost . . .

(*The* CHILDREN *stand fixed*)

Do you hear?

(*He takes a half-step towards one, who immediately draws back*)

What you need, my little zombie, is a well-placed and repetitive touch of the cane! But I suppose that anything as admirable as that is still forbidden?

(*Looking around at all of them*)

Well, close your mouths and go away, little uglies, if you won't be helpful. I am sure your doting parents are anxious for you—for some ungodly reason. Why are you all got up like that anyway? Is it Halloween? Dear Lord, don't tell me I've come back just in time for *that!* Well, I wonder then if you might interrupt your mute joke long enough to tell an old man just one thing. If only I might persuade you quite what it would mean to me . . . You see, I should very much like to know—

(*Deep pause*)

What *time* it is. You think that's silly, don't you; yes, I rather thought you would. That a chap might go off and hide himself in the woods for twenty years and then come out and ask, "What time is it?"

(*He laughs*)

But, you see, one of the reasons I left is because I could no longer stand the dominion of time in the lives of men and the things that they did with it and to it and, indeed, that they let it do to them. And so, to escape time, I threw my watch away. I even made a ceremony of it. I was on a train over a bridge . . . and I held it out the door and dropped it. Quite like—

(*He gestures, remembering*)

—this. But do you know the very first thing I absolutely had a compulsion to know once I got into the forest? I wanted to know what time it was. Clearly I had no appointments to keep—but I *longed* to know the hour of the day! There is, of course, no such thing as an hour, it is merely something that men have labeled so—but I longed to have that label at my command again. I never did achieve that. Ultimately I gave up seconds, minutes and hours, too . . . Ah, but I kept up with days! I made a rock calendar at once. It was a problem too: the wild animals would knock over the rocks. Finally, I gave up and made a game—a game, ha!—of keeping up with the days in my head. It got to be a matter of rejoicing that the seasons came when I knew they would.

(*Looking down*)

Or, at least, that's how it was for the first fifteen years. Because, naturally, I lost track. I accumulated a backlog of slipped days which, apparently, ran into months because one year, quite suddenly, it began to snow when I expected the trees to bud. Somewhere I had mislaid a warm autumn for a chilly spring. I almost died that year; I had lost a season.

(*Boastfully, for his new-found audience*)

Consequently, among other things, I expect that I must be the first adult you have ever met who did not know his age. I was fifty-eight when I went into the woods. And now I am either seventy-eight or perhaps more than eighty years old. That is why I have come out of the woods. I am afraid men invent time*pieces*, they do not invent time. We may give time its dimensions and meaning, we may make it worthless or important or absurd or crucial. But ultimately I am afraid it has a value of its own. It is time for me to die. And I have come out to see what men have been doing. And now that I am back, more than anything else just now, you see, I should very much like to know—what time it is.

(*The* CHILDREN *stare*)

Ahh . . .

(*Stiffening and shaking his finger at them*)

But you must not for one second take that to mean that I *regret* my hermitage or do in any wise whatsoever return repentant to the society of men. I return in contempt!

(*More quietly*)

And, if one must tell everything—*curiosity*. Not love! Not once, not once in all those years did I *long* for human company. Not once!

(*He flicks his fingers at them in sweeping gesture, settles himself on the ground and spreads a small cloth*)

Get along, then; go ahead: shoo! I am going to have my breakfast and I prefer privacy.

(*He first looks to the setting-out of his food and then up again to see them still standing, apparently transfixed*)

I am quite serious about it and will become stern with you any moment now! The diversion is OVER! Toddle along to your—

(*Nastily*)

—mummies and daddies.

(*They do not move*)

Do you *not* understand the language merely because it is literately spoken? I don't wonder—recalling the level of study. Shall I employ sign signals?

(*Gesturing impromptu hand signals*)

GO A—WAY! *Andale!* SCRAM!

(*They do not move, and he is angry*)

All right. But you might as well know that you do not frighten me. I shall eat my breakfast and be content whether you stay or go. And when you recover your tongues, I will accept your directions. I must confess I do not remember this plain at all. I could have sworn that the forest continued for many miles more. But then my memory has to cover a long span of time. You little folk are the very first human souls that I have seen in twenty odd years. Well, what do you think of that!

(*He points to the woods, roaring proudly*)

I've been in there, in the forest: for twenty-odd years! Deep, deep in the forest. I am *a hermit!*

(*Showing off, stroking his beard*)

What do you think of that? Just like in books!

(*To another child*)

What is your name? You look like a pupil of mine. But, I suppose he would be a little older by now. I am Charles Lewis Lawson. Professor Charles Lewis Lawson. I was an English teacher.

(*He lifts out a handful of food from his bundle— begins to place it on his cloth: as swiftly the* CHIL- DREN *throw themselves upon him and the scraps of food. In the scramble he is knocked over. Those who get some wolf it down, and the old man gets himself aright in time to see one of them gulp down the last morsel. He reaches out tentatively to the child as if, in outrage, to recover it, but the child gnashes his teeth—like a cur. Others pick up his bundle and empty it and paw about in the articles in a cruelly savage search for more food. The old man turns from one to the other frantically*)

Animals! . . . Animals! . . . I'm an old man! Don't you know anything!

(*The* CHILDREN *fall back a short distance and now lounge about, still watching him*)

Oh, all that I have missed, all that I have undoubtedly missed!—

(*Bitterly*)

—in the society of men!

(*He gathers up his things angrily*)

Well, why don't you laugh? Go ahead. Go ahead. Go ahead! It is a great game to beat up an old man and take his food from him, is it not?

(*In a curious rage about it*)

I can see that nothing at all has changed. Damn you! And damn your fathers!

(*He sinks down and pouts rather like a child himself*)

Why did I come out; why, why, why. . . !

(*The* CHILDREN *sit and watch him and do not move. Then, presently*)

Well, are you all still with me? You must be looking for your grandfather. Or Santa Claus. Well, I am neither!

(*He gathers up his things and stamps off right; the* CHILDREN *sink down where they are and freeze as the lights come down—and then up again. The old man comes on from left, having gone in a circle on the plain. The* CHILDREN *are stretched out where he left them, asleep. They rouse*)

Oh, there you are. I was hoping I would find you again. Certainly haven't been able to find anyone else. Just this interminable plain. Now, look here: I must have directions to the city. You must end this little joke of yours and talk to me. I will admit it: I am impressed that you can hold your tongues so long. Well, I will have to stay with you until you tire of it. Or, until your parents come.

(*He is mopping his brow and smiling at them. They look back at him and say nothing. He looks at each one separately*)

Listen, I happen to know that you are not mute, because I heard you screaming before.

(*He neatly arranges a pile of dry twigs, dead leaves, and begins to twirl a flint. He works hard at it and, presently, as the first thin stream of smoke arises, the* CHILDREN *silently lean forward, fascinated*)

Pretty neat, eh? You get good at it if you stay in the forest long enough. I will tell you the truth though. There was not one time that I ever made a fire like this when I did not fancy myself an Indian scout on television. My word, television! I suppose the Images walk right into the living room by now and have supper with you.

(*Dryly*)

Oh, all that I have undoubtedly missed!

(*Fixing the nearest boy with an exaggerated glare*)

Don't think that's funny, eh? What dry parents you must have! The lot of you. Speaking of your parents, where the devil are they? To tell you the truth, I was rather hoping that they might give me a lift. Ah, there we are.

(*He gives a good hard rub at this point, and a small lick of flame rises. The largest of the boys jumps to his feet and shouts*)

BOY

VAROOM!

(*And simultaneously the* CHILDREN *hit the dirt, face down, and try to bury their heads under their arms. The old man looks up from the fire*)

HERMIT

"Bang, bang!" I gotcha! Rat-tat-tat-tat!

(*He wields a "submachine gun." One of the littler ones raises his head*)

You there, step here, since you are the least dead of the cowboys. I need a bellows and you will do nicely.

(*The child does not move*)

Now listen—come here. *Kommen sie hier! Venga! . . . *
Well, I don't know Yiddish.

(*With total exasperation, he goes back to the fire, fixes a string of wild fowl he has caught on a skewer across the flames and then sits back comfortably to wait.*

The little bit of meat sends up its bouquet; the child sniffs and goes closer. The others lift their heads slowly. It is an unfamiliar smell. Then, like beasts of prey, they stealthily shift to stalking positions and start to close in on the old man—who mugs back at them, draws his "six-shooters" and stares them down as in a game)

Once upon a time there were seven little ugly, unwashed, uncombed and unmannered little children—

(*The* CHILDREN *throw themselves on his birds and tear them to pieces and devour them raw, precisely as they did his lunch the day before. The old man rises, horrified, his eyes wide, looking from child to child*)

Why . . . you're not playing . . . you *are* wild!

(*He regards them for a long time and then reaches out abruptly and pulls one of them to him*)

Are you lost children? What has happened to you?

337

(*He inspects the child's elbows and kneecaps, which
are hard calluses*)

Dear God! Calluses. You really don't understand a word
I am saying, do you?

(*Experimentally, but swiftly, expecting nothing*)

"Mother." "*Mutter.*" "*Madre.*" "*Mater.*" "Mama."
"*Bambino*" . . .

(*He is looking closely at the child and smoothing the
hair back from the face so that he can see the eyes
for any sign of recognition. The others look on guard-
edly. The youngster is motionless in his hands*)

No, words don't mean a thing to you, do they? Dear, dear
God . . . What have I found?

(*With desperate hope that he is wrong*)

Here—

(*He pulls out a pocket knife*)

—lad, What's this?

(*The boy looks but does not touch. The old man
opens and flips it into the earth; then retrieves it and
lays it flat on his palm. The boy clutches for it*)

No, not *blade* first, lad!

(*Closing and pocketing it, he sits back on his heels,
stunned, looking around at them*)

You eat raw meat, don't know fire and are unfamiliar with
the simplest implement of civilization. And you are prelingual.

(*He stands up slowly; as if to consult the universe
about his impending sense of what has happened*)

What have they done. . . ?

(*Slowly turning about; his voice rising in its own*)

eccentric hysteria, crossing down center to the audi-
ence)
What have you finally done!
　(*In a rage, screaming*)
WHAT HAVE YOU DONE!

Blackout

SCENE 2

Many weeks later. Several rather serviceable lean-tos have been fashioned, and at far right a tiny garden is crudely fenced off. The CHILDREN, *who have been combed the least bit, so that it is hardly discernible, sit cross-legged in a semicircle; the Master, in the stance of his old profession, stands in front of them.*

HERMIT

Before we go any further at all, I must distribute names. I can do that, you see, because in this present situation I am God! and you must have names. Ah, you are wondering "Why—?" Well, it is because it will keep you from having to remember who you *really* are as you get older. Let's see, quickly now, you are hereby: John, Thomas, Clarence, Robert, Horace, William. You may be Charlie, and you are henceforth Alexander.

(*To* ALEXANDER)

But may I caution you at the outset to avoid all temptations toward any adjective to follow it.

(*Indicating the little girl*)

And you—you shall be Lily.

(*Gruffly*)

Now, down the list.

(*He holds up items or gestures actions. First he picks up a piece of meat*)

CHILDREN
  Food.
     (*The* HERMIT *holds up the knife*)

CHILDREN
  Knife.
     (*The* HERMIT *holds up a crude earthenware pot*)

CHILDREN
  Pot.
     (*The* HERMIT *gestures with his cheek on his hands, eyes closed*)

CHILDREN
  Sleep.
     (*The* HERMIT *gestures*)

CHILDREN
  Drink.
     (*The* HERMIT *gestures*)

CHILDREN
  Lift.
     (*The* HERMIT *gestures*)

CHILDREN
  Eat.
     (*He has not had such a good time for twenty-odd years—though of course, if asked, he'd deny it.*

     He speaks fluently to them regardless of their only understanding a handful of words. When he wishes them to do or understand something explicitly, he speaks slowly and with abundant gesture)

HERMIT

Very good. So much for today's academic lessons. Time now for the vocational section. And all I can say is that primitive though my knowledge of technical skills may be—you had better be bloody grateful that I have at least some! In my world, certain men prided themselves on *not* knowing the things I am attempting to teach you! So, I shall do the best I can, do you hear me?

(*Under his breath*)

And when you learn to understand what the deuce I am talking about most of the time, you will also understand that you have just had a profound apology for ignorance, disguised as a boast. I was indeed a true member of the tribe!

(*Loudly*)

Now let me see . . . "Ceramics."

(*To himself*)

If only we had a manual. Does one bake the clay before or after it's dry? There is a point at which the clay must be put into—a kiln? . . . "Kiln"!?

(*He clears his throat and looks up*)

Yes, well, in any event—remember yesterday we gathered clay at the riverbank?

(*Holding up a handful of clay*)

Repeat it: "Clay."

CHILDREN

CLAY!

HERMIT

Very good. Clay. And I did this to it—

(*Holds up the clay pot*)

CHILDREN
CLAY!
(*He points again to the pot for a further answer*)
POT!

HERMIT
. . . And we sat it in the sun. "Sun."
(*He points overhead*)

CHILDREN
SUN!

HERMIT
And now, see, it is hard. And now it is possible for one to carry not only one object—but several. Now this process is called . . .
(*He makes as if he is fashioning the pot again*)
"Work." Say it.

CHILDREN
WORK!

HERMIT
And with "clay" and "work," you can make all you need of these. So that you can "use" it. "Use" it . . . "use" . . .
(*The class is puzzled. He demonstrates by putting objects into the pot and taking them out*)
Well, this, I will admit, is something of an abstract concept . . . but it is a vital one and you will have to master it quickly. "Use" . . . "use" . . .
(*The* CHILDREN *are silent; it is too abstract. And he*

goes through it again. Then, with great excitement as CHARLIE *raises his hand*)

You *got* it, Charlie? Good boy! Come and show me what to "use" something means.

(*The youngster gets up, picks up the pot and puts things in it*)

Good . . . good . . .

(CHARLIE *carries them back to where he sat and takes them out and looks at the teacher for his approval*)

Capital!

(*Pleased,* CHARLIE *puts them back in the pot and hands it back to the teacher*)

Very good, Charlie!

(*To the class*)

Charlie has "used" the pot.

(*He takes out his knife and whittles a twig*)

I am "using" the knife.

(*With a sense of urgency*)

It is such a vital verb, you *must* master it.

(*A beat*)

Well, on with the weaving.

(*He sits down, crosses his legs contentedly and picks up, as do the* CHILDREN, *the beginnings of the baskets they are making*)

Cross one over, bring the other through, then—

Dimout

SCENE 3

As the lights come up this time: stone implements, baskets and hoes as well as drying meats are in evidence. The Master and the CHILDREN *come on far right; they are rather more frolicsome than we would have supposed they could be. And, for the first time,* LILY *is the only one with long hair. The boys have been barbered and are dressed in foliage or animal skins now.*

HERMIT (*Pausing at the garden*)
By heaven, those are most attractive radishes, Thomas. Very good! Come along now, time for class.
    (*The* CHILDREN *moan*)
How quickly you learn! Come along, or you'll get a caning.
    (*They obey and take the positions of the prior scene*)
Well, now, you've made such—
    (*He considers them doubtfully*)—
—admirable progress that I think you are ready to graduate to an area of knowledge which, sadly enough, used to be known as "the humanities." And, in that connection, Charlie and I have prepared a surprise for you. A "surprise" is something that you do not know is coming and, in life, most "surprises" are quite unpleasant—but every now and then, there are those which are pleasant indeed,

345

and they generally have to do with another abstraction which you do not know how to call by name but which you have already experienced—

(*Touching one of them*)

—by your nose, your eyes, and way, deep inside you. It is called: "beauty." Say it.

CHILDREN (*Shouting, out of habit*)
BEAUTY!

HERMIT

My word, you needn't shout it! "Beauty" is just as well acknowledged softly as loudly. Say it like this so the word itself is beautiful—

(*Sweetly, lifting his head back and gesturing*)
"Beau-ty."

CHILDREN (*In dead-earnest mimicry*)
Beau-ty.

HERMIT
Again.

CHILDREN
Beau-ty.

HERMIT

Lovely. You see, your very voices have this abstraction in them. Now—

(*He picks up the pot*)

—here is our dear and useful friend the pot again.

CHILDREN
POT.

HERMIT

Which, as we have learned, "works" for us, when we have worked to make it. Now, we have also learned that we can "use" it to carry all sorts of things: the berries we have picked; the water we wish to carry somewhere . . . but also—

(*He lifts up a little bouquet of wildflowers*)

—we may use it simply to hold that which we "enjoy" because—

(*He puts the flowers into the pot*)

—they have "beauty." Like these flowers, which are almost as beautiful as our little Lily, which is why we have named her after them.

(LILY *promptly preens herself before the boys.* WILLIAM *raises his hand*)

William?

WILLIAM (*Loudly*)

USE?

HERMIT

What *use* are flowers?!

(*A bit thrown*)

Well . . . there were, in the old days, certain perfectly tasteless individuals who insisted on making wine out of them. But that was not a use—it was a violation! Ah, but the uses of flowers are infinite! One may smell them—

(*He inhales deeply, then holds them out to the* CHILDREN, *who inhale deeply in imitation*)

One may touch their petals and feel heaven—

(*He touches them*)

Or one may write quite charming verses about them—

347

(*Abruptly, to head them off*)

—now, do not ask me what verses are! When you have become proficient in language, I'm afraid no power on earth will be able to stop you from composing them! All right, now on to the surprise. I think that it will be perhaps the most satisfying thing I shall ever be able to teach you . . .

(*He turns upstage, draws himself up, makes several false starts and finally, turning back, begins to sing—horribly*)

Alas, my lo-ove, you do me wro-ong—

(*The* CHILDREN *giggle at the curious sound—he hesitates with embarrassment, but continues*)

To cast me out discourteously

When I have lo-oved you so lo-ong

Deli-ighting i-in your company.

(*They giggle again, but he presses on and at last they hush and listen, caught in the phenomenon of the human voice lifted in song. He sings crudely but sweetly, gaining confidence*)

Greensleeves was my deli-ight

And Greensleeves was all my joy

Greensleeves was my song of so-ongs

And who but my La-ay-dy Greensleeves.

(*He is momentarily overcome with the realization that such notes may never in fact be heard on this earth again. Then, recovering*)

Well, that—loosely speaking—is what is called a "melody." It belongs—well, properly sung, it belongs—to a great body of pleasure which is called "music" . . .

CHILDREN
Music.

HERMIT (*He nods*)
However, melodies do not necessarily need to be sung.
Sometimes they can provide as much beauty when . . . ah,
but that is Charlie's surprise. Charlie.
(*He beckons to the boy, who hesitates. Reassuring-ly*)
Come along, lad.
(CHARLIE *steps forward, as nervous as a performer has ever been and reveals a reed instrument which is a crude but competent flute. He lifts it to his lips and haltingly plays the first stanza of "Greensleeves." The* CHILDREN's *faces reflect the miracle. As* CHARLIE *begins the chorus, the* HERMIT *stops him*)
That was lovely, Charlie. Lovely. Now—
(*To the* CHILDREN)
—you try it with us . . .
(*He sings the melody to* CHARLIE's *accompaniment and conducts, expecting the* CHILDREN *to join in. They do not. Undaunted*)
Come on, children . . . sing! . . . sing!
(*He begins once more, louder and more urgently, as if by sheer force of will to sweep them along. There is no response and at last he stops. Helplessly*)
Try . . .
(*Silence. He turns away in defeat. Suddenly one takes up the song, then another, and another, and finally all —tentatively at first, then with growing conviction as the Master conducts, quite carried away, exultant*)

349

Good . . . good! Yes, yes . . . keep to the tempo now! Good
. . . good . . .

(*Suddenly peering forward as* LILY *raises her hand*)
Yes, Lily?

LILY

USE?

HERMIT

Use? What *use* is MUSIC???

(*At a loss for words, he gropes*)
Well, there are many uses . . . there are different kinds
of uses . . . Yes, well—

(*Decisively: an order*)
—YOU *JUST* SING!

(*As the voices rise to their fullest, he grins*)
Tomorrow—Beethoven's Ninth!

Blackout

SCENE 4

In the darkness, CHARLIE's *primitive flute begins, very slowly and haltingly, the first measures of Beethoven's Ninth, the Choral; and presently, over it, we hear the* HERMIT's *voice:*

HERMIT

Yes, Charlie . . . there! I told you you could do it! You're playing Beethoven, boy! Beethoven!
    (*The notes become firmer, more controlled, as if we are experiencing the learning process in microcosm, until finally they are rendered almost perfectly in the temper of the Hymn to Joy as we know it, the tempo addressed to the spirit of man: martial, certain, aspirational*)
. . . He couldn't *hear,* you know? But that didn't stop him! . . . We'll *do* it, Charlie! You will teach the others the melody and I shall teach them the words! Well, that is—as soon as I can recall them well enough to translate from the German—I simply have no strength left for the declensions!
    (*As the lights come up, Schiller's flash of ecstasy is shouted out by the old man, and the* CHILDREN's *voices burst forth. They are arranged in that stiff self-conscious grouping which is the style and posture of all choruses—except that* LILY *is beating time to*

351

CHARLIE's *accompaniment on a great drum of clay,
while the others add flourishes of their own on im-
provised instruments. They sing with pride and vigor
—and what we should be forced to thrillingly feel is
childhood's assumption of the inevitability of the
statement. And through it all the Master stands facing upstage, waving his hands in accurate tempo and
lacking only flowing black robes)*

HERMIT (*Shouting*)
　　Joy, thou source of light immortal!

CHILDREN
　　Joy, thou source of light immortal!

HERMIT
　　Daughter of Elysium!

CHILDREN
　　Daughter of Elysium!

ALL
　　Touched with fire, to the portal
　　Of thy radiant shrine we come.
　　Thy pure magic frees all others
　　Held in Custom's rigid rings;
　　Men throughout the world are brothers
　　In the haven of thy wings . . .

HERMIT
　Bravo, children. Bravo!
　　　(*He bows to them and they, formally, to him*)
　As the poet Emerson said to Walt Whitman upon the

publication of *Leaves of Grass:* "I greet you at the start of a great career!"

> (*The group disperses and various ones settle down to different onstage activities*)

Uh, Charlie. I should very much like to talk with you.

> (*The Master ushers* CHARLIE *into his lean-to, with oddly deliberate social mannerisms all of a sudden*)

Have a seat, won't you?

> (*This lean-to is not, of course, what man or child can stand up in fully, and the "seats" are well-placed flat rocks*)

Would you care for some water?

> (*The boy signifies "no" with his head and looks at the Master curiously*)

HERMIT (*Shoving a mug of water on him*)

No, you must say Yes, Charlie.

> (*Passing some grapes*)

Because we are not pupil and Master just now—we are friends and—

> (*Settling down on one rock after forcing* CHARLIE *to sit on another and to accept the water and grapes*)

—what we are doing now—

> (*Taking a grape himself and smacking over it elaborately*)

—is "socializing." And, you see, since this is *my* home, it is my obligation to make you feel welcome and even to entertain you and give you refreshments. And, under the last codes that I recall, it was more graceful to accept than not. Though I will admit such rules frequently reversed themselves.

353

CHARLIE

How—you—?

HERMIT

"Socialize"? Exactly like this. We sit and we look at one another and eventually begin to tell one another perfectly outlandish stories, you see. It was a kind of ritual. But I shall have to teach you quite what a joke is. The last one I recall—well—oh, yes, Why does a chicken cross the road? That is to say, Why does the wild guinea hen that we eat, you know, why does it run across the path? You are supposed to say: "I don't know, sir."

CHARLIE

Why?

HERMIT

Because if you don't say that, I shan't have an altogether logical reason to give you the answer and it was the answers, I gather, which were purportedly the point of these quite extraordinary exercises of the human mind.

CHARLIE (*Stiffly*)

"I-don't-know-sir."

HERMIT

Well, a chicken crosses the road to get to the other side.
   (*They stare at one another*)
Now you do this, lad.
   (*Holding his stomach like jolly old St. Nick in order to instruct*)
"Ho, ho, ho, ho!"

CHARLIE (*Frowning mightily and imitating with exactitude*)

Ho, ho, ho, ho!

HERMIT

Show your teeth rather more, I think. And throw back your head. Yes, very good. That will do.
(*Looking down at his hands with sudden seriousness*)
Look here, there's another reason for our little get-together this afternoon. And it has to do with something fairly serious. And this really is the proper setting, because what we are having here is a sort of cocktail party, you see, which is where most really important matters were generally decided. Under circumstances quite like this—I mean with people chatting amicably and drinking things. Be that as it may. I want to try to discuss something rather serious and rather difficult with you—and, well, the fact of the matter is that I don't really, to tell the absolute truth, know how to go about it.
(*Blurting suddenly*)
Not that I didn't know one hell of a lot about women myself, you see! But, with the young, we traditionally preferred to make an awkward process out of it. And I don't seem to know how to reverse the custom.
(*The child simply stares at him*)
What I am trying to say is: do you know why I did not cut *Lily*'s hair?
(*As quickly realizing the futility of that approach*)
Oh, no, no—! Listen, let us approach it this way: you are a leader, Charlie, and there are some things which . . . you

poor fellow, I shall have to hope that you take responsibility for when I will—have gone away.

CHARLIE (*Jumping up*)
Gone? Where?

HERMIT (*Quietly*)
That will have to be a different lesson one day soon. But, we still have time . . . and for the moment this other matter is more imperative—so that when I do go away . . . What it has to do with is—
(*Looking at the boy with serious eyes*)
—the survival of—
(*His lips fall with the weight of the impossibility of trying to suggest to a ten-year-old that the perpetuation of the human race could possibly be his responsibility.*

Throughout the prior scene the following has been occurring outside at right: of two boys making pottery, one has proven more an artist than the other, and thus the first has simply reached out and claimed one or two of the other's pots, and the other fellow has retaliated by yanking them back, for which he is socked—which now launches a grim, stark and savage fight with one bashing the other's head until it is red with blood and the other as passionately trying to choke all life out of the first. It is the fight of savages who mean to maim or destroy.

As they tussle, they crash a lean-to here and some pots there. As it is not yet spectacle or sport in their society, the CHILDREN *do not pay the fighters the least bit of attention; but merely move out of the way*

when they roll their way and go on with whatever
they are doing.

Hearing a crash finally, the HERMIT *looks out to see*
what is happening)

HERMIT (*Seeing and screaming at them*)
Animals . . . !
>(*He runs to them and tries to tear them apart; they*
>*snarl and tear at him viciously in their eagerness to get*
>*at one another again*)

Animals, I say! . . . Will you never change!
>(*Now he is also being covered with the blood of one*
>*of them as he is flung about trying to tear them*
>*apart*)

Even in your wretchedness—are you still at it!?
>(*One of them flings him to the ground.* CHARLIE *is*
>*about to come to his rescue but hesitates and stands*
>*back, frozen*)

Go ahead! *Destroy yourselves!* You do not deserve to
survive! YOU DO NOT DESERVE TO SURVIVE!
>(*The fighting* CHILDREN *do not hear him but contin-*
>*ue tearing away at each other. The others simply stare*
>*at the screaming old man with a quizzical expression*
>*on their faces.*

>*Getting up almost in delirium, rolling and slipping*
>*and falling in trying to get on his feet*)

FORGET EVERYTHING I HAVE TAUGHT
YOU—!
>(*He rises and stamps on the pots, violently tears bas-*
>*kets to pieces as the boys fight on*)

I RENOUNCE YOU AGAIN! . . . YOU AND YOUR

PASSIONS AND ALL YOUR SEED! . . . MAY YOU
PERISH FOREVER FROM THIS EARTH!!
(*He staggers with sudden pain and goes reelingly off
toward the woods. The fight continues*)

Blackout

SCENE 5

A few hours later.

Blue lights at rise. The CHILDREN *sit in a stiffly arranged group at right. With apprehension. The old man is flat upon his back in his lean-to; one hand is on his stomach, another trails to the floor.*

Each child hands CHARLIE *a flower, and he crosses from them to the lean-to of the Master. The old man says nothing. The child holds out the bouquet.*

CHARLIE (*Tentatively, expecting rebuff*)
Flowers . . .

HERMIT
If you got hungry enough you'd kill me and eat me. Go away, Charlie. I've had enough.

CHARLIE
Music—

HERMIT
I do not want flowers, music or poetry.

CHARLIE
Beethoven—

HERMIT
No, not even Beethoven . . . You want to know *why,*

don't you? Well, because I hate you. You are human, therefore you are repulsive! All of you. But *you* in particu- lar!

> (CHARLIE *looks at him curiously—but does not move*)

Now, *that* is what is known as an insult and, in the face of them, people generally go away.

CHARLIE

I don't like insults then.

HERMIT

Which only proves that you are an even more common type than I had supposed. Go away, Charlie, I have decid- ed to die and I prefer to die alone, after all. Ah, you still don't know what *that* is, do you? Well: *you just stand there and watch!*

> (*He turns his face gruffly away and* CHARLIE, *with the flowers, comes closer and peers down at him intently as if a lesson, like all others, is to be rendered pronto. The old man turns to see the earnest face above his own and shouts*)

Get out of here!

> (*Primitive or not,* CHARLIE *is hurt by the tone and starts to back out as a hurt child must*)
> (*Relenting*)

Charlie . . .

> (*The boy halts; but the old man does not look directly at him*)

When it does happen—

> (*Slowly, seriously*)

—and it will be soon now . . . not tonight, but soon enough . . . I will get cold and stiff and still and it will seem strange to you that I ever moved at all. It will seem then, boy, that I was a miracle . . . but it will happen. Because I am old and sick and worn-out—

(*A hoarse rasp*)

—And mortal. But what you have to know is this: when it happens you will all stand for a long time with your mouths hanging open with wonder. That's all right, boy, it's an awesome thing. It is in the nature of men to take life for granted; only the *absence* of life will seem to you the miracle, the greatest miracle—and by the time you understand that it should be the other way around—well, it will be too late, it won't matter then.

CHARLIE (*Smiling*)

Hen cross road.

HERMIT (*Smiling the least bit in return*)

No, it really isn't a joke. Some men, in my time, spent whole lifetimes writing books trying to prove that it was. But it isn't. The thing that you have to know is when mine is over, and I have grown stiff and quiet for a while, I shall begin to exude a horrid odor, and what you must all do is dig the deepest hole that you possibly can and put me in it. It doesn't matter which way and I don't have to be wrapped in anything. I shall be glad enough to merge, atom for atom, with the earth again. And that is all there is to it.

(CHARLIE *looks at him quizzically, mystified*)

HERMIT

Ah, you are wondering, how will I get out? I—won't! I will stay there forever. For always. For eternity.

(*Shouting irritably*)

Well, you've seen other things die! The birds, the fish we eat. They don't come back, do they? The wood we burn, it doesn't come back! Nothing comes back!

(*Looking at* CHARLIE's *puzzled eyes*)

You are thinking that I am not a bird or a fish or a piece of wood. All right—I am not!

(*Raising up on his elbow, screaming feverishly*)

WELL, I CANNOT SOLVE THE QUESTION OF IMMORTALITY FOR YOU, CHARLIE!

(*Sinking back again, exhausted*)

And you don't like that, do you? Thy name is man and thou art the greatest arrogance in the universe . . . Well—

(*He shrugs. Gently*)

—put a stone over my head when you have buried me and come and spend hours there pretending to have dialogues with me and you will feel better. It won't mean a thing to me, but you will feel better.

(*Then, more softly*)

The truth of it is that you really are going to miss me, Charlie. All of you. You will discover an abstraction that we never got to because there wasn't time. Affection. And, for some of you, something worse than that even, something more curious, more mysterious, that I shouldn't have been able to explain if there had been time. Some of you—*you* for instance, because we have been closest—will feel it; it will make you feel as if you are being wrenched apart. It is called "grief" and it is born of love. That's what I was really trying to tell you about this morning, Charlie. Love. But, you see, it wasn't a very respectable sort of business in my time; as a matter of fact we tried any number of ways to get rid of it altogether.

CHARLIE

What use?

HERMIT

Use, boy? How to *use* love? Well, we never found that out either. Mostly it got in the way of important things. And, for all I know, they did get rid of it altogether . . .

> (*Sitting up again with great determination*)

Now, look here, Charlie! Do you—do you like Lily?

> (CHARLIE *shrugs*)

Well, you will. Agh! The problem is that you *all* will. You can't imagine how glad I am that I shall be out of here before all of that confusion erupts! But that's beside the point, the point is . . .

> (*Once again lost in the Victorianism of his world*)

Well, listen, let's put it this way, boy: you've got to take rather good care of Lily. What I mean is if there should be a time when—when there just isn't enough food for all of you . . . well, Charlie, you've got to see to it that Lily isn't the one who goes without. It mustn't ever be Lily as long as there are three of you . . . Yes, I know I taught you to share; but you can't have permanent rules about things. The only rules that count are those which will let the race . . .

> (*He halts once again; weighs this thought and its persistence and decides afresh*)

. . . let the race continue.

> (CHARLIE *leans forward intently and, as if pushed by*

a compulsion to get through to the boy, the older man strains forward in turn. In its matching intensity, the child's pose takes on a startling resemblance to the old man's)

I'm avoiding a good part of the thing about Lily, Charlie. Mainly because I can't help myself. I promised myself that I would tell you only the truth. Only the truth is so damned—Well, let's have a go at it this way:

(*Slowly*)

Lily is different, you see. That is to say that someday perhaps, when one of you is feeling—well, as I am feeling now—that is to say, sick—Lily is the one who will make it tolerable by bringing you an extraordinary cup of tea and looking at you in a way that will be different from the way the others—*hang it, this is impossible!*

(*He turns away in a fury at his own inability to deal honestly with the moment.* CHARLIE *stands and waits attentively*)

The truth is, Charlie, you are right: the thing I saw in your eyes before when I was explaining death. I am nothing more and nothing less than a bundle of mortality; an old package of passions and prejudices, of frightful fears and evasions and reasonings and a conscience, and deep in my heart I long for immortality as much as you do already without even understanding it. We all did—and cursed one another for it! And renounced one another for it! That is why I went into the woods, you see: I was outraged with mankind because it was as imperfect, as garrulous, as cruel as I.

(*Turning and looking at him*)

But tell me something, Charlie, I've puzzled out a lot about you. I know that you were prelingual when I found you; you must have been perhaps five or less when—it—happened as you seem to be about nine or ten now. Can't really tell; with your diet you might be much older. But let us suppose you are ten . . . The thing is it seems strange to me that you've not seen human death before. I assumed at first that there had been more of you, some who died around you. But you don't know human death. Why were there so few of you?

    (*Raising up, and enunciating carefully as when he really means to be understood*)

How did you get here . . . ?

    (CHARLIE *begins a narrative in flowing articulate gesture*)

. . . Yes, Charlie . . .

    (*Studying a gesture which sweeps from one place to another*)

Why, you were brought here! Yes, go on . . .

    (*As a stone rolls, so did that vehicle*)

In a thing that moved! Yes, yes!

    (*Great blades of grass grew here on that day; high like this*)

Yes, there were many trees then! I understand, boy, go on!

    (*The outline of the human figure*)

You were brought here by one like you—

    (*No.* CHARLIE *points to the* HERMIT)

Like *me!*

    (CHARLIE *nods, then shakes his head. The* HERMIT *peers at him.* CHARLIE *points to him again*)

Like me . . . ?

    (CHARLIE *nods and shakes his head. The* HERMIT *is confused. The boy picks up a flower: the lily*)

. . . Ah, by one like Lily, only big! A woman. Yes, yes, go
on!

> (CHARLIE *smiles and goes to him and reenacts the
> only kiss of his memory*)

She kissed each of you . . .

> (*The sweeping gesture from one place to another*)

And went away . . . And then—and then—?

> (*A circle of the arms collapses*)

. . . "The sun fell down." Yes, I see, I see. Of course. A
woman brought you here to the perimeter of danger and
then went back. A nursery school teacher or counselor
or—some great woman had tried to guarantee the human
race and then went back for more! She *chose* to go
back . . .

> (*Throwing his head back in anguish*)

Dear God: what a strange tribe they were! Lunatics and
heroes all.

CHARLIE

"Heroes"?

HERMIT

A hero was a fool . . . No—come here, Charlie.

> (*He draws the boy to him*)

How ashamed we were of our heroes always. That one,
like Lily, who brought you here, she was like the song I
taught you. Do not ever be ashamed of what you feel
when you think of her.

> (*Lying back in obvious weakness*)

Listen, Charlie, I've not tried to weigh you down with a
lot of moral teachings; for one thing there hasn't been
time. And so much of what I would have tried to tell you

about all of that would have been absurd and obstructive,
and you will get into your own habits in time about that.
But look here, fellow, about that woman—well, for reasons that we never did agree on, the vast majority of
humankind over the centuries became committed to the
notion that—that this particular unpremeditated experi-
ment of the cosmos which was the human race—well—
that it *ought* to go on . . . It was a defiant notion, and only
something as fine, as arrogant as man could have dreamed
it up: only man could have dreamed of triumph over this
reckless universe. But the truth is, we didn't quite know
how. In the beginning, you see, we had such a little to
work with and we never quite believed our poets when
they told us that, in the main, we were doing the best we
could. We demanded more of ourselves than that; for
above all else, boy, man was valiant. Really—

    (*An admission*)

quite splendid, you know. Ah, the things he perceived!
You will be like them: heroes all of you, merely to *get on*
as long as you do.

    (THOMAS *enters with a thing: a crude wheel with little
    clay scoops attached to its spokes*)

Hello, Thomas . . . Now, what is that, boy?

    (THOMAS *brings it and puts it on the old man's stom-
    ach*)

Well, it's fetching, child, but what is it?
Look, Charlie, Thomas has made something. Now the
question is . . . what has Thomas made?

    (*He turns the thing about, utterly confounded.*
    THOMAS *races out and then back again and, mutely,
    pours water from a pot into the topmost scoop so that*

its weight forces the wheel to turn and scoop up more water)

Yes . . . yes!

(Drawing THOMAS *to him)*

I understand, boy . . . you have found the wheel as simply as this! Creation, what ignites this flame!

(Smoothing THOMAS *'s hair about his face with adulation)*

I should have christened thee "Leonardo," Thomas!

(In a rage of jealousy CHARLIE *seizes the invention and hurls it out of the lean-to.* THOMAS *'s instinctive move to seize him in return is arrested by the realization that* CHARLIE *is stronger. The* HERMIT *shakes his head in distress)*

Ah, Charlie, Charlie! You can't understand, can you, that it is something for all of you . . . Thomas saw a problem and invented something to solve it. It's all right to be jealous, in fact it's a fine thing; it means that you have placed value on something, and that is fine. But you must *use* your jealousy, Charlie. You must help Thomas to build another wheel, a bigger wheel, and then you won't have to waste all that time carrying water and can do something else, sit around and sing if you like, or make up new tunes on your flute—in the time that you used to spend carrying water before Thomas invented the wheel. Of all the things you must learn, this is the most difficult and that from which you most will profit.

*(*CHARLIE*'s face continues ugly with resentment.* THOMAS *retreats cautiously backwards and turns, when a safe few feet away, to dart towards his invention)*

But the truth is, I don't think you will learn it. The truth is, children, that I don't think you will survive at all. I have been indulging myself, no more. Engaging in a timeless vanity of man. Pretending with you that it would be possible. Pretending that *you* wild little things could conceivably raise great Egypt and China again, claim the equations of Copernicus and Newton—ha! the perceptions of Shakespeare and Einstein! Pretending that I could hand to you the residue, badly learned and hardly retained, of—five thousand years of glory!—

(*Turning gruffly away*)

—on which I turned my back with all the petulance of our kind . . .

(*Turning back and shouting*)

WHY, YOU DON'T EVEN KNOW WHAT STEAM WILL DO YET! WE DIDN'T EVEN GET TO STEAM!

(*Crying out to* THOMAS)

Steam, Thomas! A force that would make your wheel turn with revolutions undreamed of in your primitive soul! Mere simple heated water . . . You don't know it.

(*Outside, the* CHILDREN, *drawn by the excitement, come one after the other to observe* THOMAS *and his wheel*)

That foolish, foolish woman! That silly sentimental female! Why did she leave you here to torment me in my last absurd hours! It's all finished with you, the lot of you! Our little adventure among the stars is over! *Finis!* The brief and stupid episode will end now! The universe will have peace now . . .

369

(*He falls back, spent.* CHARLIE *stands and holds out the lily. The old man lifts his head*)

Use . . . What *use?* Charlie, the uses of flowers were infinite . . .

(*He lies still.* CHARLIE *gently places the flower by his face and after a moment crosses out to join the* CHILDREN *who, unaware that the old man has left them, are now clustered intently about the wreck of the wheel which* THOMAS, *squatting in the dirt, is patiently reconstructing*)

Curtain

LORRAINE HANSBERRY, at twenty-nine, became the youngest American, the fifth woman and the only black playwright ever to win the New York Drama Critics' Circle Award for the Best Play of the Year. Her *A Raisin in the Sun* has since been published and produced in some thirty countries, while her film adaptation was nominated by the New York critics for the Best Screenplay and received a Cannes Film Festival Award. At thirty-four, during the run of her second play, *The Sign in Sidney Brustein's Window*, Lorraine Hansberry died of cancer. Her death was a blow not only to the world of the theater but to the world at large, for as Martin Luther King wrote, ". . . her creative ability and her profound grasp of the deep social issues confronting the world today will remain an inspiration to generations yet unborn." Possessed of a soaring spirit and unique universality, Lorraine Hansberry eloquently articulated the aspirations of her people and at the same time embraced all humankind. In the six years since her death her stature has continued to grow as more and more of the work she left is brought before the public. *To Be Young, Gifted and Black*, a dramatic portrait of the playwright in her own words, was the longest-running Off-Broadway drama of 1969; it has been recorded, filmed for national television, published in expanded book-form, and has toured an unprecedented forty states and two-hundred colleges. *Les Blancs*, her last play, was hailed by a number of critics as the best play of 1970–71.

ROBERT Nemiroff, Lorraine Hansberry's literary executor, shared a working relationship with the playwright from the time of their marriage in 1953. Originally a music publisher and award-winning songwriter, he produced her second play, *The Sign in Sidney Brustein's Window*. Mr. Nemiroff's own play, *Postmark Zero*, was presented on Broadway in 1965, in London, and on national television. Since then his adaptations of Miss Hansberry's posthumous works *To Be Young, Gifted and Black* and *Les Blancs* have been hailed by both the critics and the public.

JULIUS LESTER is the author of three adult books, two juveniles, one of which, *To Be a Slave*, was runner-up for the Newbery Prize. He has also recorded two albums of his own songs. He has contributed articles and reviews to many publications, including the *New York Times Sunday Book Review, Evergreen Review, Liberation, Nickel Review, Black Review* and *Ebony*. He has just recently completed editing *The Seventh Son: The Thought and Writings of W.E.B. Du Bois* for which he also wrote the introduction. He has a radio program on WBAI-FM in New York, where he makes his home.